THE LANCING OF MY SOUL

A pastor encounters the healing touch of Jesus in the most troubled regions of his soul

Thomas Dages

Published by NEWW Publishing LLC
6464 S Quebec Street, Suite 600, Centennial, CO 80111

Copyright © 2019 Thomas Dages
All rights reserved.

ISBN: 978-1-7328783-2-7

Unless otherwise indicated, all Scripture quotations are from The ESV® Bible (The Holy Bible, English Standard Version®), copyright © 2001 by Crossway, a publishing ministry of Good News Publishers. Used by permission. All rights reserved.

Cover Design: Craig Pritchett

FIRST EDITION

ENDORSEMENTS

Tom's recommended practices for soul healing and deeper intimacy with God are desperately needed in the contemporary Church today. He convincingly demonstrates that the casual Christianity embraced by many church-goers today must be replaced by sober personal examination, unceasing prayer, appropriation of Christ's life, and soul-renewing disciplines. Tom also conveys bright rays of hope to those who struggle with shattered dreams, unanswered prayers, and debilitating addictions. I am pleased that this book is biblically faithful, spiritually sound, and excellently word-crafted. Tom's transparency and willingness to share his personal struggles—and God's enduring faithfulness—will prove encouraging to readers as it has been to this professor and writer. I highly commend his work for adoption and publication.

Bruce Demarest, Ph.D.
Senior Professor of Christian Formation, Denver Seminary
Littleton, Colorado

Tom Dages's book, *The Lancing of My Soul*, is a proof text of how real healing from emotional wounds is not a one-dimensional process, nor is it a journey we are meant to travel alone. Tom's transparency in describing his journey through debilitating anxiety and depression provides a window into the many facets of our being that affect our health (mental, emotional, spiritual, and physical) and how the Lord wants to meet us and heal us at every level. This book is a powerful testimony providing insight, wisdom, and hope for those dealing with internal struggles of the heart either as caregivers and/or sufferers of mental, emotional, or spiritual disorder.

Lenore T. Gray, M.Div., LPC
Clinical Therapist, Licensed Professional Counselor

This is a deep story about a man's battle and victory over the enemy of anxiety and despair. These pages are filled with both raw honesty and spiritual truths that will awaken you to both the spiritual battle and the power of the Holy Spirit through humility and prayer. Tom is not just sharing truths, he is sharing his life, and it is a wonderful gift to spiritual leaders and those who are wrestling not against flesh and blood.

Zach Bearss
Senior Pastor, ClearView Community Church
Buena Vista, Colorado

THE LANCING OF MY SOUL

For more information or to request a speaking engagement, please go to: www.tomdages.com

If you liked the cover and illustrations and wish to speak to the designer, please go to: www.brandeavor.com

Thomas Dages

CONTENTS

Acknowledgements 7
Preface 9
Part 1: The Attack 13
Chapter 1: The Night It All Began 15
Chapter 2: Getting Up After the Train Wreck 27
Chapter 3: Seeking Relief on Vacation 37
Part 2: Surprises of God's Supernatural Assistance 45
Chapter 4: Prayer Miracles Begin with the Elders 47
Chapter 5: Truth Comes Alive in the Imagination 59
Chapter 6: The Slow Return of Sleep 71
Chapter 7: Another Terrifying Night Terror 79
Chapter 8: Hit by Another Train 89
Chapter 9: Three Startling Visions 97
Chapter 10: A Great Pastor Helped Armor Up 107
Chapter 11: The Dream of a Snake 115
Chapter 12: Freedom Through Midnight Worship 121
Chapter 13: A Disappointing Deliverance 129
Chapter 14: Surprising Help from an Anglican Priest 139
Chapter 15: More Healing Grace in Denver 151
Chapter 16: A Hope-Filled Dream of Heaven 163
Part 3: More Gnarly Infections of a Soul Boil Emerge 169
Chapter 17: The Night All God-Given Helps Failed 171
Chapter 18: Severing Thick Roots of Obsessive Compulsiveness ... 191
Chapter 19: A Petri Dish of Inner Emptiness 203
Chapter 20: At the Crossroads of Decision Making 215
Chapter 21: The Final Decision to Move West 227
Part 4: Developing the "New" Me 233
Chapter 22: God Develops My Humanity Through Hardship ... 235
Chapter 23: God Develops My Security by Touching my Past Again ... 247
Chapter 24: God Develops My Inner Identity 261
Chapter 25: God Develops My Trust 273
Chapter 26: God Develops My Ability to Stand in Grace 281
Chapter 27: God Develops My Love 289
Chapter 28: God Develops My Dying to Self 299

Epilogue: My Inner Boil Now and in Eternity 309
Appendix.. 315
A Salvation Creed 317
Biblical Affirmations Concerning God and Divine Healing Today 319
Poems.. 327
Bibliography 329

ACKNOWLEDGEMENTS

WRITING A BOOK IS A GARGANTUAN TASK. I am filled with gratitude for the indispensable help from the following people.

Amy Lively, author and friend, who tackled with wisdom my initial bulky manuscript and provided priceless patience and advice in book writing.

Jon Cook from Keynote Content whose final edit helped me say what I wanted with precision and accuracy.

Julie Little and Nat Weeks for their expertise in proofreading.

Craig Pritchett, long-time friend whose illustrations often communicate better than my written words.

All the people and prayer teams who prayed for me, especially Todd Bramblett of Christian Fellowship Church, who spent hours helping me find the healing touches of Jesus.

Paul Boorujy, president of NEWW Publishing, who took a big chance on a first-time author.

The Elders of Reston Presbyterian Church for their investments of prayer and financial support for me and my family—even when they knew I was never coming back to be their pastor.

All my family and friends whose prayers and financial support during my crises helped me get healthy and get serious with my writing.

My wife Julie who walked with me so faithfully and patiently as I was buried by such a fierce life storm and slowly emerged a new man.

My three children Sarah, Allison, and Nathan who endured an emotionally absent dad for far too much of my journey.

PREFACE

EARLY IN LIFE, I was captured at heart by the sport of wrestling. Not the entertainment stuff you sometimes find while channel-surfing the TV, but the real contest pitting wit, strength, and stamina of one man versus another. In junior high school, I remember going to watch my future high school Haverford wrestle their archrival Ridley. Even though they lost 24-23, I was irresistibly drawn into the high-octane drama between the individuals and teams. I was hooked. As I ventured full-blast into wrestling, little did I know the work I would face, the joys of victory I would taste, the sorrows of defeat I would suffer, nor the life lessons which would spill over as I would learn to wrestle in future life struggles.

It was midway through college after giving up the sport of wrestling when my concentration shifted to wrestling against spiritual opponents with much higher stakes involved. The Bible says we "wrestle" against invisible evil spirits who deftly strategize to work lies into our minds, work over our wills to give into temptation, and shoot an array of painful flaming arrows into our emotions. However, these evil spirits don't attempt to pull us down to the mat for an embarrassing pin in front of a gymnasium full of people. No, the struggle is much greater as they seek to pull us down into the pit of destruction where recovery is daunting, even impossible this side of heaven. While wrestling in the spiritual realm takes place from the beginning of Genesis to the end of Revelation, most people are woefully ignorant both of the demonic force's cunning schemes and the spiritual armor God gives so we can "wrestle well" in the strength God supplies. Scripture and my own life also attest these invisible evil spirits work in concert with our natural sinful tendencies and worldly values to make our opponents often feel insurmountable.

For twenty-three years after seminary, I carried out God's clear calling upon my life in pastoral leadership to help people wrestle well against these formidable forces. While my opposition at times was fierce, even after I was thrown down hard upon the "mat of life," I continuously found myself getting up to wrestle again.

That all changed in the summer of 2010. God permitted and I allowed the enemy to get in close to my soul and launch vicious attacks against me. He launched attacks against my weaknesses, previous wounds, and pockets of wickedness in my own soul, the seriousness of which I was hardly aware. This was to be my "day of evil" about which St. Paul warns against in Ephesians 6:10-13, telling us to "put on the full armor of God," which unfortunately, I was foolishly slow to do, despite my previous encouragement to others to take that same action.

These attacks came in two waves and started one hot summer night in July 2010. The first wave hit hard. I wrestled in my own strength and failed to put on God's armor, so I was knocked out of preaching for three months as the elders saw my condition and encouraged me to get rest and needed help. The next attack exposed what felt like an "inner boil" rising to the surface of my soul, which God knew needed to be painfully lanced, but only with my full cooperation. This soul boil, which fomented for decades in my inner man, was so painful and woven so deeply into the fabric of my inner being that God set me aside from formal ministry on the East Coast.

He sent me into a time of exquisitely hard soul rehabilitation in the mountains of Colorado.

By God's gracious design, through these spiritual attacks, what I suppressed for decades forced itself to the surface of my soul and screamed for my attention through my body and emotions.

I was forced to face my spiritual infections or live with their toxins in my body, emotions, and relationships for the rest of my life. The latter was simply not an option. However, the work I faced felt insurmountable, even with the surprising and gracious ways God powerfully assists.

My soul boil consisted of formidable fears I mostly "managed" for years: performance addictions and strong, even strange obsessive-compulsive behaviors. God revealed an early life trauma subjecting me to a form of post-traumatic stress disorder. This trauma infected in me a fiercely strong coping mechanism of attempted control. My soul boil was filled with my own sinful choices from a multitude of hurts, some of which I allowed to morph into subtle hates. I discovered a plethora of lies lurking not only in my mind, but also distorting my deeper beliefs. Idols or functional gods that I hotly pursued were cutting me off from experiencing the life of God in me. I discovered that my inner man was woefully undeveloped in crucial areas outside of athletic prowess and preaching, which is where I previously poured all my life energy. All of these soul infections and more made anxiety sweep through my soul like wild currents of a swollen river.

Yes, this was *my* story as I discovered both the protection and power of putting on the armor of God. However, a deeper story unfolded as I experienced the truth and love touches of Jesus by His Spirit in the deepest places of my soul. How emotionally delightful it was to discover by His grace the "me" He masterfully created, redeemed and then made, as C.S. Lewis described, "deliciously clean."

This is even more about *His* macro story wisely woven into the fibers of mine by all three Persons of the Godhead. The Father orchestrated my season of suffering for His glory and my growth. Jesus saved me by His incredible work on the cross and powerful resurrection from the grave. The Spirit opened my eyes to the salvation riches graced to us by Jesus and the good ways God grows His life in our souls.

Isaiah the prophet spoke the truth about God's wise redemptive work centuries before the first arrival of Jesus.

"For my thoughts are not your thoughts, neither are your ways my ways, declares the LORD. For as the heavens are higher than the earth, so are my ways higher than your ways and my thoughts than your thoughts."
Isaiah 55:8-9

I invite you to join me by the fire of His fierce love so you might witness the "lancing of my soul" and experience healing for your own. Can you catch His warmth? Can you see the ways of His goodness? This is my story, but in many ways, my friend, this may be your story where you find healing of your own.

PART ONE

The Attack

"But who can endure the day of his coming, and who can stand when he appears? For he is like a refiner's fire and like fullers' soap. He will sit as a refiner and purifier of silver, and he will purify the sons of Levi and refine them like gold and silver, and they will bring offerings in righteousness to the LORD."

— MALACHI 3:2-3

"Simon, Simon, behold, Satan demanded to have you, that he might sift you like wheat, but I have prayed for you that your faith may not fail. And when you have turned again, strengthen your brothers."

— LUKE 22:31-32

Thomas Dages

CHAPTER ONE

The Night It All Began

The chilling cold of night often comes suddenly and without warning.
— *Dr. Terry Wardle*[i]

Fear, like wolves, often runs in packs.
— *Edward Welch*[ii]

IT WAS A SUNDAY NIGHT IN JULY OF 2010, and after a hard week and weekend of work, I crawled into bed to capture my much-needed sleep. As a minister, I had just completed teaching a sermon series on the challenging portion of Scripture called, "The Sermon on The Mount." Preaching faithfully these hard truths from the lips of Jesus, even to a generally receptive congregation, drained me. Fatigue flattened me, and an unusual amount fear swirled around my head as I crawled into bed. While I had learned to cope with such fear and anxiety as unwanted companions throughout much of my life, this night I sensed them circle like wolves above my head, snarling insidiously at deep places in my heart. Hopefully, a good night's sleep would send them back to the margins of my life where I could manage them better the next day.

Jesus has some tough terrain for ministers to preach in His "Sermon on the Mount." That day, I covered a portion of Scripture identifying false prophets and mentioned the name of a modern-day prophet who disturbed the Christian community by unwisely and incorrectly predicting the return of Jesus. I used this man's name as a "false prophet," believing the congregation of listeners would benefit from a concrete modern-day example. My conscience, however, accused me of "judging" this man, and I anxiously wondered if I indeed had done what Jesus warned against elsewhere in this famous sermon found in Matthew chapters five through seven. Even though this preacher's prediction was wrong, he collected lots of money, and he gave a big black eye to the church, my conscience accused me of wrongly judging him in the sermon I had just preached. "You are guilty judging this man," came this poignant ping of accusation in my conscience. As I received the feelings of accusation, guilt and shame, along with anxiety and fear, slowly filled my soul.

I turned to my wife Julie and asked her opinion as I mused on such an accusing thought. I asked Julie for her take on the credibility of such thoughts and whether I was wrong for using this man under the category of "false prophet." After listening to my account and the song of accusation now playing in my mind, Julie said, "How like the enemy to use your sermon and the truth you correctly preached to turn and twist the truth against you! It sounds like the work of the enemy to me." I should have heeded the calm and insightful response of my wife. She clearly identified the voice of the enemy active in my conscience, and her warning should have prompted me to put on God's protective armor against such fiery darts, which were now sticking and starting to burn in my soul. However, I proceeded to analyze, ruminate, stress over, and strive against the voices of fear and my guilt to my own heightened anxiety.

On top of this fear piled on a plethora of other fears. As my head hit the pillow, the gnawing sense of accusations, doubts, and guilt weighed heavily upon me. Fears like, "Your mother really isn't saved because she hasn't been water baptized as a believer," also stung my heart. The truth of her accepting Christ by faith in her early thirties and living such a godly life was very light background music to this fear playing so loudly in my head. Also howling in my heart was the possibility of having my identity stolen as I had recently sent my personal information to an insurance company. Who would see and possibly seize this information I had faxed into a corporate computer? Anxiety riddled me as I thought about having my identity stolen and all that would transpire in getting my life back.

Seemingly inane fears like, "Your daughter Allison will never hit a homerun in the travel softball league she's now playing," also grew to dominate my mind. Then came the rumination of all the small animals suffering under the weight of the pile of dirt dumped outside our lake house cottage in Pennsylvania during a construction project at our family's summer home. The possibility of frogs caught and slowly crushed under the weight of the dirt, trying to get free, started to torment my mind. The voice of accusation speaking to my mind told me, "These animals are suffering because you are responsible as the manager of this project, and you can't stop their suffering."

I took on each of these thoughts, one by one, and tried to dismiss them with my own logic. However, the more I wrestled to dismantle each fear with the powers of my reason, the greater grip they seemed to gain on my mind and heart.

As I wrestled to resist with my own rational reasons as to why these thoughts were untrue, the stress and anxiety continued escalating. Sleep that always visited me quickly was nowhere to be found. The stress ramped up to where I paced around my bedroom, long after Julie was asleep. My pacing went from around my bedroom to around the neighborhood at 2:00 and 4:00 in the morning. Yet nothing could shake my fears, relieve my stress, or help me relax. My reasoning against such a circle of wolves, only ramped up my stress and drove me further away from the sleep I craved.

As I walked up the stairs after pacing the neighborhood, I sensed something in my spirit clearly telling me, "Shut the doors." However, in my mental confusion and fatigue, I didn't make the connection that the Holy Spirit of God was telling me to "shut the doors" or entry points the demons were using to bring fiery darts to stick and burn within my soul and amp up the stress chemicals being released in my body. As spelled out clearly in the New Testament of the Bible, God has given Christ-followers protective armor by which we are to "put on" and "stand in" for our protection, when the enemy launches such fiery accusations and fear into our minds. Most of the time, the Spirit speaks quietly with such warnings, but on this night, He spoke over the fears and stress with great clarity. Yet in my stupor, I failed to heed His clear and gracious warning. These currents of anxiety releasing stress chemicals into my body only grew stronger as the night drifted toward morning.

The next day was a walking nightmare. I was filled to the brim with anxiety, fear, and fatigue, and I felt as though I were locked in a state of anxiety with no key anywhere to be found. I was locked in an emotional prison of another world, yet the prison bars were in my inner man separating me from the peace, restfulness, and sleep that now felt so far away.

Anxiety and fear were by no means new to me. I had lived with these unwanted fiends for years. On occasion, using the Scriptures, I was able to send them away. Many times, I fought against them simply to keep them at bay. Frequently, I stuffed them and occupied myself with other tasks to keep anxiety and fear under control. However, these fears were different. They were unrelenting and seemed to be burrowing deeper and deeper into my soul as I fought them with all the reasoning strength I possessed. These fears pricked wickedness, weaknesses, and wounds that opened deeper into the history of my heart.

I felt like a football player thrown into a circle of other players in practice where the coach calls out the number of a player on the perimeter to run at you and hit you as hard as they can. However, being in the center of the circle, you don't know from where the player is going to come. Your job as a player in the middle is to turn and face each opponent who comes at you viciously from an unknown place on the perimeter, so that you can stay standing.

Coaches do this drill to see if a player can stand their ground from players running at them from all directions. Sometimes, multiple numbers will be called at once. I felt like I was in the midst of such a drill, not with football players I could see, but with unseen formidable foes whom I could not see. I was deep in this drill without wearing any of God's protective armor, like a football player without shoulder pads or helmet!

The next night was full of more mental fighting with the same sleepless results. I ruminated over the same thoughts, paced the same pathways in my room, and walked the same sidewalks around my Reston, Virginia neighborhood. I found myself fighting these disturbing thoughts with the rational reasons of my own strength, all to no avail. The results were again disastrous. A night of even higher stress and anxiety, and again, not a wink of sleep. It was now 48 hours without a wink of sleep. Spiritual and emotional turmoil turned my inner man into a knot, and the tension on both sides of the knot was getting stronger.

Here is an embarrassing reality for this pastor to admit. It took me deep into the second night of sleeplessness to crack open my Bible and ask for the Holy Spirit's aid and counsel. At 4:30 in the morning, I finally got out of bed, went downstairs, and opened the Scriptures to seek God's solace and wisdom in this battle. As I sat down in my green La-Z-Boy chair, filled with hideous anxiety and craving sleep, my Bible seemed to supernaturally open to the following verses.

"Humble yourselves, therefore, under the mighty hand of God so that at the proper time he may exalt you, casting all your anxieties on him, because he

cares for you. Be sober minded; be watchful. Your adversary the devil prowls around like a roaring lion, seeking someone to devour. Resist him, firm in your faith, knowing that the same kinds of suffering are being experienced by your brotherhood throughout the world. And after you have suffered a little while, the God of grace, who has called you to his eternal glory in Christ, will himself restore, confirm, strengthen, and establish you. To him be the dominion forever and ever. Amen."
1 Peter 5:6-11

As I read these words slowly, I knew the Spirit had specifically brought me to this sacred text: these words were for me in my crisis. I was under extreme spiritual attack. The devil and his demons were out for my destruction. They were circling around my soul and attacking me where they sensed I was most vulnerable. The devil was on the prowl, I was in his crosshairs, and his voracious appetite was for my annihilation. I'm sure it wasn't the devil himself, but he has hordes of demons to work his ways of havoc. They knew exactly where and how to target my mind for stress chemicals to ramp up to dangerous levels. As long as I fought in my strength and on their terms, their dangerous attack would continue succeeding. It was up to me to humbly "cast my anxieties upon God" and "resist him," stand firm in my faith, and "in time" God would "restore" me.

I had suffered strategic attacks from the enemy and had let him get in close and stay close to my soul. Do you remember the great boxing matches of the 1970's between Muhammad Ali and Joe Frazier? Most people believe Ali was the better fighter with his incredible quickness and ability to dance. However, occasionally Joe Frazier got in close and landed punishing blows to Ali's ribs. This is where Joe excelled. When a fighter let Joe in close, he could land crushing blows that would inflict great pain, break a fighter's ribs, and take his opponent's breath away. In my case, I let the enemy in close to my mind and soul and allowed him to hit me with stronger and stronger blows. He knew both where and how to inflict the most damage.

I spent two days and nights boxing with the enemy of my soul and suffered great damage. I felt he had knocked me into the corner, but his hits were relentless. I was knocked senseless and continued flailing while my soul slumped in the corner without defense. God awakened me in the midst of this pounding, giving me sacred instruction for fighting in His strength. I had no idea how long or how hard it would be to get space from the enemy's deft blows, gain stability in body and soul, and find healing from old wounds they reopened and punished.

Although I felt gale force winds, I had no idea of the size of the storm that started to crawl slowly across my soul. I had served in the ministry for decades with lots of tape to hold me together, but the enemy, under God's supervision, was about to expose my self-reliant "fighting skills" and a huge spiritual boil that had grown in me for decades.

Practical Wisdom for the Invisible War

If we want to be battle ready, we need to know who our enemy is and the kind of tactics he employs. "Spiritual warfare" is a term we use to highlight the battle which people, especially followers of Jesus, engage in with evil, unseen spirits. In Ephesians 6:10-18, Paul highlights several dimensions of spiritual warfare, so we will fight and wrestle in God's strength and not our own. Recognizing the reality of the battle and the mind tactics the enemy employs, especially by launching lies to the mind, is essential for us to avoid serious injury.

> *"Finally, be strong in the Lord and in the strength of his might. Put on the whole armor of God, that you may be able to stand against the schemes of the devil. For we do not wrestle against flesh and blood, but against the rulers, against the authorities, against the cosmic powers over this present darkness, against the spiritual forces of evil in the heavenly places. Therefore take up the whole armor of God, that you may be able to withstand in the evil day, and having done all, to stand firm. Stand therefore, having fastened on the belt of truth, and having put on the breastplate of righteousness, and, as shoes for your feet, having put on the readiness given by the gospel of peace. In all circumstances take up the shield of faith, with which you can extinguish all the flaming darts of the evil one; and take the helmet of salvation, and the sword of the Spirit, which is the Word of God, praying at all times in the Spirit, with all prayer and supplication. To that end keep alert with all perseverance, making supplication for all the saints, and also for me, that words may be given to me in opening my mouth boldly to proclaim the mystery of the gospel, for which I am an ambassador in chains, that I may declare it boldly, as I ought to speak."*
> Ephesians 6:10-20

First, Paul states that we battle with demons who can be fierce opponents. Demons are the non-flesh invisible "rulers," "authorities," and "cosmic powers" against whom we really wrestle. Our real opponents are not intimidating people whom we can see and touch, but evil spirits working through people and apart from them against our vulnerabilities.

Demons in the Scriptures are fallen angels who followed the rebellion of their leader "Satan" in his attempted rise against God. Scriptures tell us that one-third of the angels followed Satan in his rebellion against God and came to earth to unleash their anger at God by attacking His people (Revelation 12:3-4, 12).

Second, because demons are unseen by the naked eye, they are exceedingly difficult to fight. They are much like terrorists who do their dirty work under the cover of seemingly friendly identities, so they can carry out their covert plans of destruction.

Third, while every day between the first and second coming of Jesus holds potential for conflict with the enemy, there are special days in which the enemy launches especially hard assaults against God's children. This is the "day of evil" for which Paul wisely warns us to prepare. Both Job in the Old Testament and Peter in the New Testament faced days of evil in which their souls, under God's sovereign design, were seriously tested and sifted to see of what they were made. In both Job's and Peter's cases, the devil asked and received permission from God before launching such vicious attacks against these godly men. Their respective "days of evil" were consciously plotted and carried out by the devil for their testing and possible destruction of their faith.

Fourth, God provides the spiritual armor, in the redemptive realities of Jesus and His work on the cross, that we need to "put on" in order to "stand" not only against everyday enemy arrows, but especially in our day of evil when the artillery is heavy and wickedly plotted against us. Yet during these times of attack, we must acknowledge God's strength found in each piece of armor and use this armor to neutralize the enemy's nasty schemes.

One of his favorite schemes is to plant lies in our minds. The more we agree with his lies, the more deeply he and his minions can penetrate our thinking, emotions, behavior, and will to build various strongholds of bondage in our souls. He uses subtle and blatant deception in false doctrine and laces temptations and fears with lies in an attempt to slowly gain control over the human soul. Replacing demonic lies with the truth of Scripture and learning to stand on these truths with faith is the only way we can learn to stand in God's strength.

As I learned early on in the sport of wrestling, if you can control your opponent's head, you can control where the rest of his body goes. My wrestling coach demonstrated to me early on, "WHERE THE HEAD GOES THE BODY MUST FOLLOW!" When a wrestler grabs your head and thrusts it into the mat or off to the side, or pushes your head over your body so that you fall backwards, your body must follow your head. In wrestling, the only way your body doesn't follow your head is if it detaches—and then, you are in real trouble! *So too, demons know that spiritually speaking, this same principle holds true. If they can control your thoughts and beliefs, then your emotions, behaviors, and habits will naturally follow towards destruction.*

Therefore, the biggest battleground between unseen demons and followers of Jesus focuses on the thoughts and beliefs they try to plant and grow in our minds to influence our emotions and behaviors. This is why Scripture says repeatedly that we must, with God's help, on a moment-by-moment basis, make sure our minds are controlled by God's truth and not demonic deception and lies (Romans 12:1-2, 2 Corinthians 10:4-5, Ephesians 4:22-24).

Renewing our minds with God's truth is part of daily worship. It pushes out lies so they cannot grow into strongholds and allows for God to grow His good realities in our souls.

Unfortunately for me, although I believed strongly in the reality of spiritual warfare and its focus on controlling the thoughts and beliefs of the mind, I failed to practice the principle of renewing my mind with any disciplined consistency. I didn't retreat to God and His wisdom by taking a stand with His truth against these lies until deep into my second night of spiritual attack. My "day of evil" arrived and I was unprepared. As a 50-year-old seasoned pastor, I was about to get retrained in Spiritual Warfare 101.

QUESTIONS FOR REFLECTION AND DISCUSSION

1. Do you believe the Bible's witness about demons that they are real, savvy in spiritual warfare, and an ever-present danger to a person's soul?

2. Why would God allow a "day of evil" to assault one of His children?

3. What is the difference between a "day of evil" and a normal tough season of challenge we pass through?

4. Why are the mind and getting people to live by lies the front line of enemy assault?

5. Why would demons plant thoughts in a person's mind which sometimes begin with, "You are guilty," and other times begin with, "I want..." or "I am..."? What kind of temptations might demons be trying to accomplish with each of these planted thoughts?

Thomas Dages

CHAPTER TWO

Getting Up After the Train Wreck

Thankfully I was led to professionals who believe that medication should not mask pain but stabilize a person enough to face it and the underlying wounds that need healing.
— Dr Terry Wardle[iii]

It is important to mention here that I never suggest stopping prescribed medication or interfering in any way a doctor's advice. I often work closely with doctors and therapists; after all, we are all working to the same end: healing the patient. It is extremely powerful to witness such a marriage of science and spirituality.
History and experience have shown that extremes can be dangerous in any field. In healing, it is as dangerous to disregard medicine as it is to forget that human beings are more than physiological machines. I believe that a gentle, loving, and compassionate balance benefits everyone and harms no one.
— Rev Nigel Mumford[iv]

IT IS INDEED SCARY HOW LIFE CAN SO QUICKLY CHANGE. One night you're sleeping like a baby, enjoying rest just moments after your head lands on the pillow. The next night falling asleep seems like an impossible chore. One day, fear is a wolf howling in a distant forest. The next day it feels like it is caged in your own backyard with your door wide open for its entry. One day, anxiety sends only a slight ripple across the pond of your soul. The next day it feels like it is relentlessly scratching the nerves of your stomach. As I sat on my front porch, it felt as if I had been thrown deep into an emotional prison from which only a miracle would provide an escape.

This two-night episode of spiritual attacks signified a ferocious fight for my freedom. My fight started, no doubt, with unseen forces launching their attack into the weaknesses, wounds, and wickedness of my heart and mind, but now, I felt like these dark emotions, and their twin cousin of cortisol-fueled anxiety, had hijacked my mind and body. Two practical questions arose: how could I find sleep, and how could I find freedom from such horrendous anxiety?

First on my list was visiting my medical doctor for a strong sleep aid. I had not slept in 48 hours, and the stress pulsating through my body denied sleep, no matter how much fatigue weighed upon me. It felt physically impossible for me to fall asleep. I knew the importance of sleep for staying sane, so this was my first step for survival. It was off to the doctor's office to find something strong enough to keep me on the right side of sanity.

After listening to an extremely abbreviated version of my sleep struggles, my doctor prescribed Ambien. He gave me a month's supply, which we hoped would do the trick. Ambien proved powerful enough to knock me out, one night at a time. It proved stronger than the stressors being released in my body to send me, night after night, into much-needed sleep.

However, Ambien didn't do anything to reverse the stressors cascading through my mind and body, and I found myself waking up, only after four or five hours, to the same supercharged state Ambien had overcome the previous night. While I welcomed this gift of sleep from this prescription drug, I was still sleep-deprived, and my body and soul both felt hijacked by the stressors stealing my sleep in the first place. How could I calm by mind and body, so my natural God-given rhythm of wakefulness and sleep would return? Concern of developing a dependency on such a strong drug also stirred warranted anxiety. Ambien was effectively putting me to sleep, but something deeper to calm my body and soul was desperately needed.

Every night I would go to bed and attempt to sleep without Ambien. Each night I would rest my head on the pillow at midnight and hope that sleep would naturally come. Even though I was deeply fatigued, sleep never naturally came. No matter how tired my body was, sleep was tantalizingly elusive. Each night after listening to gentle songs of worship and praise, trying hard to trust God for each area of worry which gripped my mind, only Ambien would send me into a synthetically induced slumber. However, the several hours of artificially induced sleep was well behind my needed seven. After several weeks of artificially induced sleep of only four to five hours a night, my body was horribly fatigued, and night by night, only grew worse. My sleep medication was doing nothing to calm my hyper alert state, and my acute anxiety was now spiking to frightening new levels.

The symptoms of my anxiety were working chaos on my body and soul. First, simply getting up in the morning and carrying out the basic functions of the day felt arduous. When your basic responsibilities feel arduous, then the real responsibilities of work, like taking care of people's spiritual needs, preparing and preaching sermons, and leading meetings, can feel like torture. Tending to the needs of my wife and kids was shelved. Functionally, I became my wife's fourth child.

Second, the anxiety at times felt like I had a claw tightening its grip at the base of my neck and the back of my shoulders. There were times when the anxiety was so acute it literally felt like a famished rodent was gnawing away on my stomach. I remember walking through a clothing store with my family and feeling like a rat was munching away, at will, on the inside of my stomach. I hung on for dear life, quoting Scripture, waiting for God's mercy to bring His aid. At other times, I felt like anxiety was building like a volcano, trying to erupt from my inner being, up through my shoulders, and neck into my head, only to find no exit and release point from my body.

With such ferocious anxiety, a stress-filled and fatigued body, and taking such a strong drug for artificially induced sleep, I decided to pay a visit to a Christian psychiatrist, Dr. Curt Thompson, who had previously helped me in other emotional and spiritual struggles. I made many visits with this wise Christian medical doctor, whose gentle and strong assurance of "getting my sleep back on track" brought needed hope to my quivering soul. He also assessed my situation by telling me "I had been hit by a train" and I shouldn't expect to get up and walk away from such an episode in a matter of days.

His counsel for me was to renew my mind with God's truth, and then, he prescribed a large portion of gentle sleep medication and added an anti-anxiety medication which possessed a sleep aid. He also reintroduced me to Zoloft, which had helped in years past to fight depression, obsessive compulsive disorder, and acute anxiety. This helped take the nasty edge off my anxiety and insomnia. My sleep slowly increased to six hours, the anxiety of my gnawing rodent disappeared, the claw in the back of my neck began to abate, and the intensity of the erupting volcano slowed its surging.

While I thank God for all my medications, they need to be given under the guidance of doctors who know their patients. It is also essential to seek out wise counseling so physical, emotional, and spiritual issues all might be prudently pricked and addressed. However, with the popularity of helpful anxiety-reducing medications, for many counselees, the deeper fallacious beliefs, distorted thought patterns, and deeper twisted soul desires, which are causing disturbances in the first place, are frequently left unaddressed. In my past, my symptom reduction primarily from Zoloft brought great relief, but it also allowed me to skirt past my brewing soul storms to get on with my busy life.

Yet burying issues alive only deepens them and puts off possibly more disruptive emergences from the soul issues. My clinical depression, experienced at approximately ages 20, 30, 40, and 45, should have been warnings to me to do extended "soul work" with a redemptive counselor wise in the Spirit's wisdom of soul and body and the currents of personal sin that can dangerously rip through deep places of the heart, disrupting everything in the inner man. Zoloft was great for symptom relief and keeping needed serotonin in the body, but it didn't heal the issues that were possibly depleting my body's serotonin in the first place.

Practical Wisdom for the Invisible War

Dr. Curt Thompson was the first counselor to care for me in the wake of this severe storm. His groundbreaking book, *The Anatomy of the Soul*, weaves together fascinating connections between mind and body and how spiritual disciplines can promote soul-transforming changes. His book and personal help were fascinating, insightful, and hopeful. Below are several of the most helpful tools Dr. Thompson suggested for my recovery from my "train wreck," which are elaborated more fully and insightfully in his book.

First, Dr. Thompson taught me how to do five-count deep breathing exercises. Sitting comfortably in a chair, I drew a long breath inward (for five counts) with my lips pursed until my diaphragm was filled, then I exhaled with the same five count. Our breath is symbolic of the Holy Spirit (*Ruach* in the Hebrew) who cleanses and relaxes us with His comforting presence. I started out these deep breathing exercises in small doses of several minutes and worked up to half an hour at a time.

Anxious people have a hard time simply sitting down to practice this; but practicing each day for prolonged periods of time enables the anxious person to increasingly focus on God and His gracious presence within. I found it very helpful to "breathe in" the name "Jehovah" (taking five counts) and "breathe out" "Jireh" (five counts), which means, "The LORD—who is my provider." This was a practical way for me to learn to build my trust in God and place my body and soul in such a relaxed state.

Dr. Thompson also suggests in his book to practice more diligently the biblical axiom of renewing the mind. He cites Hebb's axiom as a helpful way to remember the power of renewing our minds. Donald Hebb, a Canadian psychologist, produced neuropsychological research on learning and memory out of which grew Hebb's axiom, which states, "neurons that fire together wire together."[v] Dr. Thompson insightfully clarifies this axiom:

"In other words, neurons that repeatedly activate in a particular pattern are statistically more likely to fire in that same pattern the more they are activated. Once the initial neurons in a network fire, there is a very high probability that the related neurons will also activate and move along the same bioelectrical pathway to the end of that network without veering off to some other set of neurons."[vi]

A mini lesson from Dr. Thompson about our brain's anatomy helps us understand the influence renewing our minds can have on our brains.

"The human brain is composed of approximately 100 billion neurons, or brain cells. These cells come in different forms and serve different purposes, but their general way of functioning is similar. They communicate with each other biochemically at points of connection called synapses. Actually, a synapse is not a point of literal contact, but rather the very narrow space (called the synaptic cleft) between the neurons themselves. It is across the

synaptic cleft (each only about 20 nanometers −20 millionths of a millimeter−in width) that each neuron signals its neighbor through biochemical messengers. Each cell has the capacity to synapse with up to approximately 10,000 other cells. For you math whizzes, that means that the total number of possible connecting patterns between all these neurons is virtually infinite. Not literally so, but almost."[vii]

I knew and taught the biblical truth about renewing the mind for changes to occur in my soul, but I only practiced this exercise of wholeness and holiness on a sporadic basis. Now, Dr. Thompson gave me a lesson on the small brain changes that would result from a fastidious renewal of my mind. Every time I caught myself thinking a lie and changed my thoughts to think and practice a corresponding truth, my neural highways were microscopically rewiring in ways that promoted my soul's wholeness.

What I took from this lesson and past reading was to realize that the way I chose to think and dwell upon good thoughts not only influenced the development of wholesome neural highways, but it also impacted the chemicals releasing across my synapses! Why rely totally on medication when I could have such a powerful influence on the chemicals and neural development of my own brain?

The Scriptures teach repetitively the power of renewing our mind for transformation to take place in our souls. In Romans Paul says:

---

*"Do not be conformed to this world, but be **transformed by the renewal of your mind**, that by testing you may discern what is the will of God, what is good and acceptable and perfect."*
Romans 12:2 (emphasis mine)

Interestingly, the word "transformed" comes from the Greek word we translate as "metamorphosis," reflecting the transformation of a caterpillar changing into a butterfly. What a drastic change that takes place when a crawling caterpillar bursts forth from a cocoon into a beautiful free-flying butterfly! What a newfound freedom and beauty the butterfly possesses through this process. This is a vivid word picture of the transformative change God brings to those whose spiritual worship consists of a moment by moment renewing of the mind. Renewing the mind away from dark lies with God's truth is that powerful. Yet the change into butterfly beauty and freedom doesn't happen as quickly for human beings. **Every person will crawl like a caterpillar until the biblical process of renewing the mind becomes a God-assisted lifestyle!**

However, as Dr. Thompson suggests, to change old established thought patterns can feel like using a machete to clear away a path in a thickly overgrown jungle forest.[viii] Yet the more we use the machete to cut away lusts, worries, self-pity, pride, selfish and self-hateful thinking and replace these thought patterns with genuine love, trust, thankfulness, humility, servanthood, and self-acceptance and act upon these truths, the more the neurological highways in our brains change for the good, and the easier it becomes to think in such ways in the future.

My oldest daughter Sarah recently told me, "Dad, I wish we could design our own brains." By "design" Sarah meant enjoying greater brain capacities and choosing specialized abilities. I thoughtfully responded by telling her of the significant influence over a lifetime **we do** have on our brains through the moment-by-moment Spirit-led choices we make that can lead to brain wholeness and development. God is the designer of our brains, but with our cooperation of steadfastly renewing our minds with His truth over a lifetime, substantial brain changes to our neurological development and brain chemistry can be expected.

QUESTIONS FOR REFLECTION AND DISCUSSION

1. Are good medications prescribed under a wise doctor's care sometimes helpful and even a necessity?

2. How can medication for symptom relief, of say anxiety, sometimes obscure the deeper issues of the soul needing mind renewal?

3. What do you say to a person who says a Christian should never need or take medication?

4. Is it hopeful to realize a steadfast renewing of one's mind can help facilitate substantial brain health over the course of a lifetime?

5. If "neurological pathways that fire together wire together" are a result of our chosen thought patterns, what unhealthy thought patterns (i.e lust, self-pity, selfishness, worry, self-sufficiency) are most deeply wired together in your mind?

Thomas Dages

CHAPTER THREE

Seeking Relief on Vacation

Every man is in a war, but not every man is at war.
— *Bill McCartney*

FORTUNATELY, RIGHT ON THE HEELS of my middle-of-the-night visitation from powerful unseen enemies, propelling me into my rock-solid insomnia and off-the-charts anxiety, I was scheduled to get away on my annual two weeks of vacation. What great timing this was for me and my family.

I serve in a denomination (The Evangelical Presbyterian Church) that is very generous in work benefits for their ministers. They mandate that each church offer four weeks of paid vacation to their teaching elders. When I had proposed to my wife Julie nearly 20 years earlier, I promised her I would take all the vacation offered for the sake of our family. I had stayed true to this promise up to this point and was even more than eager to do so again this year. I saw this summer's vacation as a chance to get back a good portion of my emotional and physical health that was stolen in my "train wreck."

So, it was off to our lake house in the Endless Mountains of Pennsylvania. My parents purchased this idyllic mountain cottage on Lake Mokoma when I was just six years old. A cottage on a lake peninsula, great blueberry picking, pies and pancakes, swimming, hiking and boating, and last but not least, fishing. Over the years, fishing became my momentary escape ticket away from stress and ministerial responsibility and into the beauty of God's wilderness creation. Coaxing and catching fish and wrestling them into the boat provided relaxing competition, which I could do for hours at a time. Arriving at the cottage and dipping into the many refreshing activities, you can feel anxieties lift off your shoulders and dissipate into the refreshing mountain air. My parents (Dr. Robert and Phyllis) and my siblings (Bill, Sue, Dave, and Bob) and many other families and friends have used this cottage as a place of deep soul restoration for the nearly half-century we have owned it. My pending vacation at our lake cottage seemed like just what the Great Physician had ordered.

The lake cottage was not only a getaway from escalating tensions in our frenetic society, but it was also a place to hide away and get lost in a good book. My mother accumulated many soul-nourishing books over the years, and the quietness of the cottage enabled me to hear much more easily the whisper of God to my soul. Whether it was reading sacred Scripture, savoring one of the plethora of soul-stimulating books Mom acquired, or cutting across the lake quietly in our canoe, the gentle voice of God seemed much more audible in this holy place of restoration.

When our family finally arrived after our four-and-a-half-hour drive from Northern Virginia, we greeted my mom with generous hugs. I crashed into one of the many chairs in our living room surrounded by fifteen windows, letting in the beauty of the lake and its pine forest perimeter. It should be no surprise that a new book Mom had purchased entitled, *Spiritual Warfare: Terms of Engagement* by Dr. David Jeremiah piqued my curiosity as it sat out by itself on the table next to me. While I didn't hear God say, "Take up and read," as Augustine did, the book did stir my curiosity as to what this well-known pastor and preacher had to say about a topic in which my soul was deeply engaged. By the second or third day of our cottage stay, my leafing through its pages turned into serious reading. As I read, the Spirit seemed to impress upon my spirit concrete ways of putting on God's armor for my spiritual protection. As Dr. Jeremiah wisely says, "God provides the armor, but we provide the putting on of the armor. Not even God's armor can be a defensive weapon if we go into battle without it."[ix]

He also summarizes the power of God's armor this way:

"As we get further into the details of the Christian's armor, it will become apparent that to put on the armor of God is to put on the Lord Jesus Christ Himself. Paul wrote in Romans 13:14, 'But put on the Lord Jesus Christ, and make no provision for the flesh, to fulfill its lusts.' Everything the armor represents, Christ is: truth, righteousness, peace, faithfulness, salvation, and the living Word of God. The seven verses describing the armor of God (Ephesians 6:11-17) are a commentary of the first seven words of Romans 13:14. Clothed in the Lord Jesus Christ, we are clothed in the armor of God. But it is our responsibility to make sure that we have put on Christ, put on the armor, and that we stay clothed continually in order to remain protected."[x]

This vacation was to be not only a time of relaxation, but a crash course in practicing "putting on" God's protective armor, both to regain ground lost to the enemy and to fortify me for future battles.

It is startling to think that 60% of professing Christians believe Satan is only a symbol of evil and not real.[xi] Such people are easy food as Satan's prey. This was not me, however, I have always believed Satan and his minions to be a real, personal, and present danger. My weakness lay in failing to practically wrestle in God's strength by putting on Christ to stand against the devil's exceptionally crafty schemes.

My vacation for restoration also took me an hour's drive north to visit dear friends, Jim and Cynthia Eckert. Jim and Cynthia faithfully served at Reston Presbyterian Church, and our terms overlapped by three years. They decided to retire on a farm owned by Cynthia's side of the family. The elders at Reston decided to give Jim the title of elder "Emeritus," and I took this vacation opportunity to take in their wisdom for the seismic battle engulfing my soul.

Jim and Cynthia listened well and prayed compassionately for my healing. They both could see how emotionally distraught I was, the weight loss I had suffered, my craving for natural sleep, and how deeply I was locked behind bars of anxiety and fear that I desperately wanted to escape. The last day I spent with them, Jim read to me excerpts from the spiritual giant A.W Tozer and encouraged me to win back lost ground to the enemy by a steadfast renewing of my mind with God's truth.

Two incidents occurred on this vacation excursion to the Eckert's farm, giving me deeper insights into the depths of God's mercy and how deeply I was wounded in my current spiritual attacks.

First, God revealed His mercy while I was on a walk around a rather long rural block in the Eckert's neighborhood. It was an unusually sunny day and about halfway around this mile or so block, as I crested a hill, a cloud of deep depression fell suddenly upon me. It fell upon my mind and heart with such a deep and sudden darkness and touched my heart with a previously unknown and frightening depth of despair. The darkness of this cloud with its strength upon me contrasted with the bright sunshine, penetrating my whole body. The strength of this cloud falling upon me was eerily overwhelming. It was like a dark cloud of depression suddenly ensconced me and plunged me into its low-pressure center. Never have I felt engulfed in such intense blackness. How would I fight such a stubborn deep darkness and prevail? The intensity of such blackness made my other times of depression feel like light inconveniences in comparison.

However, after a moment in such hell, the depression lifted and left as quickly as it had landed. In my spirit, I sensed God's mercy and the intuitive message that "this is how bad it could be," and that

God was showing me the limitations he was placing on the enemy's assaults.

On top of this grace awakening, on a stroll around this farmland neighborhood came an experience that demonstrated just how my "train wreck" was taking its toll on my physical health. On the next afternoon as I lay in bed trying to sleep, I began to hear what sounded like an electrical current zapping in my head. It was like the electrical current in my brain suddenly came out of its normal silent mode to let me know things were out of order and I was running on too many RPMs. This popping sound started slowly, but then increased so that the popping was very fast, with little time between pops. It then settled into a constant flow of firing with no intermittent pauses. This popping noise probably lasted only for a few minutes. However, as I wondered what was happening, it seemed frighteningly long. Fortunately, it did die down so that again the work of my brain was peacefully quiet.

As I drove back to our lake house for the rest of my vacation, it became apparent that finding rest and sleep on my vacation, no matter how long or how idyllic the place, "vacation" was not going to bring me back to find the rhythms of sleep and peace for which I longed.

Practical Wisdom for the Invisible War

I'm convinced that if you asked most confessing Christians today to tell you the pieces of armor that God gives to us for our protection in the fight against evil, most would not be able to list them, and more importantly, would not know how to practically put on their armor.

I had a good friend and fellow elder in the first church where I served at Bear Creek Presbyterian Church, whose name was Mike Bahm. Mike prayed for me on many occasions when I found myself fighting deception and temptation, exacerbated by the enemy. Mike's most important line to me was, "I see a soldier fully dressed and ready for battle!" By saying this, Mike was both reminding me of where my strength lay (fighting in God's armor) and calling me to put on God's armor. What a great way for a friend to call another friend to put on the armor and stand in God's strength and protection.

I knew a few pieces of armor and used the Scriptures as "the sword of the Spirit" to fend myself from temptation and mind deception at critical junctures in life, but my knowledge and use of all the armor was sporadic at best.

The first piece of armor given by Paul in Ephesians 6:14 reads, "Stand, therefore, having fastened on the belt of truth." What is this belt of truth, and how do we put it on to stand firm in God's strength?

Dr. Jeremiah has an insightful explanation for this belt of truth. Picture a Roman soldier with a long garment falling down near his feet. He also has a belt around his waist that he could use to tuck in the extra material, pulling it away from his feet so that he can advance into battle without tripping. This belt is, therefore, a picture of gathering in the loose thoughts of our minds that cause us to stumble in spiritual battle. If we live according to demonic lies directing our thoughts, it will greatly cripple how we fight and cause us to stumble on the battlefield of life. In the New King James version, Peter puts it this way: "Therefore, gird up the loins of your mind…" (1 Peter 1:13).[xii]

My first two nights of battle I lived as though the accusations, condemnations, fears, anxieties, and false guilts were true and didn't tuck them into the belt of truth to live according to the reality of my redemption in Jesus Christ taught in Scripture. Therefore, I was stumbling as a soldier all over the battlefield of life! Fighting in the strength of my own logic simply opened more doors to let the enemy burrow deeper into my mind and emotions, sending stress chemicals careening through my body.

As Areon Potter has pointed out:

"Bear in mind it is not God's job to gird the believer's mind with truth. That is the job of each individual. When Peter talked about girding up the loins of the mind, the sentence structure is in the imperative; we are to do the girding."[xiii]

Therefore, the first piece of armor commanded by God for the believer to put on as they advance into battle is a mind guarded, protected, and saturated by the redemptive truths of our Lord Jesus Christ.

QUESTIONS FOR REFLECTION AND DISCUSSION

1. Why is it essential to know the redemptive truth each piece of armor represents and how to put it on in battle?

2. Why is self-reliance so ineffective in spiritual warfare? What spiritual vice is underneath self-reliance?

3. Why won't God put the armor on for us?

4. Why do you think the belt of truth is given as the first piece of armor?

5. Does God expect us to renew our minds with His truth: (1) at Christmas and Easter, (2) once a week, (3) daily, (4) moment by moment as needed? What is your practice?

PART TWO

Surprises of God's Supernatural Assistance

"Now to him who is able to do far more abundantly than all that we ask or think, according to the power at work within us, to him be glory in the church and in Christ Jesus throughout all generations, forever and ever. Amen."
— EPHESIANS 3:20–21

Thomas Dages

CHAPTER FOUR

Prayer Miracles Begin with the Elders

Nothing sets a person so much out of the devil's reach as humility.
—Jonathan Edwards[xiv]

николай **EARLY ONE MONTH PASSED** after the onslaught of my spiritual warfare sent my life spiraling down class-five emotional, spiritual, and physical rapids. I was caught in these rapids with a paddle of faith but didn't know how to negotiate my way safely to the riverbank. Yet I was trying feverishly to do so. It became clear my healing was going to be an extended season and God would use all kinds of prayer to bring the flow of His healing grace to my heart. The people and their prayer care, which God raised up for my help and healing, were nothing short of amazing.

I needed to humbly admit my needs to the elders and the congregation. Soon after this spiritual hurricane hit, I shared with the elders how I was suddenly derailed. I explained what transpired in my all-night spiritual stressors, how long it took me to put on God's armor, and how God had spoken so clearly through 1 Peter 5 about the spiritual attack on my soul. They listened carefully, non-judgmentally, and compassionately. We decided I needed some time of concentrated prayer. According to the book of James, elders of faith and godliness are to anoint with oil and pray over God's sick people as they are requested (James 5:13-16).

I had prayed over many ill-struck people for healing during my ministry; however, now as a suffering elder, I was in need of this prayer and promised healing for myself. According to James, my responsibility was to confess any known sin that may have been a genesis or an open door for my current state of illness, the elders were to pray in faith, and the resurrected Lord Jesus would bring His power to heal. **Through this process the Lord Jesus was about to flex His healing powers in ways delightful and novel to my soul.**

The first healing movement of His Spirit occurred in the basement of our associate pastor's home. It was during the prayer time of our monthly business meeting when we decided my life needed the lion's share of our prayer efforts. James is clear that if we pray in faith, meeting the conditions set forth in James 5:13-16, we can expect healing to come. He doesn't promise when or how the healing will come, but healing, in His time, is nevertheless promised.

I reflected on my life and confessed any known sin God brought to mind. Not only did I confess my self-reliance in spiritual warfare, but I also confessed a work ethic that too easily got sidetracked and distracted by computer non-essentials on Saturday nights. By this, I mean that I found myself frittering away precious time by tracking football games and hockey games on Saturday nights when all focus was supposed to be on finalizing and praying over the all-important sermon the next day. I wasn't involved in anything as serious as internet porn, yet this habit of tracking sports results and games eroded my work ethic and interfered with preparing for worship the next day. If I counted up the hours during the month that my computer took away from loving God and people, it was a fairly substantial issue.

At this point, I admit I may have been "belly gazing" and hypersensitive to my possible sins, but I didn't want to leave any rock unturned and miss anything the Holy Spirit was gently urging me to confess for my cleansing and healing. Failure of specific confession can be a serious roadblock to divine healing, and I didn't want to miss anything God was bringing to my attention.

Confession of sin, especially public confession, is humbling. It was hard to open up and share with the elders where a lifestyle of laziness was secretly living, a lifestyle that drained the very spiritual vitality needed to nurture souls. Unfortunately, because of possible pride and discomfort, this all-important principle of confession of sin is often skipped when elders anoint with oil and pray over God's people. While it is hard to raise the issue of possible sin as a causal root in people's sickness, nevertheless, it needs to be sensitively done. As elders, we shouldn't be shocked when sin in all its ugliness comes forth from the lips of confession, and if people fear judgment from those who are listening, they might stay closed and fail to come clean and stifle the healing process God may be stirring.

Oil was placed on my forehead, and I felt their hands rest lovingly upon me. Then, I heard each of their voices ask Jesus for His healing power to flow into me. While they all prayed insightfully, each petition was full of faith and compassion. After each elder prayed to God through Jesus, the Spirit unquestionably moved in my inner man. I felt a knot of anxiety untwist in my gut as though someone was pulling on just the right string to undo this knot. As this knot of anxiety suddenly released, I felt something slip away from my soul. A small yet palpable release of anxiety ensued.

From my knees I spoke up to the men who were surrounding me and told them what had just occurred. I also sensed a quiet but clear message in my mind to "pray more." However, I was so relieved by the sudden release and departure of this anxiety knot, I didn't communicate to the elders this "pray more" message. We would pray for a little while longer, and as it turned out, this was just the beginning of many more sessions of prayer with a variety of teams.

Several weeks later, I had an "epochal" encounter with God. Once again Jesus moved overwhelmingly through the elders' use of oil, love, and prayers of faith. This time, we met at my church office.

I vividly recall fighting fatigue as I drove myself to church on that hot August Saturday afternoon. I arrived before the other elders did, and I found a piece of mail addressed to me from Dr. Jeff Jeremiah, the Stated Clerk of the Evangelical Presbyterian Church. How encouraging to read the following words as I prepared for another prayer session with the elders: "Tom, as I've been praying through our church directory for all the ministers of the Presbytery of the East, The Lord has continually brought your name to my mind. Let me know if there is anything I can pray specifically about for you..."

Wow! What a surge of encouragement to know the good Lord was prompting another elder to continually pray for me, one who was 3,000 miles away and hadn't heard from any human being what I was presently encountering. As our elders arrived for our next prayer session together, I communicated what Dr. Jeremiah wrote, which encouraged us all that God was stirring behind and through our prayers.

We followed the same general procedures as in our first formal prayer time together. I again confessed any known rebellion in my life that could have opened up a door and given opportunity for demonic harassment in my life. I again took a kneeling posture, the elders gathered around me, and anointed my head with oil.

THE LANCING OF MY SOUL

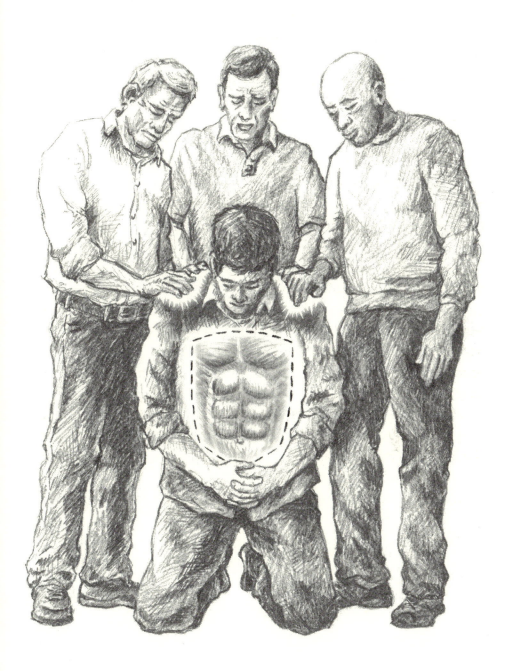

As the elders prayed, one of them, Larry Simpson, vocalized a specific prayer request from Paul's prayer in Ephesians 3:14-19, "that you, being rooted and grounded in love, may have strength to comprehend with all the saints what is the breadth and length and height and depth, and to know the love of Christ that surpasses knowledge." Larry prayed the gist of this prayer that I would know and be filled with the love of Christ in my inner man. As he prayed, I suddenly felt an incredible strength well up inside me. It felt like the borders of my entire inner man were traced by the finger of God. With this "tracing" The Holy Spirit identified my inner me and filled me with incredible power. I once again told the elders what I was experiencing as it was happening.

I previously experienced encounters with God's supernatural peace, overwhelming love, and deep joy in the past, but I had never felt such an encounter with tremendous strength marking out what felt like borders of my inner man. It all happened so quickly, powerfully, and definitively as the elders prayed over me. While I didn't sense any "deliverance" as in our last encounter, I did sense His powerful presence on the outer borders of my inner man. It was as if God, by His Spirit, was marking out the territory of my soul as His and laying the groundwork of His powerful presence for where He was going to strengthen my inner man.

Practical Wisdom for the Invisible War

The last piece of armor in Ephesians 6:11-18 that Paul delineates is called "all prayer." Paul says in Ephesians 6:18:

> *"Praying at **all** times in the Spirit, with **all** prayer and supplication. To that end keep alert with **all** perseverance, making supplication for **all** the saints"* (emphasis mine).

One kind of prayer James teaches is corporate prayer for healing of the sick. James tells us if we seek healing for an illness, we are to call for the elders of the church for their anointing with oil, and the laying on of their hands with prayers of faith.

> *"Is anyone among you suffering? Let him pray. Is anyone cheerful? Let him sing praise. Is anyone among you sick? Let him call for the elders of the church, and let them pray over him, anointing him with oil in the name of the Lord. And the prayer of faith will save the one who is sick, and the Lord will raise him up. And if he has committed sins, he will be forgiven. Therefore, confess your sins to one another and pray for one another, that you may be healed. The prayer of a righteous person has great power as it is working."*
> James 5:13-16

This passage calls for at least three conditions to be met for sick people to find healing in the name of our Lord Jesus.

First, the sick must humbly call on the elders for their prayers of faith. Understandably, in this age of science and medication, doctors are often depended upon solely for healing through medication and surgeries. This is unfortunate and can be one reason that deeper soul healing is not experienced by more Christians seeking help. While I have found my share of great help through surgery for cancer and a hip replacement, we must ask ourselves why we so reflexively and exclusively go to physicians for help. In doing so, we may miss the cleansing of sin and healing of the soul, which in some situations can be the deeper issues of the afflicted body-soul matrix.

Let me say it again, I'm not against doctors and helpful medications and surgeries to manage illness and cut out cancers and bad joints. I had been prayed for by elders on several prior occasions with positive healing results that brought medical realities to bear on my healing. On one occasion, at my first church in Lakewood, Colorado, where I served as an associate pastor, I endured ten years of excruciating hip pain and felt on the edge of desperation. I needed pain relief and needed it fast, so the elders gathered together to pray over me for my healing. It was later that week that the name of an acupressure therapist came across my desk whose therapy significantly reduced my acute pain. This kind of therapy managed my pain until a doctor, some 20 years later, cut out and replaced my bad hip! God uses doctors and physical therapists as His instruments of healing.

Second, godly elders must pray in faith to God for healing. Our elders need to pray in faith, expecting the resurrected Lord Jesus to heal, but they first must be clothed by faith in the righteousness of Christ as the foundation of their righteousness. After this, they need to practice the kind of righteousness life James and all the biblical authors command. A lifestyle of practical righteous living (faith, works, love, prayer, justice for the oppressed, honesty, non-hypocritical living, and self-control over the tongue and lust) need to be evidenced in their lives. Too often, churches choose elders because of their business acumen and success or worldly leadership tactics and miss out on the foundational and practical godliness elders **most** need to qualify for leadership in God's house.

Finally, the sick person needs to confess any sin which may be the cause of their intense or extended suffering. This question needs to be dealt with very delicately. On the one hand, telling a suffering person that their suffering or sickness is due to their personal sin can be cruel and as wrongheaded as Job's "friends" who were convinced Job's sin lay behind his massive misfortunes. A person's suffering may have NOTHING to do with their sin, and everything to do with Adam's sin and death leading to decay and disease, which touched all humanity. It may also be due to a divine mystery, like Job, which may not be known this side of heaven.

Also, examples in church history abound of saintly people who carry suffering as an instrument of witness and soul refinement for God's glory. Joni Erickson Tada is one of many saintly sufferers who apparently will have to wait for full sight of Jesus to end her pain and suffering. Paralyzed as a teenager in a diving accident, Joni believed and prayed for physical healing. Yet her soul healing and radiant joyful testimony of God's enabling presence has drawn scores of people either to come to saving faith in Christ or to give courage to saints living under the fire of their own suffering for the fulfilment of divine purposes.

To see and hear Joni is to get a clear glimpse of Jesus living through her suffering. Shame on the Christians who have said she lacks healing simply because she lacks faith! God is doing bigger things in the lives of His blood-bought children than to bring immediate relief from the suffering we may despise, yet which may be the very tool God uses for others' salvation and for our own shaping into the image of Jesus.

Elders who pray in faith and people who penitently confess in humility must be wise in the full view of such redemptive dynamics in suffering and illness. Answered prayer for healing and suffering can look vastly different in the lives of the saints He loves and whom He chooses to uniquely chisel.

On the other hand, it is equally foolish to pray over a person who may be living under God's direct chastisement for their flagrant rebellion against God and skip the possibility of personal sin altogether. Sensitivity to the Holy Spirit and the one being prayed over is of utmost importance, as many of their sin issues may be wrapped up in deep heart issues, which have been covered over and hidden away for decades. Suffering is one of the ways God can get our attention and force us to face these issues that would otherwise go unaddressed.

I have found, personally, to take prayerful reflection of sin seriously in my own life. On many occasions in my depression, anger, and self-pity, unwholesome thinking like worry, false guilt and unhealthy control were playing a definitive part. Asking God for guidance and strategic repentance has opened doors of refreshment to my life. While sensitivity needs to be practiced, the questions of sinful attitudes and practices need to be asked, in love, by wise and discerning and humble elders (who have been humbled sufficiently by their own sin).

QUESTIONS FOR REFLECTION AND DISCUSSION

1. Have you ever called upon the elders to pray over you? If so, describe your experience.

2. Why can prayer and confession be considered acts of humility?

3. What is the significance of faith, elders of godly character, and anointing with oil for healing to occur? Is any one of these more important than the others?

4. If the sickness is due to the consequences of sin in one's life, and one doesn't confess in humility, can that person still expect God to heal them?

5. Why might "more prayer" be needed in cases of deep emotional healing or where spiritual strongholds might exist?

Thomas Dages

CHAPTER FIVE

Truth Comes Alive in the Imagination

The soul without imagination is what an observatory would be without a telescope.
— Henry Ward Beecher[xv]

...Imagery enriches our grasp of reality.
— Bruce Demarest[xvi]

The imagination has gotten a bad rap in the Christian community.
—Peter Kuiper

*For this reason, because I have heard of your faith in the Lord Jesus and your love toward all the saints, I do not cease to give thanks for you, remembering you in my prayers, that the God of our Lord Jesus Christ, the Father of glory, may give you a spirit of wisdom and revelation in the knowledge of him, **having the eyes of your hearts enlightened**, that you may know what is the hope to which he has called you, what are the riches of his glorious inheritance in the saints, and what is the immeasurable greatness of his power toward us who believe, according to the working of his great might...*
— Ephesians 1:15-19 (emphasis mine)

PRAY MORE was the clear word the Holy Spirit laid on my heart the first time the elders prayed over me—and pray we did. The elders, my immediate and extended family, friends past and present, and people of Reston Presbyterian Church, all amped up their prayer petitions for my embattled soul.

God in His mercy moved me into the prayer-care of two other churches experiencing the healing touch of Jesus in their healing prayer ministries. My prayer experiences were previously limited to personal time with God, lifting up people for initial salvation and the immediate physical hurts they suffered. Now, however, God was raising up faith-filled churches to extend this prayer power of the Holy Spirit to move His present healing touch into my past traumas with truth in picture form through my right-brain imagination for a deeper integration and healing in my soul. The touch of Jesus upon my hurting history was about to open up a new chapter of healing in my life, and my old wounds were about to be touched with the redemptive realities of Jesus like never before.

I had minimized and marginalized such workings of the Holy Spirit in the past and the need for such emotional healing, but now with my own hidden wounds being exposed and God communicating such grace to me by His Spirit, through my own imagination, these fresh "healing" ways of God could not be denied. Our small, conservative group of elders had seen God move in fresh and powerful ways in our own corporate prayer times, and now they were willing to hand me off to other prayer teams more seasoned in these fresh ways of the Spirit to which we were all unaccustomed.

These two evangelical churches (one Anglican and the other a large Community Bible Church) were geographically located in two entirely different directions from my home in Reston. The Falls Church was located directly east, just inside the Washington Beltway, and took me 45 minutes fighting through northern Virginia traffic. Christian Fellowship was located directly west in Ashburn, VA, about 25 minutes through traffic. These two churches were like specialty hospitals that would focus their faith through sessions of healing prayer over my soul. Both "healing prayer" ministries relied entirely on the Holy Spirit, for only He can best expose hurting pasts that were buried alive and reveal redemptive truth in word pictures to ignite healing and wholeness through Christ's power in our heart's deepest places.

Ron Huggins was my contact at the Falls Church. He and his prayer partner, Chuck Cook, met with me on several occasions to listen and pray over me in regard to the serious issues that suddenly seized me. Both Ron and Chuck were well seasoned in praying for people in their church and had seen God's strong healing touches in people's lives. I went away from my meetings with them often sensing new direction, fresh breezes of grace, and powerful periods of peace. As I would learn, answered prayer does not always end our problems abruptly, but often it gives the momentary provision we need to keep moving forward in faith and divine insights into the deeper problems of the soul.

These two men were willing to continue praying with me, as Ron had actually built a prayer chapel on top of his garage for such purposes. Yet the travel distance and my already meeting regularly with another geographically closer prayer team, along with the encouragement of one of our own elders to focus on one group, moved me to concentrate my efforts with Christian Fellowship.

Todd Bramblett was my contact with Christian Fellowship Church in Ashburn. Todd was leading a burgeoning "healing prayer" ministry in which God was working with His powerful presence. Todd and his prayer partners spent hours praying with me. It is not an overstatement to say I was desperate. Desperate for God to clarify my heart issues and touch these areas of trauma, stubbornness, and twistedness with His healing grace. Often, we don't come to God in desperate prayer until we feel we're going to crack under life's pressure, or in my case, until we feel at the breaking point of anxiety and insomnia. I was in prison for sure, but I was carrying this emotional prison in me wherever I went. Healing prayer is the cry of the heart for God to touch the sore areas of our soul, the depths where human means cannot reach with human touch, talk therapy, or medication.

Shortly after the elders prayed over me for the second time and my inner being felt suddenly surrounded by His incredible strength, I attended a healing prayer seminar at Christian Fellowship Church where the teacher taught on God's movement in the life of Gideon from the book of Judges (chapters 6-7). Gideon was an Old Testament judge called and empowered by God to be a valiant warrior. Yet he felt anything but a valiant warrior! He needed the courage of God to venture out, against great odds (humanly speaking), to lead God's army into victory. However, with Gideon's eyes of faith focused on God, God used Gideon's leadership to defeat the Midianites with an army purposely pared down to 300 soldiers. God ministered courage directly into Gideon's inner being despite the overwhelming logic of man.

While the Friday night teaching was insightful, nothing dramatic happened. Nevertheless, I made sure to have a group of people pray over me before leaving the seminar and heading home to Reston.

That was when the move of God's Holy Spirit was deliciously released in me. I arrived at my home and retreated to my couch. As I thought about Gideon's story and how the Spirit of God moved upon Gideon, the Spirit moved mightily in me. It was like God's Spirit started to massage my inner man with the touch of His strength and love, which literally began absorbing my anxieties. I didn't do anything except receive and enjoy His love and strength as God's Spirit rested upon me and released Himself into my inner being. It was as if I were hooked up to a love IV drip, drop by drop releasing liquid love and strength into my soul. The drops of liquid love and strength not only deposited God's presence but absorbed the anxieties they touched.

I wasn't seeking God on my knees in prayer. I wasn't reading my Bible. I wasn't obeying God in some act of sacrificial service. I was simply being passive and receiving God's love and strength being released and massaged into me one love drop at a time.

This palpable presence of God's Spirit releasing into my soul happened dozens of soul delightful times over the next few years. It was as if the incredible strength God released in me, through the healing prayers of God's people and Gideon's story, was now on time-release tablets working in my heart. Each time it happened it worked its way more deeply into the fabric of my soul. While the strength of the experiences waned over time, these "love drip" experiences brought a more settled experience of God's love, presence, and strength to my inner being. God was working His strong presence into the deepest places of my inner man, and it was happening over time and through prayer and going deeper than anything professional people could perform.

As much as I enjoyed these love drips, I couldn't regulate when they came or how long they stayed. Sometimes they flowed during personal times of prayer and worship; however, most often they would be released in me during the mundane experiences of life: driving a car, taking a shower, or watching my son's baseball game. Sometimes they would happen at more consciously "spiritual" moments like prayer meetings at our small church. These touches of God were pure grace to my soul, and yet the expectant prayers of His people played a mysteriously significant role.

Some people call these "saturation" prayers where the love of God saturates more deeply into the soul. Whatever they are called is secondary to the reality of God working His love more deeply into the experientially empty and hurting places of the heart. Maybe this is a piece of what Paul had in mind when he prayed for the Ephesians "that according to the riches of his glory he may grant you to be strengthened with power through His Spirit in your inner being, so that Christ may dwell in your hearts through faith" (Ephesians 3:16-17a).

After all, this was the passage of Scripture elder Larry Simpson had prayed over me several months prior. I also had one of the more spiritually minded ladies of our church tell me, unsolicited, that God had laid this precise prayer on her heart to pray for me!

The prayer I was receiving from Todd and His prayer partners came in one-hour increments and was accompanied by counsel as we learned to listen to God's Spirit for guidance and direction. Todd and his prayer partners learned there were obstacles in people's lives to hearing God, as well as "open doors" the enemy could enter through specific areas of disobedience, which needed to be closed through confession and repentance. While God was massaging me with His love and strength, we also kept our ears open to areas of disobedience in my life that needed my attention to close off the enemy's entrance, which would cut off his torturous touches.

Christians can give ground for the enemy to torturously play on the turf of our souls through our disobedience to the clear teaching of God's Word. I had failed to fight in God's strength when the enemy attacked, and we were to find several other "open doors" that gave him freedom to play hard-ball on the contours of my soul. Over time, God would show me areas of unforgiveness, idolatry (looking for affirmation and validation in the opinions of people) and living by fear instead of faith as wide-open doors that needed closing. These and other areas gave demons permission to play baseball with track spikes on the sacred ground of my saved soul.

One of the areas of my soul that God began to cleanse and speak through more consistently was in and through my right-brain imagination. Because the imagination can be used as a tool for the enemy and because God communicates primarily through the rational truth of His Word and since many modern Christians only use the filter of left-brain logic to analyze truth, we have little to no expectations of God reinforcing left-brain truth with right-brain imagination experiences. Seeing God communicate truth through redemptive pictures in my imagination was new ground for me, but as it would happen, this new way of communicating became powerfully transformative and helped me immensely in fully integrating God's truth in both hemispheres of my brain.

After all, why would God give us two hemispheres of our brain, a logical and experiential side, and only limit His communication to one half of our brain? God can and does move deeply in the imagination with word pictures that coincide with Scriptural truth, and when He does, He deepens our experience of redemptive realities. God was about to pry open my imagination and plant healing movements of the Spirit, and He would do so like a new gentle stream finding its way by an abundance of rain into an already established brook where nurturing water now flows with greater abundance.

As we prayed together, God began to touch my right-brain imagination more and more frequently. This was new terrain for this conservative Presbyterian who had previously never ventured into this "taboo" territory. I was a man who lived and preached from my left-brain logic. I had lots of passion at times (unfortunately also fused with anger), but my God-given imagination was largely dormant and honestly close to being dead.

The first time God spoke to my imagination was through the symbol of a lion walking in my imagination. The Bible does call Jesus "the lion of the tribe of Judah," so this picture could be trusted as a Biblical image planted by the Holy Spirit. As our prayer team composed of Todd Bramblett and Fred Clark prayed together and expectantly waited for God to move, I saw a clear picture of a powerful lion walking slowly toward a beautiful city, which was obviously heaven.

The city shined as brightly as stars on a dark night, but even more so because the lights were brighter and closer and bigger. Heaven was our clear destination. As we walked slowly together, I saw a picture of my inner man's muscles that God wanted to strengthen in me. This picture in my imagination, of a lion walking next to me, wanting to strengthen me, was a clear picture of what Jesus wanted to do in me as we walked together to my salvation destination. The only other obvious teaching symbol that came in this imagination vision was the fact that as we walked together, we walked very "slowly" towards heaven. It was slow because it was going to be a life-long journey, which wouldn't end until Jesus and I reached heaven together.

This vision occurred as I prayed with Pastor Fred and Todd, as we simply waited expectantly in silence for God to move. As the Holy Spirit revealed these transforming truths, I described to them what I was seeing. Such rich truths about my journey and what God was doing was powerfully encouraging as my soul lancing was occurring. No words, ideas, or suggestions prompted this Holy Spirit picture in my imagination, just quietness in expectant prayer, and an openness on my part to the Holy Spirit communicating healing truths in ways to which I was unaccustomed!

THE LANCING OF MY SOUL

Practical Wisdom for the Invisible War

Should Christians use their imagination in prayerful meditation? Many sincere conservative Christians are leery of using their imaginations in biblical meditation and prayer because of its susceptibility to the demonic, and the potential of using mental images to falsely represent God. These concerns are legitimate. Nevertheless, a mind surrendered to the Spirit of God and saturated by the truth symbols used in Scripture will be enriched by God, more open to communication with Him, and help the soul to experience redemptive truth much deeper than pure logic.

In his insightful book *Satisfy Your Soul*," Dr. Bruce Demarest defines imagination as "the God created capacity to form mental images of what is real but not immediately present."[xvii] He also points out through Evangelicals such as Eugene Peterson and Alister McGrath that Christians have used "the imagination in meditation for centuries."[xviii] He quotes Francis Schaeffer on the Christian's use of the imagination by saying, "The Christian is one whose imagination should fly beyond the stars."[xix]

We rightly employ our imaginations when we take time to reflect on the variety of symbols God uses in Scripture to portray salvation realities. When reflected upon in meditation, these truths become more alive to both our minds and hearts. For instance, God presents Himself in Scripture as a shepherd (Psalm 23, 1 Peter 5:4) who provides, guides, protects, and directs His people. He presents Himself as a lion (Hosea 5:14) and as streams of living water bubbling forth from inside the believer (John 7:38-39). He also presents Himself as a living stone and cornerstone for His people who in faith become His Holy priesthood (1 Peter 2:4-5).

Yes, we need to read and study the entire Bible so our minds may be fully informed, and our doctrines may be accurate and precise. God's Word should inform us as to what we must believe about God, ourselves, our responsibilities to Him and fellow mankind, and His grand rescue plan to save people through faith in the Lord Jesus. In this way He protects us from erroneous ideas offered by legions of false religions which challenge the exclusivity of Jesus (John 14:6).

However, Scripture must also be read slowly (via meditation), so the Spirit can use God-given propositional truths and biblical symbols to speak more richly and deeply into the deepest fabric of our beings. Learning to read the Scriptures slowly and asking God to protect and speak to our hearts through our imaginations can help connect the mind and heart and bring a fuller experience of God, which many hyper-rational Protestants sorely lack.

I would also learn to re-imagine the powerful redemptive pictures which the Holy Spirit planted in my mind. I would imagine the lion figure of the tribe of Judah that represented Jesus and the muscles of my inner man that God was working to strengthen in me. The acts of reimagining these redemptive pictures which the Spirit graciously planted in my mind helped grow these truths as palpable experiences in my soul.

While I had to persist in catching lies, I was living by and replacing them with the truth of Scripture. Meditation on these God-inspired symbols representing realities of my salvation in Jesus Christ was taking the renewing of my mind to the deepest level.

Dr. Demarest also adds this helpful clarification: "The purpose of imaginative meditation on Scripture is not to create reality, which is impossible. It is to open new windows of the soul to revealed truth. The sanctified imagination, working on the words and symbols of Scripture, leads believers to deeper and more relevant dimensions of spiritual understanding. God expects us to use every created capacity---our reason, intuition, imagination, and affections."[xx]

QUESTIONS FOR REFLECTION AND DISCUSSION

1. Dr. Demarest says the imagination is "the God created capacity to form mental images of what is real but not immediately present." What do you think about this definition?

2. Does God expect us to use our imaginations to help picture truth?

3. What does it mean to read Scripture slowly and deeply?

4. Do you agree with using both hemispheres of your brain for the deepest integration of truth in your soul?

5. How can we protect ourselves from the enemy abusing our imaginations?

CHAPTER SIX

The Slow Return of Sleep

We must depend upon God to do for us what we cannot do for ourselves. We must, to the same degree, depend on Him to enable us to do what we must do for ourselves.
—Jerry Bridges[xxi]

Anxiety does not empty tomorrow of its sorrows, but only empties today of its strength.
—Charles Spurgeon[xxii]

As I closed out my healing prayer sessions with the men at Falls Church to focus with my new team at Christian Fellowship, I distinctly remember my prayer partners telling me, "Your sleep will return as your heart issues are revealed and healed." This statement would be true. However, I had no idea the time it would take or the heart issues which God was taking aim at to lance in my soul.

I started realizing the soul can be as complex as the body is intricate, and God needed to be in charge of this process for the deepest healing to occur. I was like a patient lying on an operating table with a doctor about to perform exploratory surgery to see just how far my cancerous infections spread. Unlike surgery of the body, though, soul surgery takes our deepest cooperation with Jehovah-Rapha (God our healer) for wholesome results.

Over the next year and a half, emotional healing slowly settled into my soul and my sleep rhythms started returning. My responsibility was to catch lies I was living by and replace them with the truth of God's Word (by putting on the "belt of truth" over my mind), practice my deep breathing exercises, receive more hours of healing prayer, reimagine God-given redemptive truth pictures, and simply receive and enjoy when God's Spirit would give me His deep inner love massages. This healing was truly a cooperative effort between God, me and many caregiving people.

I was able through this healing process to cut back my sleep medication from three Trazodone (my sleep aid) and two Clonazepam (my sleep and anxiety aid) to half a Trazodone. While I don't advocate taking oneself off any medication without a doctor's supervision, I felt like my sleep rhythms, after being shot out of orbit like a spacecraft, were now on their return trip with their parachutes out, gently floating me down towards the sea.

I was practicing what counselors today call REM (Rational-Emotive) or cognitive therapy, which teaches what the mind thinks greatly influences how we feel. However, Scripture has taught this for thousands of years and adds the importance of right behaving or living for God's peace to settle more fully into our souls. This invitation to find God's peace is found in Philippians:

"Finally, brothers, whatever is true, whatever is honorable, whatever is just, whatever is pure, whatever is lovely, whatever is commendable, if there is any excellence, if there is anything worthy of praise, **think** about these things. What you have learned and received and heard and seen in me—**practice** these things, and **the God of peace will be with you.**" Philippians 4:8-9 (emphasis mine)

This must be why God makes guarding our minds with His true and wholesome thoughts our first piece of armor that we put on in battle, for this is what putting on "the belt of truth" commands. Yet thought patterns of lies (about God, false gods, self, others, the security of salvation) grew up like strong weeds choking my inner being. God was revealing to me a plethora of thought patterns and deeper beliefs that needed my rock-solid commitment of replacing with His truth for deep healing to occur. My learning to think, meditate, and behave according to God's ways opened the door to His gift of peace growing in my inner being.

"What if" worries breeding "future fears" were at the top of my list for catching and changing. "What if" worries breed anxieties because they focus on the worst-case scenarios happening to me. This leads to what counselor Dr. David Burns calls "catastrophizing" as our minds focus on worst case scenarios coming true, which naturally become great disturbers of our personal peace. My mind was filled with worries like these:

- "What if" I lose my job and can't find another one?
- "What if" my thyroid cancer comes back and the doctors can't stop it?
- "What if" a line drive takes out my son's front teeth?
- "What if" my wife gets pregnant again when she's in her mid-40's, and I'm in my 50's?
- "What if" I touch something at the hospital and become a MRSA carrier?
- "What if" I've blasphemed the Spirit and lost my salvation?

My natural thought patterns were strongly structured with these and other "what if" worries, and I spent time living as though these worries were going to happen. I lived so frequently as though these worries were true, that God's peace only frequented my soul like a distant relative visiting for Thanksgiving dinner and leaving soon after arrival.

The phrase "what if" should be a loud warning siren telling us that what is lurking in our minds should be traded out with truth. My thinking needed to be changed from "what if" worries to, "'Who is in complete control?" My mind needed to be saturated with God's powerful control and His good plans for my life:

- Who is in control and can be completely trusted, if I lose my job and struggle to find another?
- Who is in control and can be completely trusted, if my thyroid cancer comes back and doctors can't stop it?
- Who is in control and can be completely trusted, if a line drive takes out my son's teeth?
- Who is in control and can be completely trusted, if my wife gets pregnant when she is in her mid- 40's and I'm in my fifties?
- Who is in control and can be completely trusted, if I pick up MRSA and become a carrier?
- Who is in control and can be completely trusted for my salvation, if Satan makes me think I've done the unthinkable?

I had to train myself to trust God for **today's** troubles, so that my future fears would eventually fizzle. I had to work by faith to "fence in today" and commit myself to live one day at a time with trust in God's care for me and complete control over everything, from the bacteria I couldn't see to every future event I would face. I learned to stand by faith on statements like, "The God who cares for me will take care of me," and "I fence in today and commit myself to trusting You for today only." I prayed these prayers from my heart, sometimes numerous times in one hour. When anxiety would strike, catching my unhealthy thoughts and prayerfully trusting God was my surest pathway to peace. As I practiced such godly thinking, praying, and behaving, God's peace began to make more frequent, deeper, and longer-lasting visits to my soul.

Sometimes it takes episodes like the one I faced to cause one to come "face to face" with our strongest, unhealthy thought patterns and deeper beliefs so we can restructure them.

Interestingly, my mom taught me Philippians 4:6, the first verse I had memorized as a child. However, it had lain dormant for years and now was called out for active duty with its surrounding verses (which I later memorized) and put into practice on the front lines of my soul. For God's peace to make its home in my soul, I needed to practice the principles of right living outlined in Philippians 4:4-9, including (1) rejoicing because of God's nearness (4:4-5), (2) praying in faith instead of worrying (4:6), (3) dwelling on God's wholesome thoughts (4:8), and (4) practicing a godly lifestyle (4:9).

As I persisted in these practices of renewing my mind, God's natural peace began to slowly grow in my soul. One of the most exciting times for me was to fall asleep naturally without any sleep medication. I had tried many times without success for almost two years., but it finally happened on our summer vacation in 2012.

As a family, we traveled to Denver. I found myself fishing all day into the evening with a fishing friend. We cast our flies, waded and slipped on rocks in the water, and hauled in beautiful rainbow trout for the better part of 11 hours. Because of our fishing success, we kept going from morning until early evening. I did fall asleep that night with my medication. However, the next afternoon, I felt unusually fatigued from my fishing the prior day and thought I would give sleeping naturally, yet another try. So downstairs to my in-laws' basement I went. I crawled in bed and noticed the clock registering 2:00 p.m., and before I knew it, I found myself awakening one hour later.

Nearly two years had gone by since my train wreck, and my sleep rhythms finally returned after a long, exhausting day fishing and hours of renewing my mind and trusting God!

Practical Wisdom for the Invisible War

Scripture teaches that God gives Christians at least two kinds of peace. The moment we are saved we have peace **with** God. This peace comes only by the blood of Jesus shed on the cross. The sacrifice of Jesus satisfied God's justice against our sin and grants us peace with God. However, Christ followers are then recipients of the peace **of** God. This peace of God can be supernatural, given directly by the Holy Spirit through faith in crisis situations, but it can also be a natural peace grown in our hearts by the Holy Spirit through the believer's practice of trust and righteous living.

Other pieces of armor vital for Christians to put on in spiritual struggle are "shoes for your feet, having put on the readiness given by the gospel of peace" (ESV).

Shoes for a soldier are essential in battle. They prepare us to walk wherever our commander tells us to fight. Without a good pair of shoes, a soldier's walking and fighting are deeply impaired. Fighting becomes much harder than it already is. Areon Potter says, "Having our feet shod with the gospel is like having new tires on our car. New tires will provide confidence as we drive on muddy or snowy roads."[xxiii]

Being at peace with God is absolutely necessary for a Christian in preparation for fighting evil. Yet knowing the peace of God's Holy Spirit in pitched conflict with the enemy and feeling His homegrown peace in our hearts is also essential for standing and fighting well—and in my case, enjoying sleep again!

"How beautiful upon the mountains are the feet of him who brings good news, who publishes peace, who brings good news of happiness, who publishes salvation, who says to Zion, 'Your God reigns'" (Isaiah 52:7).

QUESTIONS FOR REFLECTION AND DISCUSSION

1. How certain are you that you are at peace with God? Why?

2. How is peace with God accomplished according to the Bible?

3. What is the peace of God, and how does worry rob us of this type of peace?

4. How does what you dwell upon in your mind influence your body and emotions?

5. When you worry, how often do you stop to identify what issue(s) are bothering you and trade worry with thoughts of trusting God's control and care for you?

Thomas Dages

CHAPTER SEVEN

Another Terrifying Night Terror

And he said to them, "I saw Satan fall like lightning from heaven. Behold, I have given you authority to tread on serpents and scorpions, and over all the power of the enemy, and nothing shall hurt you."
— Luke 10:18-19

Blackness like blindness, a loss of hearing, a loss of contact with the real world, time standing still. He could feel himself dying. An image, a hallucination, a vision or a real sight broke through for an instant: two ghastly yellow eyes full of hate. His throat began to compress, squeezing shut.
"Jesus!" he heard his mind cry out, "help me!"
His next thought, a tiny instant flash, must have come from the Lord: "Rebuke it! You have the authority."
Hank spoke the words though he couldn't hear the sound of them: "I rebuke you in Jesus' name!"
The crushing weight upon him lifted so quickly Hank felt he would sail upward from the floor.
— Frank Peretti[xxiv]

I'M SURE THAT WHEN I MENTION "NIGHT TERROR," different kinds of night frights pop into people's minds. Periodically, since early childhood, I had encountered a kind of terror which brought me to a fully awakened state, yet struck me with total paralysis, making any physical movement impossible. I would awaken from a nap or from sleep, and not be able to move an inch of my body. Of course fear would surge through me, and there were times when other terrifying phenomena would accompany these terrors.

I emphasize that I was fully awake, because I've been told there is a phase of sleep where the body has difficulty moving, and it was possible these "terrors" were simply times of slow emergence from my sleep. While I do not doubt emerging from sleep's depth can have effects on the body, I was fully awake and accosted by too many other frightful phenomena to make emerging from "levels of sleep" the sole or even primary reason for these aberrations. On top of this, as I will explain, simply using the powerful name of Jesus would always bring an immediate end to these "night terror" encounters.

These terrors would come upon me strongly, suddenly, and without warning. They happened to me several times soon after receiving Jesus at age six. They continued in high school and college, and happened with less frequency, but with more ferocity in my 20's, 30's, and 40's. When my later occurrences hit with more intensity, they were mixed with more obvious flavors of demonic harassment.

In college, at Taylor University, I skipped chapel one day for a wanted nap. Unfortunately, skipping chapel for these wanted naps happened too frequently, causing me to forfeit lots of spiritual growth opportunities. On this day, I awoke from my nap and realized I couldn't move. There I was on my bed, knowing exactly where I was, and where I had to go next, but absolutely stuck in this fearful state of paralysis. After struggling for a few seconds (which seemed like minutes), I called on the name of Jesus, and the bondage was **immediately** broken. I was totally free from my temporary paralysis and free to go about my student duties.

Fortunately, at an early age, when these terrors started, I instinctively (by God's grace) drew on Jesus' strength for help and victory. Because the name of Jesus worked so powerfully every time, I didn't feel a need to talk about this with my parents or get any doctor's or counselor's advice on the matter. These terrors would happen only sporadically, with no rhyme or reason, but every time I would draw on Jesus for His strong deliverance, I found instant and decisive victory. My faith in Jesus and His delivering power was built, one strong delivery at a time.

My Three Worst Night Terrors

At age 30, after thinking I helped a man out of demonic bondage (he later apologized and confessed he was part of a Satanic Coven planted in our church to harass unsuspecting pastors like myself), I was accosted by one of my worst night terrors. I invited this young covert Satanist, who I will call Timothy, to stay in my apartment. Thinking he was delivered of foul spirits, I thought he was free and therefore, I was safe. That night, however, with Timothy staying in another room adjacent to mine, it seemed like all my worst weaknesses were being played upon. My lusts and angers raged with hideous strength, and I struggled with unusual nightmares. I say unusual nightmares because nightmares were rare occurrences for me.

This night as I awakened from my nightmares, I found I could move neither my body or lips! How frightful this was to find myself in complete paralysis, and not even able to call upon Jesus for His deliverance. To make matters worse, as I lay paralyzed in limb and lips, I felt raw hatred slide over my soul. In my mind, I called out frantically to Jesus for his help. I don't remember the exact words I mentalized, but in prayer where my lips didn't move, I called out in frightful desperation to Jesus with all my heart. In an instant, I became free. My body could move, my lips could speak, and raw hatred lifted off my soul. As much as I believe our body's chemicals can influence our emotions, it is hard to pin such strong spiritual dynamics on items like caffeine, stress, or levels of sleep, as some do with night terrors.

Since childhood I have also been accosted with fears of condemnation for committing the unpardonable sin. For many reasons, my hypersensitive soul found it difficult to rest and find security in my heavenly Father's redeeming love, and my soul has been an easy target for doubts about committing unforgivable sins. Many times, I had to quote Scripture of my "righteous" standing in Christ, so the fires of condemnation would stop burning in me.

To overcome this fear of condemnation, it has also been helpful for me to "preach" to myself the biblical logic that true blasphemy of the Spirit, whatever dreadful sin that entails, is always accompanied by a full and final departure from the faith, which is what the Bible calls apostasy. If I had committed "blasphemy of the Spirit," which is what the enemy wanted me to think, I would have turned from the faith with finality with no more interest in walking with Jesus. This was obviously not the case with me, as this fear of blaspheming the Spirit would torture my tender soul. This torture of the soul was the enemy's intent.

However, there is a lot of truth to the idea that people who worry about committing the unpardonable sin don't have to worry they have done it. If a person is walking with Jesus, his current walk of faith is a sure sign that God's grace still has His grip on his soul. This biblical logic of my current tenderness towards Jesus informed me that I was nowhere near apostasy, and that realization brought much comfort to my soul.

Yet the evil one and his minions knew where to launch their fiery darts. As bad as these described "night terrors" were, my worst night terror assaulted me soon after being married and living in our first apartment. This was about a year or so after my harrowing experiences with Satanist Timothy. I was sound asleep next to my wife, when suddenly I awoke from sleep and sat up in bed. Then frightfully out of my own mouth came the start of the blasphemous words I always dreaded saying. As I sat up in bed, the words slowly, mechanically, and uncontrollably began to slip from my lips. I knew exactly what I was saying, and didn't want to say them, but I couldn't stop them. It was like I was a puppet being controlled by a ventriloquist.

The words H-O-L-Y S-P-I-R-I-T, came out of my mouth slowly and mechanically, and on the tip of my tongue, waiting to come crashing out of my lips, was the worse curse I could utter.

However, by God's sheer grace, the Holy Spirit inside me shut this demonic dictation down before I could finish the sentence. One moment I was uncontrollably saying what I never wanted to say, and the next moment someone had turned me off or shut me down, so I couldn't finish this venomous speech. I felt like a faucet which was suddenly turned off, preventing me from pouring out the words which I hadn't been able to stop. As ferociously as the enemy awakened me and dictated through me, God strongly intervened to shut this torment down. As a pastor whom I confided in later comfortingly reminded me, "Greater is He who is in you than he who is in the world." God was greater in me than the enemy was upon me! The enemy is crafty and knows when and where and how to attack in ways that can do serious spiritual/ psychological damage. I don't believe that even if I had finished this dreadful sentence it would have been true blasphemy, because it didn't represent my heart. Yet God in His grace shut the demonic dictation down, knowing how hard it would be for me to psychologically recover if my lips actually finished saying the very words I dreaded saying. God is truly rich in mercy!

Another night terror "leapt" upon me about five years into my marriage, again in the middle of the night. We were living in Michigan at the time. This time my wife, Julie, heard the attack coming from my side of the bed. The sensation of something jumping on me and wrestling with me had happened on several occasions prior to this, and I had conditioned myself to counterattack by speaking the name of Jesus and telling a demon of fear to leave. However, on this occasion Julie was awakened by this sudden commotion on my side of the bed. The demon's attack stopped, as always, the moment I took authority in the name of Jesus over it and commanded it to leave. Yet his departure this time had another tormenting twist. As it departed from me, it let out a bark that came out of my own mouth and was suddenly gone. Julie lying next to me startlingly said, "What was that?" We didn't yet own a dog, yet the noise was so animal like! We both knew what it was but had never heard such a noise in a demonic departure. The fact that it came from my own lips made it even more unnerving.

In my current crisis, the enemy did visit with another night terror. It was late September, a little over two years after my crisis had begun. I was lying in bed fast asleep with my wife when I was suddenly awakened by what felt like something jumping on my body. I woke up and felt like I was in a fight. I wrestled to get something off me, but of course, there was no one to see. After an initial and quick fight for freedom I realized what was happening and wanted my reliance to be completely on Jesus. I ceased striving in my strength and called out with the name of Jesus and commanded, "You evil spirit of fear, I command you in the name of the Lord Jesus to leave me alone."

In an instant the opposition stopped. Yet to my surprise, on the heels of that same instant, a demon appeared directly in my face. It was so indescribably ugly and wicked looking, as though right out of a Stephen King horror movie on hell. I had witnessed demons respond immediately to the name of Jesus, I had sensed "darkness" on many occasions, even heard them on occasion using my very own tongue. However, in my over four decades of being a Christian, I had never once had one manifest itself to my eyes, so that I could see its presence. Yet it did this as it was leaving, and in an instant as fast and furious as it had come, it was gone. As I sat there peacefully in bed, I wondered why such a pouncing attack had come and why it showed itself to me. It was a scare tactic for sure, and a reminder that although things were getting better for me, I was still on enemy radar.

"It" would come back again in overt fashion about a month later, waking me up and speaking frightful lies to my mind. However, this night, I could rest easy and go back to sleep, knowing I had used the authority of Jesus and won another great victory in His powerful Name. The demonic force punched hard, but I counter punched in the name of my Lord and Savior Jesus Christ and sent it scurrying away.

Practical Wisdom for the Invisible War

The verse quoted in the beginning of this chapter was spoken to the followers of Jesus, whom He would equip with His authority and power to fight and defeat the enemy. As they went forth preaching the good news of new life under His rule, healing diseases and casting out demons in His name, they could expect all kinds or enemy ire and fire. Yet followers of Jesus need to know our authority and exercise that power for our protection when the battle gets heated.

Jesus spoke prophetically in Luke 10:18-19 about Satan's fall, which would come decisively by his crucifixion and resurrection from the dead. Jesus' victory at the cross would cause Satan "to fall like lightning from heaven." Then, Jesus would clothe his people with His authority and power both equipping and protecting them as they went forth, ministering in his name. The promise of "no harm" for his followers should be taken as no "ultimate" spiritual harm as to take them to hell, but it also presupposes Jesus' followers would fight with the authority and power He would supply. If the followers of Jesus advance into spiritual battle only partially clad in their armor or fighting in their self- strength that they muster, deep wounds, and serious injuries will follow.

The "serpents" and "scorpions" Jesus referenced are no doubt demons deceitfully doing the dirty work of their leader Satan. They look for opportunities to hurt to God's people, especially Christian workers (both clergy and laity) laboring hard to advance God's gracious rule through the works and words of the gospel. These demons are bondage makers and want to hold people in the prison of unbelief, the tyranny of sin, and the torment of all kinds of harassments and fears.

When Christians feel the opposition of the enemy trying to hurt them, either in the context of doing ministry or the demonic spirits bringing the battle to them at night, we have the authority of the highest officer in the universe to step into the conflict, and command them in the name of Jesus to stop! Yet we must exercise this authority by speaking in the name of the Lord Jesus to see the power of Jesus work!

If the enemy comes pouncing like a lion, take your authority in Christ and command him to leave. If he comes roaring like a lion to paralyze you with fear, take up your shield of faith and quote Jesus' faithful promises. If the enemy approaches you with deft deceptions, expose his lies and counter with the truth of God's Word.

If you are being harassed by a demon, he will leave, and when he does, don't be surprised if he tries to scare you as he departs.

QUESTIONS FOR REFLECTION AND DISCUSSION

1. Have you ever felt you were under attack from evil spirits? How did you respond?

2. How did the death and resurrection of Jesus disarm the power of Satan and his demons?

3. Who are the biggest targets for demons to strategically attack? Why?

4. Can a Christ-follower expect the protection of Jesus if they are not living life with God's armor on?

5. What is the difference between possessing authority and exercising His power in demonic conflict?

Thomas Dages

CHAPTER EIGHT

Hit by Another Train

Lord, we are weak and frail,
Helpless in the storm
Surround us with your angels
Hold us in your arms
Our cold and ruthless enemy
His pleasure is our harm
Rise up, oh Lord, and he will flee
Before our Sovereign God
—Fernando Ortega

It happened again. I suffered another demonic late-night attack, and instead of immediately putting on God's armor (as my sticky note on my bathroom mirror instructed me to do), I fought way too long in my own rational strength. I suffered horrible emotional, physical and spiritual fallout because of that mistake. However, the enemy did use a slightly different tactic. He is very crafty and knows the battle tactics that will have the greatest success to bring about the most collateral damage in the people he attacks. After all, he has been up to these battle tactics for thousands of years and knows how to create the most havoc and chaos in our souls, families, and churches and every other God-created institution.

He not only knows our weaknesses, but he also has become craftier at his cruel trade. There is no other created being in the universe trickier than he. Instead of slowly feeding me lies and ramping up my stress as I engaged him with my own logic and rationale (as in the first attack), and instead of an obvious frontal attack, which I successfully fought off in the name of Jesus, he plunged ahead with raw rage into a specific fear with which I was currently struggling.

At about 3:00 a.m., I woke up suddenly to clear, concrete thoughts that shot raw fear throughout my body. "The ringing in your ears will never stop, and the only way to stop it is to kill yourself," were the clear thoughts echoing in my head. I didn't hear these words audibly, (the enemy typically doesn't speak that way), but these fiery words echoed and burned through the corridors of my soul. I immediately resisted them. "No, this is not true!" "This will not happen to me!" "I will never do such a thing!" I pounded the enemy's thoughts with the heavy artillery of my self- strength and resistant thinking. I wasn't going to give into these fears. No matter how hard I wrestled and battled, they wouldn't leave me alone. I twisted and turned in bed, trying with all my effort to fight them off. I'm not sure how long the mental battle raged, but it must have gone on for at least half an hour. Again, I was wide awake physically, and this time I knew it was the breath of the dark one. He was the one speaking such words into my mind, but I wrestled in all the strength I could muster.

A little background about my tinnitus is in order. This loud ear ringing developed on the heels of my first insomnia and anxiety crises. As we traveled back from our mountain house in August 2010, I noticed this new ear ringing. It started out lightly but then grew into a consistent loud ringing that sounded like the high-pitch noise made by jet engines on a runway. While millions of Americans struggle with and tolerate this phantom noise, my tinnitus accompanied by all the other soul-stressing issues at times felt like "the straw that would break the camel's back." More will be shared about my tinnitus struggles and the significant relief I found, but at this time the enemy of my soul used it to wake me up in the middle of the night and shoot raw fear through my body/soul.

Suddenly it hit me—the enemy was speaking his lies (Scripture says lying is his native language, John 8:44), yet I was countering his lies with my wisdom and energy and not the absolute truth of God's written Word. I was not yet wielding the Sword of the Spirit, the written Word of God, in this fight.

Philippians 4:13 popped into my mind. "I can do all things through Christ who strengthens me." I spoke this verse out loud, relying completely on the veracity of His Word—and amazing, good things immediately happened. A supernatural peace **immediately** flooded my soul, pushing out completely every vestige of fear in me. The ear ringing was suddenly silenced, as I quickly slipped into sleep. Sleep that was so torturously difficult swept suddenly over me like an anesthesiologist giving me medication before surgery. It happened that quickly. Where paralyzing fear and loud ear ringing and a dark presence with suicidal thoughts once crippled me, it all was swept away and replaced by peace, quietness, and a rush into instant sleep. It all happened immediately upon quoting Scripture when I leaned completely upon the Lord Jesus for my strength.

The Word of God quoted and relied upon is powerful to silence demons and push away quaking fear. This is why Jesus met the temptations of Satan when sparring in the wilderness, with the Scriptures Jesus had hidden in his own heart since childhood. (See Matthew 4:1-11.) Every time the Son of God responded to Satan's temptations, it was with, "It is written..." and what followed was the power of God's sharp two-edged sword. This is why the Sword of the Spirit is to be wielded wisely as a vital piece of armor when the enemy comes, day or night, with deceptive attempts to cripple us with his lies. When we rely totally on the veracity of God's Word, we are resting in His strength and not fighting with our own. It was as if the Spirit of God inside me was waiting for me to take up and wield the sharp sword placed in my hands. Demons hate the sharp edges of the Word of God wielded in faith.

Fortunately, this time it didn't take me almost two whole nights to pick up Scripture and wield it as it did during my first attack. Although I waged war in my strength for a good half-hour, my learning curve was considerably cut down. Yet I was still far too slow in relying completely on the trustworthiness of God's Written Word. While high school and college wrestling trained me well in self-effort, God was in the process of training me how to rely immediately and totally upon Jesus and His weapons to simply stand in His strength.

In my first train wreck, the enemy attacked with subtle fears. When I responded with my mental reasoning, the reaction sent stress chemicals cascading through me, piquing both outrageously strong anxiety and rock-solid insomnia. The demonic forces crept in close and were able to continue to land these stress punches until I took my stand in the truth of Jesus. This time, however, the enemy hit me with raw fear, shaking me out of my sleep and sending me immediately into an intense fight-or-flight response. And wow, did I fight, with every ounce of strength I could muster!

When I awakened the next morning, I felt like I had been through World War III. Thankful for the night sleep and remembering the battle and my decisive victory by quoting Scripture, I wondered where the supernatural peace, rest and quietness had gone. As I slogged into my bathroom, my anxiety was heightened and ear ringing was singing substantially louder in my ears.

I didn't realize it at the time, but not only would this setback with the enemy would be used by the Lord to remind me once again to fight in His strength, but in a new onslaught of anxiety and insomnia, God would surface an inner boil buried alive in me for decades. God was using the attacks of the enemy to place me willingly on His operating table, where He would place surgical scalpels in my hand and strategically guide me to where He needed to cut into my boil.

I didn't know it at the time, but the hardest part of my healing journey was before me. God was going to go after the oldest, deepest, sorest infections in my inner being. He was going to use the claws of the enemy to masterfully bring these infections to my attention.

Practical Wisdom for the Invisible War

Paul tells followers of Jesus to put on all the armor, including "the sword of the Spirit, which is the word of God" (Ephesians 6:17b). This is another piece of vital armor Christ-followers need to become adept at wielding.

The Scriptures of the Old Testament and New Testament are clearly the sword of the Spirit, which He places in our hands to wield against all kinds of enemy attacks. If we learn to listen to the Holy Spirit in times of warfare, He will direct our minds to pick up the verses we need most to fend off the variety of attacks which demons craftily bring to our minds. After all, it was the memorized Scriptures Jesus used in His encounters with the devil in the wilderness.

I can recount many times in my life when fear immediately and completely vanished upon wielding God's Word. Let me recount my favorite.

About 15 years ago, while vacationing in Denver, my wife and I were fast asleep in her parents' basement. This basement is very dark with only one window in the bedroom in which we slept. I remember being awakened to a greater darkness which seemed to fall upon and cover me with heaviness and smothering fear. In the darkness, I felt blackness fall upon me. The words of Isaiah 26:3 immediately came to my mind, "You keep him in perfect peace whose mind is stayed on you, because he trusts in you." When I quoted this verse out loud, the spiritual darkness and fear hovering over me was ripped off like a heavy blanket as fast as it fell upon me. Immediately, God's peace filled me up so fully I felt weightless on my mattress. That is the power of the sword of the Spirit when wielded by God's people in faith. The enemy, as strong as he is, is no match for the truth of God's Word as the Spirit puts it in into our hands. Yet we must memorize it and quote it in faith when fear falls upon us.

How well do we know Scripture? How well have we memorized Scripture in the areas where our soul is weak and most susceptible to enemy attack? As we read God's Word daily, it's helpful to write down and memorize the Scriptures for bringing God's strength into our weaknesses. How well do we listen to the Holy Spirit's promptings in the heat of battle and stand by faith on the verses He brings to mind? How often do we saturate our hearts with God's truth and love in Bible meditation, so these realities sink into the deepest places of our souls?

QUESTIONS FOR REFLECTION AND DISCUSSION

1. Why might demons like to assault people at nighttime?

2. What do you think it means that demons and their attacks are opportunistic?

3. Do you know your greatest weaknesses and Scripture to help when attacked in those areas?

4. Why is it significant that Jesus Himself fought the devil with Scripture?

5. Can a person tell if his thoughts are unhealthy, coming from his flesh, or if they are planted by demons? Does the origin of your thoughts change your response?

Thomas Dages

CHAPTER NINE

Three Startling Visions

And it shall come to pass afterward, that I will pour out my Spirit on all flesh; your sons and daughters shall prophesy, your old men shall dream dreams, and your young men shall see visions. Even on the male and female servants in those days I will pour out my Spirit.
—Joel 2:28-29

WHILE THE ENEMY WAS CERTAINLY MOVING at me in harassing and harrowing ways, the Spirit of God was also communicating to me in ways which were novel, powerful, and exceedingly helpful. The Holy Spirit was speaking to my imagination and directly to my emotions, which were deeply transformative. Neither my imagination nor my emotions were emphasized in my conservative Presbyterian heritage. Now, God gave me three visions in a short period of time in which truth pictures appeared seemingly outside myself to enhance my understanding of what was going on inside me and around me in the spiritual realm, and where God wanted me most to heal and grow.

The words written in the beginning of this chapter by the prophet Joel were possibly scribed some 500-600 years before the first coming of Jesus. The prophet Joel describes some of the influences God's Spirit would have upon old and young, sons and daughters, and male and female servants of God. In other words, age, social class, and gender would not be an impediment to God's Spirit falling upon and working special graces of His Spirit through His people.

The Spirit works supernaturally through all of God's people and in sometimes surprising and supercharged ways.

This outpouring of God's Spirit on His people occurred at Pentecost (fifty days after the resurrection of Jesus), and continues until Jesus returns the second time. There is much stronger biblical support for the continuation of God's surprising works of His Spirit until the return of Jesus than there is to support a cessation of these works when the New Testament was completed.

Augustine (died 430 AD), arguably the greatest theologian of the early Church, originally believed God gave supernatural works, such as healing and other extraordinary gifts, to get the church started on a solid footing, but then, those gifts ceased when the first apostles died. However, after witnessing dozens of healings himself among the people of his parish, he was compelled to change his perspective. Three years before he died, in his essay called "Retractions," he wrote of this change of perspective.[xxv]

The great devotional writer of the 19th century, Andrew Murray, also supports the continuation of the miraculous by the Spirit throughout church history. Dallas Willard cites Murray's convictions on this matter: "Basing my views on scripture, I do not believe that miracles and the other gifts of the Spirit were limited to the time of the primitive Church, nor that their object was to establish the foundation of Christianity and then disappear by God's withdrawal of them…the entire scriptures declare that these graces will be granted according to the measure of the Spirit and of faith."[xxvi]

I grew up in a church and went to a seminary that for the most part didn't teach these fresh, powerful gifts of the Spirit were still active in the church. Therefore, there was not much faith or expectation to see the surprising works of God manifest among His people. Understandably, many church leaders want to keep people in line and on track with what God already spoke in sacred Scripture, but there was little to no room for the Holy Spirit to give spontaneous "words," "visions," "dreams," or fresh applications of truth for what may be helpful in particular oppressive circumstances accosting God's people.

God can and does speak powerfully through sermons, but the Spirit has a variety of other ways of communicating truth about the seemingly impervious circumstances of our churches and the wounded and stubborn places of our hearts. Nothing given by the Spirit, of course, will ever contradict the principles of truth taught in Scripture.

The first vision occurred as I was simply pondering while sitting at my desk in my church office. Suddenly I saw a picture of myself—outside myself. I had never "seen" such a picture of my soul outside myself with my mind's eye. However, this was not a mental picture conjured up in my mind, but one given suddenly, appearing for me above my right shoulder. It was a picture of my soul filled with abject terror. It was a picture of my heart controlled by and exuding fear. Both my fists and teeth were clenched; my face quivered with fear radiating from every feature. The Spirit used this clear vision of myself outside myself, which probably lasted no more than a few seconds, to powerfully communicate how deeply my heart was controlled by fear.

I was already convicted of sins like anger, lust, and greed by reading Holy Scripture or by listening to sermons, but never had I been given, supernaturally, such a quick and potent picture of my attempted control of life, which spawned so much fear and anxiety through the entire fabric of my being. I had never seen a picture of the strongest posture of my fearful heart until this point. It was going to be a long, hard process to let go of my attempted control over what only God could control, and to trust Him with all the details of my life, family, future, and ministry.

The second and third visions also happened in my church office and came several months after the first vision. This time, however, I was on my knees praying while kneeling beside my office couch. I don't remember how long I had been in prayer, but suddenly I was aware of a being in the form of a stick figure, which came from behind me and over my shoulder and landed right in front of me. As I saw it come over my shoulder and land in front of me, I knew intuitively that this being was sent to oppose me.

While the presence of a being opposing me was no surprise, never had I been shown pictorially a stick figure coming over my shoulder to symbolize such opposition. In my five decades as a follower of Jesus, I had believed in unseen spiritual opponents and had felt their opposition in some crazy ways, but had never seen their opposition in a symbolic picture. I would learn in a few moments why this stick figure appeared through another supernatural vision, after I ended my prayer time and returned to my desk. However, for now, the clear message through this symbolic picture was a confirmation of direct demonic opposition in my life.

Moments later, as I returned to my desk to sit in my chair, with my eyes open in a state of thoughtfulness, suddenly I saw before my face an ever-enlarging water drop. As the edges of the water drop enlarged, a picture of a person in my congregation emerged and filled up the enlarging water drop. Inside the water drop appeared the clear picture of a person in our church, who resisted help I had previously attempted to give him. His picture inside this water drop was unmistakably clear, as if his colored picture had been taken and placed in a church directory opened right before my face. However, his face was the only picture in this water drop and given with such clarity.

Although I had previously tried helping him, my counsel had not been received well. I had sensed his anger towards me surfacing in a variety of ways, but now the Lord was showing me the spiritual opposition working him over that was now coming against me. As I involved myself in his life, I seemed to catch the harassing opposition that was making his life miserable!

We often don't realize the deepest wrestling matches in which we engage are not against the people with which we have conflict but against the spiritual forces gaining control over them and who then come after us.

Dr. Rebecca Brown, in her insightful book *Prepare for War*, sheds light on how the enemy can use hate as a powerful fulcrum in our hearts in spiritual warfare. While Dr. Brown's specialty is understanding Satanism and helping people out of unimaginable bondage, her words about hate are sobering for everyone.

"Hatred is a conscious sin. As such, it gives Satan legal ground in our lives if we permit it to dwell in our hearts. If you hate someone, Satan can step in and use your spirit body to attack the person you hate. Such an attack can produce all sorts of illness, accidents, emotional problems, and even physical death. The person doing the hating usually is never aware that Satan is using his spirit body. The person being hated usually has no idea where his trouble is really coming from."xxvii

While I confess much ignorance in helping people out of Satanism and how the enemy can use a person's "spirit body" in spiritual attacks, I believe the stick figure in my case represented spiritual opposition that came off someone who hated me to afflict me. My response was to prepare myself in prayer and love. Interestingly, while I knew this person resisted my counsel and probably didn't like me, there were others in the congregation whom I would have associated more quickly with such contempt. It was also humbling to discover hate at times existing in my own heart and wonder how the enemy might be using me as an instrument of spiritual warfare against others.

I was also reminded of how the prayer teams assisting people with healing prayer need to cover themselves with warfare prayers of protection before and after such engagements. After all, if you minister to people and help them find freedom where the enemy has built a nest of his presence, like angry bees, you should expect them to come after you as well.

My platter was full of my own heart's issues and harassment from wicked spirits. Now another was added to my wrestling, and the Lord was again graciously telling me to "armor up" for my protection. Paul the apostle reminds us,

---

"for we do not wrestle against flesh and blood, but against the rulers, against the authorities, against the cosmic powers over this present darkness, against the spiritual forces of evil in the heavenly places."
Ephesians 6:12

These three visions were power pictures from God. While the spiritual warfare and wrestling with demons and my own heart had never been so intense, God had never spoken to me with so much clarity. The Spirit of God was using new ways that were fully in line with Scripture both to teach me to "armor up" and train me in battle tactics the enemy was using against me.

Practical Wisdom for the Invisible War

It is amazing the frequency with which God used visions to guide His people in both the Old Testament and throughout the New Testament. Even though the Bible is completed and closed to new books being added and is the only authoritative rule for faith and practice for Christians to follow, it makes sense that the Spirit of God would still use "visions, dreams, and power pictures" to open our eyes to spiritual realities taught propositionally in Scripture. When we see with the eyes of our hearts what is going on in our hearts and in our relationships and churches, it gives us new impetus to "wrestle" in God's wisdom and strength.

Scripture, however, does not teach us to seek visions, but to seek the Lord who chooses to reveal Himself and His wisdom when and how He desires. Jesus promised that if we love God by obeying Him, God will reveal Himself to His people.

"Whoever has my commandments and keeps them, he it is who loves me. And he who loves me will be loved by my Father, and I will love him and manifest myself to him."
John 14:21

Jesus is promising His followers that as we love God by obeying His clear commands, He will disclose Himself and His wisdom to us, as He chooses. As we seek God's presence, worship Him with the entirety of our lives, trust Him with all our hearts, and obey the clear teachings of His Word, He will disclose Himself to us in sometimes surprisingly fresh and helpful ways.

QUESTIONS FOR REFLECTION AND DISCUSSION

1. Should we expect God to communicate to us in the same manner He did in Bible times? Why or why not?

2. Why is studying Scripture the surest safeguard to discern what God is saying or not saying to our soul?

3. Have you ever had a time when God spoke directly to your mind or Spirit when not reading the Bible, yet you were convinced it was God speaking? What did He communicate? How did you know it was God?

4. What does it mean to seek God, and why is it important to seek Him and not visions and dreams?

5. Why might God turn up His ways of communicating as we pass through especially deep seasons of darkness?

CHAPTER TEN

A Great Pastor Helped Armor Up

A stronghold is anything that exalts itself in our minds, "pretending" to be bigger or more powerful than our God. It steals much of our focus and causes us to feel overpowered. Controlled. Mastered. Whether the stronghold is an addiction, unforgiveness towards a person who has hurt us, or despair over a loss, it is something that consumes so much of our emotional and mental energy that abundant life is strangled—our callings remain largely unfulfilled and our believing lives are virtually ineffective. Needless to say, these are the enemy's precise goals.
—Beth Moore[xxviii]

WHEN I WAS YOUNG MY OLDER BROTHER Bill took great joy in tying me up with wrestling holds to torture me with tickling. Since he was six years older, much stronger, and a more adept wrestler, he could place me on my back, wrap his legs around mine, and tie up my arms so I only had one free hand to protect my ticklish spots. During these times on the floor, I felt overpowered and almost helpless. Bill laughed and laughed while he playfully tormented me. Of course, because he was my brother, if I protested too strongly, he would relent and let me go.

Demons, however, don't let people go when we protest strongly. They torment people by tying up our minds with lies to slip their grips over our wills and emotions to torture us in the areas where they know we are most vulnerable. As they gain strongholds over us, we can feel as overpowered and helpless as I did on the living room floor with my big brother. Yet God gives us weapons that when used wisely and persistently can break us free from such tormenting strongholds.

Since my second train wreck occurred, anxiety began torturing me again in powerful ways. There were times when it slipped over me or fell upon me to the point where I felt almost helpless. God was in the process of teaching me how to use His weapons of warfare to break enemy strongholds. By His grace, He would use a pastor to help me armor up and fight for freedom with the weapons God supplied.

I met Pastor Dan Hotchkiss through a family attending our church. Dan and his wife would come at Christmas to visit their kids and grandkids and worship with us on Sunday mornings. When they visited during the summer or Christmas, Dan and I often enriched each other through Jesus talks, fellowship, and prayer. Dan's Christmas visits in 2011 and 2012 turned out to be strategic for the support, growth, healing, and help I needed to break strongholds in my soul.

When I visited with Dan for Christmas 2012 in his daughter's home, it didn't take long for me to share what had transpired in October during my second round of spiritual attacks and the fierce fight that was currently engaging me. He and his wife came to my assistance with listening love, prayer, and seasoned advice, all wrapped up in the gift of their presence. They did all this while "on vacation" from their own pastoral duties on the West coast, making room for me in their schedules as though I was a wounded and embattled sheep from their own flock.

Today, we as a church frequently define great ministers by their possession of exceptional speaking gifts that can hold or attract a crowd of people or numerically grow a church. However, Dan highlighted to me the greatness of what it meant to simply "be with me" and "walk with me" through my intense darkness. Pastor Dan personally and powerfully communicated the presence of Jesus more eloquently than any sermon ever could. For God's people to be ministered to most effectively and deeply, maybe we need our churches to be smaller and led by more pastor-teachers instead of exceptional speakers! They are the ones getting to know well the sheep who come limping into their churches.

Pastor Dan gave me spiritual warfare prayers to pray as we both sensed there was more to this battle than psychological struggles and chemical imbalances. Dan not only shared these prayers but took time to pray them with me. He prayed in such a way that demonstrated he wasn't worried about time but concerned about helping me find freedom from the foes of anxiety and insomnia throttling me. We talked and prayed together at our kitchen tables several times in the weeks preceding and following Christmas. We ate lunch at the Reston Chick-Fil-A and prayed together in the restaurant. As Dan gave me advice, he gave it as a seasoned pastor with his own weaknesses and wounds from many of his own wars.

I formulated the following prayer when anxiety would rise to almost out of control levels.

"In the name of the Lord Jesus Christ, I command any foul spirit who is causing anxiety in me to leave me alone. I put the blood of the Lord Jesus between me and you and command you to stop working your tormenting ways against me. I cast all my anxieties upon you, Lord Jesus, because God cares for me."

Many times, after using such a prayer, I would feel the anxiety abate —sometimes significantly. If it felt like there was a demon attacking my anxious spots, prayer in the name of Jesus broke off its oppressive ways. However, my anxiety would not completely dissipate because there were many spiritual and emotional and physical issues contributing to my anxiety complex.

Pastor Dan also encouraged me to relentlessly wield my sword of Scripture. When God puts a verse of Scripture on our hearts to combat incoming temptations or help us break free from enemy oppression and affliction, we must wield His sword and stand in faith. We must believe His words are completely true, especially when we don't feel their realities in our emotions. As a faithful pastor, Dan persisted in coaching me to fight in God's strength with God's weapons and to keep standing on His truth, regardless of how I felt. Dan knew there was nothing in Scripture that promised an easy battle. Sometimes, to gain back territory where demons have slipped their torturous grip into our souls, we must pray boldly and speak Scripture relentlessly to break free.

The verse that we both sensed God was calling me to fight with most intensely was 2 Timothy 1:7. Here Paul tells his protégé Timothy, "for God gave us a spirit not of fear but of power and love and self-control," or as the New King James Version translates: "of a sound mind," which is the phrase I used in battle when quoting the verse. Young Timothy had a propensity towards fear in the ministry to which he was called by God. Whatever those fears might have been, persecution by Roman authorities, imprisonment, death by martyrdom, people who looked down upon his youth, comparing his gifts to other preachers like Paul, or whatever vulnerabilities his unique make-up opened him to, Paul wanted him to fight and stand in God's immovable "power and love and self-control."

The two-edged sword of God's Word slowly cut the grip of fear and anxiety upon me and brought to my soul an eye of peace in the center of this hurricane. Yet it had to be wielded persistently. The enemy loves to haunt and taunt God's people with fear, especially those who possess propensities towards fear, like young Timothy. At 51, I was no longer considered a "young" minister; nevertheless, the enemy seemed to be viciously attacking my vulnerabilities. I had to faithfully quote Scripture to stand and find my way through these squalls of anxiety and fear.

This verse helped me stand strong while under oppressive anxiety as I counseled someone in my congregation. I was in a young man's home trying to listen and counsel as anxieties gripped me ever so powerfully and pressed upon me like a heavyweight wrestler upon my soul. It took everything I had to not crumble under it. Mentally, I rehearsed this verse over and over in my mind just to keep the full weight of anxiety off me. I would later confess to this person how divided my mind was at this time due to this anxiety battle, and he graciously understood. All throughout this counseling session as anxiety seized me with its vice like-grip, the only thing I could do was repeat silently, over and over, the words of 2 Timothy 1:7: "For God gave us not a spirit of fear but of power and love and self-control."

Pastor Dan also shared his own battles with fear, and how listening to soft worship music helped his soul relax and find sleep. Some musicians, with their voice tone and music, have a special way of gently and graciously opening up hurting hearts to make special deposits of soul soothing truths, helping to calm our inner storms. While Pastor Dan's favorite musician was the pianist Dino, my favorite became Fernando Ortega, whose soothing voice, music, and comforting words help bring calm to my quaking heart. At nighttime especially, Fernando was an instrument used by God to sing comfort into my tumultuous soul.

Pastor Dan gave me a personal example of what it means to be a pastor in time of deep need. He helped me pray, stand on Scripture, and use the gift of music to help me find freedom when my stronghold of anxiety tightened its grip.

Practical Wisdom for the Invisible War

Demonic deliverance for Christians is quite the hot-button issue for the Christian community. While Jesus and his disciples delivered many afflicted people from demonic bondage, they exclusively were dealing with people outside the family of faith. This is one reason why many Christian counselors today understandably don't use deliverance tactics with believers, but counsel followers of Jesus to fight with the full armor of God, with what Dave Powlison calls "The Classic Mode of Spiritual Warfare," over against power encounters or casting out the enemy.[xxix]

"Demonization" is a word many healing prayer counselors use for the different levels of influence which demons can have over people. Terry Wardle, citing Charles Kraft, believes the Greek word in the original language of the New Testament often translated "demon possession" could better be translated "demonized," inferring different levels of influence or domination demons display over the lives of people.[xxx]

While full-blown demon possession (the most extreme forms of demonic domination) is limited to individuals outside the family of faith, more and more counselors today believe varying levels of demonization can occur among God's people. Terry Wardle gives four different levels of demonization that he has witnessed in his counseling experience. I'll quote him at length from his book *Healing Care, Healing Prayer*.

"Harassment. Much the same as a hornet flies around a person's head, annoying and distracting him, so it can be with this level of demonization. The demon does not keep the person away from his or her appointed course, but does seek to bother or discourage him.

"Oppression. This level of demonic activity is much like a fog that settles in upon a person. The individual finds it more difficult to stay on track, and often battles varying levels of emotional and spiritual oppression. It can be more difficult for a person to keep focused on what is true and right.

"Affliction. Jesus often cast out demons when people suffered from physical sickness. At this level of activity, demons seek to bring emotional, spiritual, and physical suffering to a person in an effort to defeat and demoralize them.

"Bondage. The demon spirit is exercising a certain level of control in an area of a person's life. This demonization is possible because of personal choices that give room for this type of bondage. Despite personal efforts to move beyond the problem or sinful behavior, the individual finds it difficult to resist and repeatedly fails to find freedom."[xxxi]

Wardle goes onto say, "The caregiver should realize that demonization usually occurs without the person knowing that the source of the problem is demonic. People can exhaust themselves chasing down other causes without considering any involvement from evil spirits."[xxxii]

I don't doubt from reading seemingly sober testimonies from seasoned counselors that there are times, especially when a Christ follower has come out of an occult background, that a form of deliverance may be necessary. Dealing in the depths of the occult and the influence of the demonic upon a saved soul is indeed mysterious business. Yet after such a deliverance, learning to put on the armor is then necessary for staying free.

No matter the level of demonization, learning to pray prayers of self-deliverance can be helpful. Self-deliverance is not delivering yourself from demonic influence by your own power or depending upon a group of people praying over you (which is sometimes necessary), but instead making choices to pray prayers based on the authority of Christ and His blood. The freedom that can come from quoting Scripture, praying prayers of Christ-based authority, and singing truth can be exceedingly liberating. Pastor Dan helped me strategically fight with all three of these weapons. He helped me pick up and wield these weapons so I could wield them on my own, as a soldier using God's armor.

QUESTIONS FOR REFLECTION AND DISCUSSION

1. Why can a person who is not a follower of Jesus be fully possessed by an evil spirit(s)? How would involvement in the occult be open doors for this to occur?

2. Do you believe a Christ follower can struggle with different levels of demonic control that fall short of full possession? Why?

3. Why do you think the control of demons over a person's mind and will might happen slowly?

4. Why do you think Dr. Wardle believes many demonic problems occur without the person knowing that the source of the problem is demonic?

5. How might the constant putting on of the belt of truth prevent a demonic stronghold from developing in the first place?

CHAPTER ELEVEN

The Dream of a Snake

When God spoke, people knew that it was the Lord; they knew what He was saying, and they knew what He expected them to do.
— *Henry T. Blackaby and Claude V. King* [xxxiii]

Although battling to fall asleep was my new norm, this night a verse of Scripture popped into my mind, and after quoting it and mixing it with faith and prayer, I was sent quickly off to sleep. "Submit yourselves, therefore, to God. Resist the devil, and he will flee from you" (James 4:7). This was the verse the Holy Spirit put on my heart. I said something like, "Alright, Lord, I humbly submit to what You're taking me through, I resist the devil in Your strength, and You promise to make him flee." This was humbling on two fronts. I humbled myself under God's plan to submit to His painful training and teaching, and I humbled myself to resist the devil by relying totally on God's strength.

That night, God powerfully communicated by giving me a dream deeply informative as to what was happening in my soul, and the next night He spoke a specific "word of encouragement" that would remind me of the process of healing and deliverance we were working on together.

Up to this point in my life, I wasn't big on dreams as tools for divine communication. Once or twice in my life I had awakened on the heels of a dream with a strong sense of God's message for me. When dreams are divinely sent to help us in our turbulence, and we are spiritually awake, their intended message is typically crystal clear. Most dreams, however, are the result of our subconscious thoughts coming through our relaxed state of sleep. This night God blessed me with one of those divine dreams where His intended meaning was impossible to miss.

I dreamed I was at our lake house in Pennsylvania. I was standing next to our boathouse facing the water. Our house was on my right and our neighbor's house, just a quarter way around our cove, was on my left. Our lake usually has water in it, but at the time, and in my dream, much of the water had been drained for a dam renovation project. As I looked out into our dry lake, I saw a huge snake slithering towards the other side of our boathouse. This snake was not an ordinary 2-3 foot northern water snake, but it must have been 25-30 feet in length, and huge in its girth. To avoid its gaze, I walked over to our neighbor's property on the far end of our cove to get a look at it from another angle. From this angle I saw the snake slowly slither away from me down into a huge dark hole. What a huge snake it was, but how comforting it was to see it disappear down into a huge black hole. When the snake disappeared, I woke up. I believe this dream was given me very late in the morning, just prior to waking up, so I would remember it with such vividness.

THE LANCING OF MY SOUL

Surprisingly, the next morning after waking up, I noticed a huge break from anxiety. I felt a measure of freedom I hadn't felt in months. In fact, my anxiety seemed to have lifted like a blanket. My wrestling opponent seemed to have let go of his smothering grip of me and walked off the mat and out of the gymnasium. I was so excited this beast was gone and overjoyed at my newfound freedom. I felt something like Charles Dicken's Scrooge after his visits by three ghosts and waking up the next morning to see he was still alive and could live with a new, joyful generosity. My surge of new freedom from anxiety and depression made me wonder if my ordeal and "trial by fire" was now over.

However, while God clearly spoke through this dream and touched me with sudden sense of freedom, He was going to speak sobering words again that same evening as I proceeded to bed. As I climbed the stairs that night to head towards my bedroom, the Holy Spirit spoke to my mind the following words, "This was just the first step."

Without being audible, His voice was clear and distinct, as the time He spoke the first night of my ordeal that I was to "close the doors." This time, however, I was much more spiritually awake to receive what He had to say. By "this is just the first step," there were many more steps for me to take in my healing/freedom process.

This dream of the snake and its departure, I believe, was God's way to reward me this night for fighting with the Scripture which He brought to mind as I submitted to Him and resisted the devil in His strength. Yet the clear message the next night was that many more steps of faith and fighting in God's armor needed to take place to emotionally secure my full freedom.

Practical Wisdom for the Invisible War

Dr. Bruce Demarest puts forth an interesting discussion on dreams in his book *Satisfy Your Soul*. He distinguishes between two categories of dreams, which he calls dreams of special revelation, which contribute to the message of salvation in the Bible, and which ceased when the Scriptures were completed, and general revelation dreams, which "represent the emergence of unconscious images when our conscious controls are relaxed during sleep."[xxxiv] He believes the latter dreams can have at least two special functions.

"First, through a dream God may disclose His will for our lives."[xxxv] He then shares quite a vivid story of how God gave him specific guidance through a dream when he was in a quandary about his future. I will quote him at length because his dream is such a good example of how God disclosed "His will" to Dr. Demarest.

"After college Elsie and I volunteered for a short-term mission opportunity in Nigeria. Four years later, I began a doctoral program in theology with Professor F.F Bruce at a university in England. At the end of the year we

planned to return to missionary service in Africa and to continue research on the side. As the year wound down, Professor Bruce informed me that research in Africa was not feasible. He said that if I wanted to continue the doctoral program I must remain in England. Our plan suddenly was blocked! Should we remain in England, or should we return to Africa and forget about the doctorate? I had no idea what to do.

"The following Saturday, I took a walk in the English countryside to contemplate our options. As the warm sun broke through the thick clouds, I sat down against a stone wall. Tired from a busy week, I dozed off for a few moments and experienced a dream. A male figure stood before me in the dream and said in plain words, 'Stay in England and work with international students.' The dream ended as abruptly as it began. Nothing like this had happened to me before. But I was certain it was God who had spoken!"[xxxvi]

"Second, God uses dreams to disclose the state of our souls."[xxxvii] This was how God was using dreams in my life. The uptick of dreams and visions God was now giving me at this critical juncture of my life not only shed light upon the state of my soul but gave me great encouragement of God's purposes for me in my spiritual warfare. My dream of the snake's departure encouraged me to continue to use Scripture and fight in God's strength for more and more personal victories.

As God gave dreams in both the Old and New Testaments to contribute to the salvation story delivered by Jesus, why wouldn't He still give general revelation dreams today at critical junctures to immensely help us walk wisely in the salvation stories He is working out in our lives?

QUESTIONS FOR REFLECTION AND DISCUSSION

1. Do you agree most dreams are simply the result of what is in our unconscious minds?

2. Do you believe God occasionally sends dreams for our guidance and encouragement?

3. Have you ever had a dream you believe was divinely sent with a clear message from God? What was the message God was clearly communicating?

4. Why might God graciously communicate through vivid dreams?

5. How might our state of "spiritual wakefulness" help us perceive what God is communicating to us in a dream?

CHAPTER TWELVE

Freedom Through Midnight Worship

Through him then let us continually offer up a sacrifice of praise to God, that is, the fruit of lips that acknowledge his name.
—Hebrews 13:15

GOD DELIGHTS TO MOVE MIGHTILY in the lives of His children, especially as we obey Him. This holds true in the realm of worship as we learn to give "sacrifices of praise" when most inconvenient for us! God gently called me to worship Him at midnight when I was trying to sleep. When I did love Him this way, He moved mightily in my soul.

There I was, lying on my bed listening to my soothing Christian music with sleep nowhere in sight. Truth be told, I was more than frustrated and bordered on fuming with anger in my fight to find sleep. What was behind my sleeplessness? Why weren't my increased sleep medications working? Why was I slowly needing to increase my medications again? In rage, I threw my iPod, with all my wonderful worship music, across my bed and against my bedroom wall, exasperated that my music therapy wasn't working. I don't remember the exact words I expressed, but I'm sure God didn't count this as one of my better moments of oration.

Then a strange idea popped into my mind for such a fuming state. The idea suggested that I go downstairs to our basement…and worship! This was strange because I was deeply angry: it was a little past midnight and I was "trying" to fall asleep! How would a midnight worship session help me get my needed sleep? After a slight deliberation, I thought I would give it a try and love God when I least wanted to. I trudged downstairs where my family couldn't hear me and began a song and praise session to the Almighty. I was fatigued from fighting insomnia, but something stirred deep within me to heartfelt praise. Out of my heart and through my lips came words from old choruses like these:

What can wash away my sin?
Nothing but the blood of Jesus;
What can make me whole again?
Nothing but the blood of Jesus.[xxxviii]

I love You, Lord, and I lift my voice
to worship you, O my soul, rejoice!
Take joy, my King, in what you hear:
May it be a sweet, sweet sound in Your ear.[xxxix]

Jesus, name above all names,
beautiful Savior, glorious Lord,
Emmanuel, God is with us,
blessed Redeemer, Living Word.[xl]

Songs like these started out softly but gained intensity as I sang and repeated them. Surprisingly and frighteningly, the deeper the worship that came from the springs of my soul, the more I felt a resistance pushing back against my songs! There was a definite growing resistance to my songs, and it wasn't a resistance to singing coming from my heart. I had already overcome that resistance when I got out of bed and went down the stairs for my midnight worship session.

I was enjoying this worship, but something was rising, seemingly in me, against my worship. Interestingly, the more I repeated the name of Jesus in a song, the stronger the resistance came against my voice. There was a definite third party getting involved in my worship, which didn't like it at all—especially the name of Jesus! The more I ramped up my singing, especially naming Jesus and singing about His precious blood, the more I felt this resistance intensify.

I turned up the worship and began to sing with all my heart almost as loud as my breaking voice could go. This certainly wasn't aesthetically beautiful, but it was from my heart, focusing on my Savior—and engaging my entire being! Since I sensed a spiritual being not liking it, I sang with my greatest gusto. My kids and most of my congregation would have most certainly cringed at the broken noises coming from my lips if they didn't know the context of my soul battle. However, I could tell a war was raging in and around my soul, and my worship was intensifying the battle.

Then it happened. Probably no more than fifteen minutes into my middle of the midnight night worship session, as I was belting out songs in the name of Jesus and singing about His precious blood, a deep, hideous voice began to actually interrupt my own singing voice. This hideous voice actually garbled my words as I sang to Jesus about the blood of Jesus.

I purposely amped up love songs to and about my Savior. I realized it was a critical moment of a critical wrestling match. As I attempted my greatest worship fervor, at the highest pitch of my singing, I suddenly let out a huge, unexpected sneeze, and my warfare suddenly stopped. It felt like with one huge sneeze, the enemy, who so fiercely opposed my worship, suddenly stopped its resistance.

This same kind of worship opposition occurred against me the following Sunday afternoon as I worshipped privately again in my basement. This time, however, there was no hideous voice pressing back against my voice, but something which made me feel like vomiting. Yet the vomit would only come halfway up my throat. No release came during my Sunday afternoon worship session, but only the feeling, "What in the world is this thing that feels like it is being pushed up and out as I worship?"

These dark shades of spiritual warfare were new ground for me. As you might expect, leaders in the Christian community gave me different views as to what transpired with my "sneeze." Some who had worked in deliverance ministries were convinced that God delivers the "demonized" through such worship and the "sneezing" and "vomiting" is a sign of the enemy's departure. Another counselor, very wise in deliverance ministry, believed demons go to great lengths to make Christians think they are inside them to try frightening them. Making Christians think they are on the inside is part and parcel of their tormenting tactics. Another friend who heard much of my story seemed to chalk it up to my overactive imagination. My imagination was definitely alive in a good sense during these trials, but too much was happening in body and soul in the midst of my passionate worship to say my overactive imagination was getting the best of me.

It is not my intention to figure out if demons were on the inside getting worked out of me or if they were harassing me from the outside. Truly, only God knows. What the Almighty highlighted for me was the importance in spiritual warfare of worshipping Him from my heart, and how He does work freedom through passionate worship. Demons hate the passionate worship of Jesus, and it is a powerful way to work freedom into our souls. Their harassment was at least temporarily broken through fervent worship. That night, worshipping in the name of Jesus won a great and encouraging victory. I went upstairs and eventually fell asleep.

Reinhard Bonnke said demons are like flies and "Flies can only sit on a cold stove, and on a cold stove they can sit very long! Get the fire of the Holy Spirit into your life, and that dirty demon will not dare to touch you, lest he burn his filthy fingers."[xli] I would add, "Nothing turns up the heat of our souls like personal, sacrificial fervent worship!"

Practical Wisdom for the Invisible War

God often moves powerfully in and for his people through worship. Worship from the heart is one way we can put on God's armor and watch Him fight on our behalf.

My brother in law, Dan Heise, a man wise in his knowledge of Scripture, called me and passed along an Old Testament story that he thought might be helpful in this time of amped-up spiritual battle, illustrating how God fights on behalf of His worshipping people. The story is that of King Jehoshaphat, who led the nation of Judah against threatening nations as told in 2 Chronicles 20. The fact that a King of Judah went to war against an invading nation was not the big story. It is the methods he used to fight the war that are so intriguing.

When King Jehoshaphat was informed of the imminent peril, he first humbly admitted his fear. He called a great fast throughout Judah so the nation could ask God for help (vv. 1-4). Fasting and prayer is a great way to communicate our helplessness to God and our need for His intervention in the face of great danger. Second, Jehoshaphat praised God publicly and recounted God's great actions on their behalf in the past (vv.5-9). Third, he specified, in prayer, what he needed in the form of deliverance (vv. 10-12).

God responded to their humble cries by falling upon Jahaziel (a priest from the Levites) in power, informing the people the fight was His to win, and giving them promises and instructions for their deliverance (vv. 13-17). In response, the people, including the priests, responded to such divine promises with great thanksgiving and praise (vv. 18-19). In this case, prayer and praise were the actual instruments God used to come alongside His people and fight their battles for them. **God worked their deliverance as they praised Him.**

---

*"**And when they began to sing and praise,** the LORD set an ambush against the men of Ammon, Moab, and Mount Seir, who had come against Judah, so that they were routed."*
2 Chronicles 20:22 (emphasis mine)

Today, God can drive away our greatest enemies, unseen demons, through the act of fervent worship! When worship is accompanied by fasting and heartfelt fervency, and when done at times of inconvenience, it can speed up deliverance and victory. The very act of heartfelt, sacrificial worship in times of inconvenience can not only be used by God as an instrument of deliverance from demonic harassment but can be the best cure for soul sluggishness, which God is deadly serious about curing in His blood-bought children.

QUESTIONS FOR REFLECTION AND DISCUSSION

1. What does the Bible mean by giving God "a sacrifice of praise"?

2. How would you describe "soul sluggishness"?

3. How does fervent sacrificial praise heal soul sluggishness?

4. Why might God choose to win battles for us during praise and worship?

5. What are some sacrifices of praise you might make in personal or corporate worship?

Thomas Dages

CHAPTER THIRTEEN

A Disappointing Deliverance

Can a Christian have an evil spirit? I am not sure I have the answer to this, but I would raise this question: Can an evil spirit have a Christian?
—Henry Wright[xlii]

WITH ALL THE OVERT SPIRITUAL ACTIVITY HAPPENING in and around me, I sensed I might have demons from which I needed deliverance. Over the past year and a half, demonic forces certainly had reared their heads in some frighteningly ugly ways so that I felt the opposition in sometimes harrowing ways. Feeling such strong resistance during worship and in my throat is more than unnerving. The depths they can penetrate into the soul of a true believer, while God keeps our spirits safe with His sealing, is one of the many great mysteries of the Christian life. While I don't have certitude in my answers, I knew evil was stirring in and around my soul. All these events were making me think I might need to be the subject of an old-fashioned deliverance from demonic spirits that somehow had found a way through my armor into a nook and cranny of my inner man.

I called my good friend and prayer partner Todd Bramblett from Christian Fellowship and told him of the ugly internal events that had transpired in my midnight and Sunday afternoon worship sessions. Todd's response was one of deep concern, and he set up a meeting with Pastor Fred Clark, a very discerning and loving pastor, with whom I had prayed with Todd on several occasions. I had been impressed with Pastor Fred since the day we first met. His genuine love for God's people, as well as for me, and his sensitivity to the moving of the Spirit were very evident. It was Todd and Pastor Fred who were praying with me the first time when I sensed Jesus powerfully walking with me towards heaven as a lion in my imagination. I trusted these two men with my life as I sensed the Spirit of God was deeply at work in and through them. Todd also demonstrated his love for me by telling me he was going to pray and fast (go without food) for me until we could get together in our prayer session. These men could be trusted as loving and discerning agents of God's healing prowess.

Several days later, the three of us met at Todd's office in Herndon, Virginia. Todd wanted Fred Clark present not only because of his godliness and insight, but because of the spiritual authority he possessed as an ordained pastor. Since we had not been with each other as a prayer team for several months, I took the time to fill them in to the many disturbing experiences I had endured since we had last met.

We took time to pray together, and then Todd took the lead by addressing any demons who might be inside or around me. Todd tried to get any demons to identify their presence as he asked questions and I listened to their possible answers in my own mind. I must confess some dishonesty on my part (I confessed this to Todd at a later date), that the thoughts which came to my mind were probably more of my making than any demonic spirit. I wasn't purposely dishonest, but I was so eager to get these things identified, and away from me, that I "helped" the process along by telling him more of what I thought should be said, rather than what evil spirits were actually saying in my mind.

Overall, I was deeply disappointed in both what didn't and did transpire during this "deliverance" session. First, nothing dramatic in any way occurred as always seemed to happen when Jesus and his disciples "delivered" people in the New Testament. There were no voices resisting the authority of Jesus. There were no shrieks from demons who were forced to leave. There were no ugly voices giving names or reasons why they had moral ground to infest my inner being. There was no sense of sudden freedom on my part, and I sensed nothing in any way depart from me. There was nothing that indicated anything foul was in or around me or anything foul had departed from me. I am a man who is highly sensitive (probably overly so) to what goes on inside of me, and there wasn't even the slightest hint of anything departing from my life, not even a small sneeze!

What did happen, however, was even more disappointing than what didn't happen. A host of ugly emotions, all wrapped together so no one ugly emotion was identifiable, seemed to bubble to the surface of my soul. It was like a painful boil suddenly emerging just below the skin, but in my case, the boil seemed to slide to the surface of my inner man. It was painful, complex, and stubborn. It emerged from the deepest places of my heart.

From watching my roommate in college and listening to his deep groans of pain, I knew how painful boils are when they emerge to the surface of the skin. Brett Cowell, my roommate in college, played football his freshman year at Taylor University, and on several occasions he found boils underneath his skin, just below his knee. Somehow, he would contract this staph infection (maybe from scraping his knee on the football field), and he would go to great pains to cajole it carefully to and through the surface of his skin. As he studied at his dorm room desk, with his face in his books, his hands and fingers worked with a warm washcloth to gently and carefully bring the boil up and out. I could tell by his deep groans and painful sighs that the process was exceedingly painful. This process could take several days and several sets of focused hours at a time to push the boil out. Once the boil surfaced, he would take what was like a hard ball of pussy infection, place it in paper towel, and dispose of it carefully, so the infection wouldn't spread to someone else. Boils are highly contagious, and Brett, thankfully, didn't want me or anyone catching what would grow into another torturous infection in someone else.

While I'm not an expert on boils of the body, I felt like what was exposed in my inner being that day was a spiritual boil emerging out of deep places in my soul. While I'm unsure whether boils in the body can have multiple strains of infection, my soul boil was festering with multiple infections of sin, trauma, lies, coping mechanisms of attempted control, and buried emotional pain. This all morphed into a painful inner boil deep within my soul. While my life was crippled with anxiety and insomnia and attacked by nefarious forces of evil, these simply served to surface and expose other, deeper infections growing and building into a spiritual "mass" in my inner man.

Sitting there in Todd's office, an inner mass of infections seemed to rise full strength to the surface of my soul. It was like the worst of me that was churning and hiding in my heart's deepest places surfaced to let me know it was present and needed expulsion. **This boil wasn't a demon needing to be cast out. It was my heart history needing to be massaged out by the love of God and deep renewing of my mind.**

A physical boil can be removed by a person who gently cajoles it to the surface, but this boil was so wrapped in my history of heart idols, angers, anxieties, coping mechanisms, insecurities, and even imbedded into the neural highways of my brain, that to exorcise it as a boil, if possible, would have destroyed me. It was during this attempted deliverance when this boil made itself known with all it stubborn, steely strength.

Prior to my crisis, if someone tried explaining to me the emergence of such a boil in their inner being, I would not have understood and would have probably encouraged them to simply "push through it," or "get over it." Of course, I would tell them lovingly to "push through it," and then think silently to "get over it." Yet now the stubborn, inextricable pain was in me, and extricating this mass was not so simple.

I can only imagine the frightening strength of others' boils worse than mine. Sexual abuse stuffed and then revealed. Levels of PTSD from seeing wartime atrocities triggering deeper and more frequent anxieties than my own. Or repeated battering from an alcoholic father. Such traumas can severely damage trust, set in motion mechanisms of attempted control, release poisonous toxins of an unforgiving spirit into our hearts, and develop inner boils of horrific strength. When my inner boil emerged, I became a "believer" in a dimension and depth of emotional pain of which formerly I was intellectually and experientially unaware.

Through my emerged inner boil, God would now set me on a new slow framework of healing (as opposed to quick fixes) and would begin to develop in this extended season of suffering and healing a new depth of mercy and sensitivity towards others who had old, deep, and menacing inner boils. I would become as Henri Nouwen coined a "wounded healer" myself, not because I had all the answers, but because I could now feel more deeply the stubborn emotional afflictions of others and more effectively communicate the deep compassion and slow healing of Jesus in those boils.[xliii] The emergence of my deep, stubborn boil was the genesis for me to start thinking differently about my healing and the healing of others.

Sitting there in Todd's office, I first recognized the hideous strength and complexity of my spiritual boil. It would be expelled, but not in one push or exorcism, but over time with many strategic surgical cuts of the Great Physician and many acts of faith and obedience to the Spirit's promptings on my part. God simply used demons and their sharp claws to bring this boil out of hiding.

I remember Todd commenting on the light of God's presence being sensed in the room during my attempted demonic deliverance, but for me, the darkness and stubborn strength of my soul boil was much more keenly felt.

It took several months for me to realize God's plan for my healing was not in a sudden deliverance through commanding demons to leave. This inner boil was not going to be cast out instantly or cajoled out in a matter of hours, days, weeks, or even months. This boil was old and an intrinsic part of me. It needed cleansing and transformation by the Spirit of the living God as He empowered me to repent and renounce and renew my mind from many different soul infections. If there were demons harassing me, the best way to rid myself of them was to "close the doors" of disobedience through which they were entering. Dr. Terry Wardle, insightfully citing Charles Kraft, suggests, "...demons are like rats. They are attracted to garbage. If you kick out the rats but leave the garbage, they will come back."[xliv]

In several weeks, I would find myself in the loving care of an Anglican priest who specialized in helping pastors entrenched in such spiritual warfare. In this, God in His mercy gave me more wonderful tools and insights for my healing journey and the "lancing of my soul." My freedom would come, but it would be a much deeper and slower process than I envisioned.

Practical Wisdom for the Invisible War

Only God can make us what C.S. Lewis references as deliciously clean inside, yet it takes seasoned wisdom to know what part we play in this process of change and healing.

Paul seems to capture God's work and our response to His work, when he says in the second chapter of Philippians,

> *"Therefore, my beloved, as you have always obeyed, so now, not only as in my presence but much more in my absence, work out your own salvation with fear and trembling, for it is God who works in you, both to will and to work for his good pleasure."*
> Philippians 2:12-13

This salvation Paul tells us to "work out" is our sanctification salvation. Sanctification is the growth process of being made into the likeness of Jesus, a process that commences immediately upon the event of our justification. Justification is a legal term referring to the positional righteousness of Jesus given to us the moment we believe Jesus as our Lord and Savior. Notice that Paul doesn't say we are to work "for" our salvation, but "work out" our own salvation. This type of salvation isn't the positional righteousness received by faith, but is the practical righteousness or process of spiritual growth into the image of Christ. God works in us, and we demonstrate our faith and obedience over a lifetime. He works it in by His Holy Spirit, but we work it out by our trust and obedience.

God is the One who causes the growth, change, healing, and cleansing within us, but we must participate and "work out" what He "works in." Paul's language is strong, even motivating us with godly fear to make sure we pursue obedience, assuring us that God is working in us "to will and to work for His good pleasure." God has saved us for more than simply giving people a ticket to heaven. He has saved us so that even in this life our lives will be truly shaped into the image of Jesus Christ. This shaping in the image of Christ not only involves the entirety of our inner man, but also the cleaning out of our inner infections. It also often involves the power tools of suffering, and God knows which suffering tools are best suited to uncover, cleanse, change, and heal our inner beings.

C.S. Lewis illustrates how this process of change occurs by God's grace and through our obedient submission to His working. In *The Voyage of the Dawn Treader*, the boy Eustace becomes a dragon through his disobedience, and he wants to rid himself of his dragon skin and change back into a boy. He has to be "undressed" and "undragoned" of his dragon skin by the Christ figure Aslan. After Eustace scratches and peels off a layer of ugly scales and skin, he finds through his reflection in water that his dragon skin is still on.

> *"Oh, that's all right, said I, it only means I had another smaller suit on underneath the first one, and I'll have to get out of it too. So I scratched and tore again and this under skin peeled off beautifully and out I stepped and left it lying beside the other one and went down to the well for my bathe.*
>
> *"Well, exactly the same thing happened again. And I thought to myself, oh dear, however many skins have I got to take off? For I was longing to bathe my leg. So I scratched away for the third time and got off a third skin, just like the two others, and stepped out of it. But as soon as I looked at myself in the water I knew it had been no good.*
>
> *"Then the lion said---but I don't know if it spoke-----You will have to let me undress you. I was afraid of his claws, I can tell you, but I was pretty nearly desperate now. So I just lay flat down on my back and let him do it.*
>
> *"The very first tear he made was so deep that I thought it had gone right into my heart. And when he began pulling the skin off, it hurt worse than anything I've ever felt. The only thing that made me able to bear it was just the pleasure of feeling the stuff peel off. You know – if you've ever picked the scab of a sore place. It hurt like billy oh but it is such fun to see it coming away..."*
>
> *"Well, he peeled the beastly stuff right off—just as I thought I'd done it myself the other three times, only they hadn't hurt—and there it was lying*

on the grass: only ever so much thicker, and darker, and more knobbly looking than the others had been."[xlv]

Lewis' metaphor of soul change and healing highlights both our need for total dependence upon Christ and our obedient submission to lay before Jesus so He can make the cuts. Eustace says about his encounter with Aslan, "So I just lay flat down on my back and let him do it." While this may sound like a sort of passivity not taught in Scripture, this surrender is the first step of necessary obedience in a direction of many smaller steps that must follow for lasting change to take place. Lewis also wonderfully brings out the desperate state we often need to experience after all our self-efforts fail.

Ask yourself the following soul- searching questions:
- Have you chosen to turn from your lifestyle of sin to trust in Christ alone as Savior and Lord? This is the start of the Christian life, yet it is only the beginning. However, a believing choice to trust and follow Christ must be made!
- Is your grand life goal lining up with God's great plan for you, to become like Jesus in purity of thought, inner strength, radical love, and obedience to your heavenly Father's will?
- Are you growing in your dependence upon God for His strength to do what He directs, or is your life set on self-effort and self-reliance to get things done?
- Have you ever in desperation and defeat thrown yourself at the feet of Jesus in full submission to do what only He can do? In the case of inner healing, the process takes time, and our dragon skin doesn't come off in one surgical cut!

QUESTIONS FOR REFLECTION AND DISCUSSION

1. What is the difference between justification salvation and sanctification salvation?

2. How is sanctification salvation related to inner healing?

3. How might wounding of the heart mixed with an unforgiving spirit slow down or stagnate the growth process?

4. What do you think it means to demonize sin? How could blaming sin on a demon hurt the process of growth and healing?

5. Why might God allow demons to scratch and claw at our soul infections?

CHAPTER FOURTEEN

Surprising Help from an Anglican Priest

To each is given the manifestation of the Spirit for the common good. To one is given through the Spirit the utterance of wisdom, and to another the utterance of knowledge according to the same Spirit, to another faith by the same Spirit, to another gifts of healing by the one Spirit, to another the working of miracles, to another prophecy, to another the ability to distinguish between spirits, to another various kinds of tongues, to another the interpretation of tongues. All these are empowered by one and the same Spirit, who apportions to each one individually as he wills.
—1 Corinthians 12:7-11

For if I pray in a tongue, my spirit prays but my mind is unfruitful. What am I to do? I will pray with my spirit, but I will pray with my mind also; I will sing with my spirit, but I will sing with my mind also.
—1 Corinthians 14:14-15

IT WAS NOT THAT I DIDN'T EXPECT HELP in my trip to Christ the King Spiritual Life Center in Greenwich, New York. It simply came in a different form than I expected. God has a way of breaking into our lives in fresh, unexpected ways, especially when we pursue Him in faith.

With this category five hurricane crawling slowly across my soul, and my life beaten with winds it never before experienced, I again contacted my good friends, Jim and Cynthia Eckert. I wanted to give them a progress report and share some of the frightening spiritual experiences that battered me and the frustration of nothing happening in my deliverance session. Cynthia, now well-seasoned in healing prayer ministries herself, was aware of the center with weekly healing prayer sessions. She thought they had a minister who was experienced in helping ministers like myself, entangled with the demonic, to help them find freedom. Cynthia contacted Christ The King Spiritual Life Center and set an appointment with Reverend Nigel Mumford, who would advise and help pray me through such spiritual darkness.

The trip was planned for late January. I would travel up to Jim and Cynthia's farm once again, and we would travel several hours together from northern Pennsylvania to eastern New York for God's assistance through this unique prayer warrior of God.

The Rev. Nigel Mumford's life and gifting is a beautiful demonstration of the grace of God cited in the above Scriptures. He tells his story of his conversion to Christ, his reception of a gift of healing, and many episodes of miraculous healings God worked through him as shared in his autobiography, *Hand to Hand, From Combat to Healing*.

Jim Eckert accompanied me as a loving friend in my meeting with Nigel and as someone who could remind me of key insights I might easily forget. A bucket was on hand next to Nigel in case a demon was present and was expelled in vomit. Fortunately, the bucket wasn't needed! Rev. Mumford listened well as I attempted to share highlights (or rather lowlights) of the past two-and-a-half years. After the better part of 45 minutes, Nigel shared with Jim and me that in his prayer preparation for our meeting together, God had given him a picture of what was going on in my life. This vision was a picture from above me, looking down upon my life, where he saw demonic spirits attacking me from behind.

When he first gave me this perspective of demons attacking me from behind, I interpreted this to mean that demons were literally finding their harassing way into my life through my back. Since none of God's armor explicitly covers the backside of a soldier, I wondered how I could fight in God's strength against such attacks! "All prayer," the last piece of armor given by Paul in Ephesians 6, was the only piece of armor that could cover me. Nigel gave me the prayer of Saint Patrick to pray, which I prayed sporadically for several weeks:

Christ be with me
Christ within me
Christ behind me
Christ before me
Christ beside me
Christ to win me
Christ to comfort and restore me
Christ beneath me
Christ above me
Christ in quiet
Christ in danger
Christ in hearts of all that love me
Christ in mouth of friend or stranger
-Saint Patrick

However, before leaving our meeting with Nigel, I shared with him about demonic opposition that I had wrestled with from an early age, and he called this new information "doorknob" information. This is information you share with a counselor when leaving, which radically changes how the counselor looks at a situation. This demonic activity had been coming against me in surges of fear and anxiety since childhood, and his vision was now better understood as demons attacking me **through my past**.

This latter understanding was, no doubt, the better understanding of my attackers from behind, as I realized my attackers were playing torturously in many old wounds in my soul. It became apparent the Great Physician was going to have to take me back to past issues of my life that were open and still festering for deep healing and cleansing to occur.

Nigel's advice to me in these times of gripping anxiety was to take my position in Christ and take authority over them by commanding them to go. As Christians who are in Christ, we have His very authority and can command demonic forces to stop their torment and leave us alone, when we exercise, verbally by faith, the authority Christ vested in us. **Nigel was strong with me to be strong in Christ and not to take any unnecessary torment.**

THE LANCING OF MY SOUL

Although I had used the authority of Christ in the recent past with extreme bouts of anxiety, this insight was really the start of my consistent usage of such a weapon when things got bad with my anxiety. It felt at times that demons were playing torturously in my already anxious heart and commanding them to go in the name of Jesus at times alleviated serious oppression. Even if the relief was only temporary, the short-lived relief brought great hope, refreshment, and encouragement to continue wrestling in faith. Faith in such instances is not passive but very active and demands that a soldier learn to fight in the power and authority given by God.

About halfway into our prayer session together, the door on the other side of the chapel suddenly flew open as a huge gust of wind blew into the chapel. Nigel looked at me and said, "That didn't happen by chance!" It was as though the Spirit of God had burst upon us in this chapel in a similar way as at Pentecost, when the Spirit formally fell in power on God's people in Jerusalem.

A little bit of background is in order at this point. I have had many "charismatic" friends who prayed over me in the past to receive the gift of speaking in tongues. Yet I was always more than hesitant in receiving such a gift. Most of my pastoral peers and teachers taught me that tongues had ceased with the closing of Scripture and today, tongues were at best a psychological aberration and at worst the influence of the demonic upon us. However, over the years I slowly came to believe charismatics are correct in teaching that tongues and miracles and healing would cease at the coming of the "perfect" in 1 Corinthians 13:10, which more naturally refers to the return of Christ than the completion of Scripture. Paul says it this way in his teaching to the Corinthians:

> *"For we know in part and we prophecy in part, but when the **perfect** comes, the partial will pass away. When I was a child, I spoke like a child, I thought like a child, I reasoned like a child. When I became a man, I gave up childish ways. For now we see in a mirror dimly, but then **face to face**. Now I know in part; then I shall know fully, even as I have been fully known."*
> *1 Corinthians 13:9-12 (emphasis mine)*

Scripture also teaches there are many kinds of tongues (1 Corinthians 12:10, 12:28, and 13:1), expressing themselves both as ways of sharing the gospel in unlearned languages in Acts, and as prayer and even praise languages in Corinth. Although prophecy or speaking truth to many edifies more, Paul adds that tongues can be a form of personal spiritual edification (1 Corinthians 14:4).

Nevertheless, even though my Scriptural convictions grew over the years that tongues today are authentic expressions of God's grace for the good of His church, my secret fears of demonic counterfeit made me extremely resistant. My "What if?" fears strongly overruled my growing theological convictions.

Yet God was softening me to receive such a gift. He was softening me theologically to see my charismatic brothers and sisters were on stronger grounds biblically for their continuation, and he was softening me experientially by helping me to see the fruitfulness flowing through many charismatic healing prayer ministries. He was also softening me through His voice to fully trust Him as my heavenly Father who would only give me what was good for me.

One day, several months prior to this prayer/counseling session with Nigel Mumford, as I traveled home from my own healing prayer session at Christian Fellowship, God brought to mind these words from Luke 11 about trusting Him to only give me good gifts.

"What father among you, if his son asks for a fish, will instead of a fish give him a serpent; or if he asks for an egg, will give him a scorpion?"
Luke 11:11-12

I found myself sharing with God in prayer that if He did indeed decide to give me the gift of tongues, I would not fear that it was a "snake" or "scorpion" but would "trust Him and receive it as a good gift from my heavenly Father."

Now fast forward to my closing time with Nigel Mumford. The wind blew the door open and Nigel was standing behind me, laying his hands upon me, anointing me with power for my own healing ministry, for healing in my own life, and for spiritual protection. He stood behind me and told me to raise my arms and as he anointed me under my arms, he spoke words like, "May you be carried forth on angel's wings." He would tell me later that he had never anointed and prayed for a person in such a way. Amazingly, something would happen in Denver the following month that told me God had honored this unique prayer of being "carried forth on angel's wings"! However, that amazing story is for the next chapter.

Now, God had another gift waiting for me before this session was over. As Nigel then sat across from me, he told me to open my mouth and begin moving my lips, so I could start praying in tongues. My first thought was, "Ok Lord, what do I do?" I had frowned upon others who used such apparent gimmicks to pass along the gift of tongues. After all, we don't have any explicit examples in the New Testament of people learning to speak in tongues in such a manner. Yet, I had recently told the Lord I was willing to trust Him as my heavenly Father with any good gifts He wanted to give me, and trust was what I most needed right now. How like God to humble me and use a methodology I once almost mocked.

Taking a tiny step of faith, I **barely** opened my mouth and moved my lips. Nigel told me to speak louder. I spoke just a tiny bit louder, and as I did, a beautiful unknown language came flowing gently and softly from my lips. I had given up full control of my tongue and lips to God, trusted Him, and He had given me a good gift from above. After a minute or so of speaking in tongues, Nigel told me, "You were not speaking in tongues, but praying in tongues." He went on to tell me that I was praying for my children in this new language, for he had been given interpretation from God.

A month later at a charismatic prayer meeting, I was tempted to give into my "What if?" fears, and as I trusted God and prayed in tongues, these "What if" fears in regards to praying in tongues by demonic influence suddenly vanished. With my eyes of faith focused on my Heavenly Father's heart of trustworthiness, my "What if?" fears, like a heavy, wet, suffocating blanket, suddenly ripped off my soul. I was now free to fully exercise my prayer language without fear and at times for great spiritual edification.

While God would remind me that tongues were the least of gifts and apparently not given to all (1 Corinthians 12:27-31), and true spirituality is to be driven by divine love (1 Corinthians 13:1), nevertheless, various tongues had a powerful place in the evangelism and worship of the early Church and apparently the Church spanning the ages into today.

After all, why would God remove spiritual gifts from His church if the demonic opposition and people's healing needs were exactly the same as they were in the early church? The giving of the Scriptures sets us a standard of objective truth to follow without taking away the gifts His church would need to move ahead in full power of the Spirit.

My visit with Rev. Nigel Mumford reinforced the existence of God's present healing graces, prepared me for my upcoming necessary journey into my past, added the protection of angels through prayer, and furnished me with a new gift of the Spirit for a new dimension of prayer. God wasn't suddenly taking away my inner issues. He was equipping me with gifts, experiences, wisdom and sensitivity so I could be changed and cleansed as I cooperated with Him in this deep renovation project of my soul.

Practical Wisdom for the Invisible War

In his book *Satisfy Your Soul*, Dr. Bruce Demarest wisely challenges Evangelicals (gospel-believing Christians) to pursue correct knowledge or doctrine in Bible study, but to not stop at building our minds in doctrinal truth.

Orthodoxy, or right belief, is essential to entering into Christ and the Christian life, and to going on to live one's life in fair territory. If we believe false doctrines, our lives will eventually be blown off course and our faith may even become shipwrecked on the rocks of heresy. Believing false doctrine may end up steering us into eventually justifying lives lived in gross immorality. However, the Christian life is much more than professing and teaching what is right to believe. Jesus is to be obeyed and experienced in the head and heart.

Christ-followers also need the humility to understand that some of our dearly held non-essential beliefs may indeed be wrong (e.g., what we've been taught about spiritual gifts and healing, what we believe about The Lord's Supper, or how end time events may really unfold). As we study Scripture, we need to be open to God bringing us to theological repentance (a change of perspective and beliefs) and be open to how He might speak through believers of other denominations to more than tweak our own doctrines. Careful study of Scripture is essential to building right beliefs. Yet, if we are not careful, we can find ourselves in self-made theological straightjackets, which don't let us take in the fresh winds God's Spirit wants to breathe into our souls.

Not only do we need to be open to tweaking or radically changing dearly held wrong-headed beliefs, but we also need to make sure that our doctrine is influencing how we actually carry out the commandments of God. This is called "orthopraxy" or acting upon what we believe.

For too long a period in my life, I believed I was a healthy Christian because "all" my beliefs were safe and sound (or so I thought), and my sermons fell in line with biblical truth. However, as A.W. Tozer points out, "You can be straight as a gun barrel theologically and as empty as one spiritually."[xlvi] We need to pursue God in such a way that we believe with our minds and obey with our hearts. In the Christian community and in my own soul, there was a huge gap between what I formally believed and what I actually practiced. I knew the truth about forgiving from the heart others who hurt me deeply. I preached this many times from the pulpit and confronted people on holding onto hurts. However, truth be told, I retained an unforgiving and soul-poisoning spirit on far too many occasions. God, in His grace, was determined to make me a doer of the truths I believed!

However, Dr. Demarest introduced me to a third term also essential to my spiritual vitality. This third term was "orthopathy," or right passions in my inner being.[xlvii] My orthopathy was not growing deeply in my delight for God or for His people. My delight in God was running near empty. One of the reasons King David in the Old Testament was considered a man after God's heart was David's passionate pursuit of God in prayerful worship. My orthopathy would deepen as I followed in David's footsteps of personally engaging in passionate, heartfelt worship.

QUESTIONS FOR REFLECTION AND DISCUSSION

1. Have you ever changed what you believed because the Holy Spirit helped you see Scripture differently?

2. Is evidence of spiritual gifts a sign of spiritual maturity? Why or why not?

3. According to 1 Cor. 13, what is the greatest indication of spiritual maturity?

4. What are some harmful things that happen in church life when evidence of miraculous gifts become more important than Christ-driven love?

5. How would you explain the differences between orthodoxy, orthopraxy and orthopathy? What are the dangers of being stuck in only orthodoxy?

CHAPTER FIFTEEN

More Healing Grace in Denver

Grace, we must learn, is opposed to earning, not to effort.
—*Dr. Bruce Demarest*[xlviii]

I can do all things through him who strengthens me.
—*Philippians 4:13*

Grace is not only pardon of sin, but also power over sin.
—*Andrew Murray*[xlix]

AFTER MY ENCOUNTER WITH GOD'S GRACE through Nigel Mumford, I returned to the Eckerts' farm where I spent the night and left the next morning for my home in Northern Virginia. I had made this same trip down Route 15 through Maryland and into Pennsylvania several years earlier when my life was sent into a tailspin. However, God now equipped me with more wisdom to face my heart issues coming to the surface of my soul.

One of the new stressors in my life, discovered while making my first trip home down Route 15 from Pennsylvania after the onset of my crises, was my new nemesis of near-constant ear ringing. To go through everything swirling in my soul and add near-constant ringing in my ears made me wonder how I was going to survive. Making matters worse, with this second round of spiritual attacks my ear ringing seemed to ratchet up several volume levels. Nigel Mumford prayed for God to heal this audiological condition but with no observable results of miraculous healing. Nigel told me as he prayed for me that God had recently healed someone through prayer with this condition of tinnitus. However, God didn't have the same plans for my immediate healing!

My father-in-law Ron Rankin suffered from ear ringing and told me about a hearing clinic in Denver helping people reduce and better manage their tinnitus. My case of ear ringing elevated to the point where I was willing to try this new therapy, even if it was new and expensive. If something could decrease the noise level and help reduce this significant stressor, it would be worth the time and expense.

When I arrived back in Reston, I weighed my options carefully and after discussion with Julie, I decided to take a trip out west. I called the Colorado Tinnitus and Hearing Center and made my appointment for late February.

Four Experiences of More Healing and Encouraging Grace

My trip to this hearing clinic would prove fruitful, yet it took much longer in treatment for me to get significant results. Dr. Patty Kalmbach took significant time to listen to how my tinnitus developed. Being a follower of Jesus herself, she was quite interested in the spiritual warfare dimension of my battle and was all "ears" to my story. She put me in a hearing booth to analyze my tinnitus severity (loudness) and capture the pitch of ear ringing I experienced. My loudness was gauged at moderate to severe, and my pitch resembled the whirring noise of jet engines, revving up on a runway. She then built in white noise and music in a neuromonics device, which would cover over much of my tinnitus. For the first several months of therapy, I listened to soft music with this white noise embedded in it.

This therapy would both cover up my tinnitus and train my brain to block it out. My limbic system in my brain, caught up in a cycle of fear, received a much-needed break from the constant noise in my ears and helped ease my fear that I would never get a break from this ringing. For the "in control" person I was, the fear of being "out of control" and not being able to stop or escape the ear ringing was at times a near-crippling fear in and of itself. My tinnitus training was a refreshing break from the noise and helped me escape the fear cycle in which I was caught.

Dr. Patty also gave me a book on cognitive therapy entitled *Feeling Good* by Dr. David D. Burns, M.D so I could learn to mentally respond differently to my ear ringing when the noise was more than a nuisance. Cognitively training our brain to respond and think differently with unwanted ear ringing is another effective way to calm the brain and corresponding fears. Dr. Burns highlights ten cognitive distortions that we need to replace with rational truths for emotional calmness to prevail. The cognitive distortion that was most disturbing me was "magnification" or "catastrophizing" my problems (making them much worse than they were).[1] Through this reading I could continue the process of renewing my mind and replace my cognitive distortions with calming biblical truths of God's control and His care for my life.

Interestingly, while God did reduce this ear ringing stressor, He also used this stressor to gently break my attempted control of life and strengthen my soul in complete reliance upon Him. His healing and sanctifying grace were so evident in this unwanted stressor. How good of God to reduce the tinnitus noise in my ears (using 21st century technology), train me to untwist cognitive distortions, and break me of unhealthy control as I learned moment by moment to trust Him.

My trip to Denver would have been worth it simply for my tinnitus reduction and soul training alone, but God had deeper surprises of grace for my battle-weary soul.

The next surprise of grace occurred as I prayed with three friends at the first church where I served. I showed up at Bear Creek Church on Monday evening after just finishing my first four-hour usage of my neuromonics device. If the truth be told, I was showing up at this prayer meeting more to see my old friends than expecting to see God move powerfully upon me.

After greeting my old friends, Bob and Debbie Sandberg and June Torborg, and giving them a brief synopsis of my tinnitus distress and therapy, we prayed together for the church, its ministries, and for people the Lord brought to our minds. However, it didn't take long in this prayer meeting for spiritual activity to stir. As we were sitting in prayer together, suddenly anxiety, emotionally crippling anxiety, fell upon me. It was like a strong wrestler suddenly dropped on my shoulders from above, placing a vice-like squeeze upon my soul.

For several minutes as we all prayed, I silently did what I could to fight free...without any results. If anything, the pressing, gripping nature of the anxiety only worsened. In the informality of the meeting, I shared with my friends the fierce anxiety battle in which I was engaged. They immediately gathered around me, laid their hands upon me, and prayed for my freedom. As they prayed over me, June, sensing guidance from the Holy Spirit, dropped a bomb on me. She sensed a word from the Lord that an unforgiving spirit or malice was the reason for my oppressive anxiety!

My response to this word from God about my anxiety being rooted in unresolved bitterness was mixed. Theologically, I knew the symptoms of anxiety could often be rooted in an unforgiving spirit, which both poisons and imprisons the heart. An unforgiving spirit, when left unchecked, can morph into even uglier sins, like bitterness, hatred, and malice. I also knew from Scripture, through the "Parable of the Unforgiving Servant" found in Matthew 18:21-35, that refusal to forgive from the heart can be a huge "open door" for demons to torture our hearts. The hypocrisy of not extending forgiveness, as it was lavished upon us in Jesus, is huge. Demons have the freedom to torture people until we forgive from the heart as the parable poignantly teaches.

My problem with this revelation by the Spirit, however, was one of frustration. I was dealing with forgiving people in my church who had deeply hurt me and who I thought I had already forgiven. When I had first dealt with these issues several years back, I deeply wrestled in fasting and prayer to forgive them, and so I thought I was finished with this spiritual fight. Yet here was an old friend telling me, apparently by the Spirit, there was more forgiveness to be done in my soul. Apparently, I was being pinned with anxiety in a prayer meeting so I would get this work of forgiveness done! I wondered, "God, what do I have to do to really forgive these people from the heart to close these open doors and find the freedom true forgiveness brings?"

I confessed, once again, my hurt and apparent hate towards these people. This time, however, I sensed a need not only to forgive, but to renounce this unforgiving spirit for the sin that I had committed. I had used the words "I forgive" on many prior occasions, but I had never renounced and repented of the unforgiving spirit and malice that fomented in my heart. An unforgiving spirit, after we are forgiven, is a truly despicable sin. I had never really seen the ugliness of this sin in my own heart. As I confessed my unforgiving spirit and verbally renounced these sins **with all my strength**, the anxiety began to abate. Sensing the freedom occurring incrementally through these verbal renunciations, I continued my renouncements **with all my heart**.

As it turned out, I'm glad this meeting was small, because my spiritual ugliness was great and my emotions were very strong. By the time our praying and my confessing, renouncing, and repenting were done, the oppressive anxiety was completely lifted and left. How awesome were the palpable results of confessing and renouncing this unforgiving spirit with my whole heart?

This prayer meeting highlighted that our wrestling with the enemy has to be done in God's strength, but it also highlights the efforts necessary to put forth serious soul work in the growth of sanctifying grace. I did make an effort of going to a prayer meeting to meet with God. I did make an effort of humbling myself to be honest before my friends about this stubborn sin of an unforgiving spirit. I did make the effort confessing and renouncing sin onto which I was stubbornly hanging. God in His wisdom led me to the prayer meeting and permitted a nefarious force to be planted upon me with great force and slowly shut the door on its harassments through my efforts of obedience.

I found this process of forgiveness when bitterness had set in to be extremely painful. Not only do we need to take our hearts to the cross of Christ for empowered forgiveness and cleansing, but when unforgiveness is old and deep, often the Holy Spirit needs to take us back to specific hurts to confess and renounce for full freedom to set into our hearts. If we pay only lip service in this process with a paltry "I forgive," bitterness bondage will stay deeply rooted. We need to allow the Holy Spirit to show us specifically where forgiveness needs to be granted and then by the grace of God we need to renounce with our whole being! Freedom will come when repentance is genuine and deep.

Yet God had even more healing grace to pour on me during this trip out west. His next move would be through a prophecy meeting in a big charismatic church.

Judy Bahm, a dear friend of mine from my years at Bear Creek Church, invited me to a mid-week worship session at her new church where she served in Littleton. I became great friends with Judy and

Mike Bahm after graduating from Westminster Seminary in Philadelphia and moving to Lakewood, Colorado, in 1990 to be an assistant/associate pastor. This was where I cut my teeth in ministry in my first pastorate. Mike became a close friend of mine, a fishing partner, and he and Judy were used by the Lord in many ways to help me grow in grace, both as a young man and a young minister. Several years back Mike was diagnosed with brain cancer, and God took him home at the young age of 56.

Judy, however, continued her nurturing ways and knowing of my seismic spiritual and emotional battles, she invited me to her church for an inspiring evening of worship and prayer. However, the music was way too loud for my ears, and we decided to slip downstairs to find help in a prayer and prophecy meeting that was running concurrently with the worship.

This was new turf for me. I was used to preaching God's prophetic Word of Scripture to a congregation of people, but this was a small group of people gifted in hearing prophetic words God was speaking to individuals who came forward for encouragement from the Lord. I figured it couldn't hurt as long as what was told me didn't contradict Scripture, and the Lord might have something fresh to tell me in this behemoth battle I was facing. God had already stretched me in the new ways He was communicating through various dreams, visions, and "words" from the Lord given in prayer meetings. Maybe He would do so again.

Without knowing a word about me, these people spoke encouraging truths from the Lord and were spot on in regards to me and what I was experiencing. The information they gave me about myself and my struggles and the word pictures they used to describe my journey paralleled my life beautifully. After probably 20-30 minutes or so of prayer and prophecy, they gave me a tape of all that was said, and we departed. It was a very encouraging time, but what

transpired just moments after the meeting was the most energizing and comforting of all.

One of the ladies who ministered to me came out of the room with a look of surprise. She said she had to tell me what she saw during our time together. She said as they listened to the Lord about me, she looked up and saw two angels just behind my arms, one on each side of me. She emphasized these two angels were huge. I smiled at the thought of what she said and remembered Hebrews 1:14 concerning angels, "Are they not all ministering spirits sent out to serve for the sake of those who are to inherit salvation?" Wow! How this affirmation of hope lifted my soul in encouragement.

I was also reminded of the words of Nigel Mumford just one month prior as he anointed me under both arms and prayed "that I would be carried along on angel's wings." God did exactly as Nigel prayed and sent two gargantuan angels to help carry me through this battle, and God opened someone's eyes to see this and communicate it to me!

To cap off this week, on my plane ride home to Reston, I sat next to a pastor's wife. She listened to snippets of my story, and I confided that it took everything in me to override my anxiety to even get on the plane and fly home to Reston. She told me of some of her husband's brutal battles serving as a pastor for ten years in Utah. He stepped down from the pastorate and went back to seminary for a time of refreshment. If I remember correctly, he now served as a chaplain in a retirement community and ministered to people at the critical time of death. She said, "He is a new man through the battles he went through and relishes to be with older people in such a sacred moment of death."

When she stood up to exit the plane, she looked at me and said with soul-stirring power, "God never, ever, ever takes anyone through hardships that He also doesn't provide strength to endure." Her words, spoken with such authority, echoed down through the deepest corridors of my soul and stirred me with courage. I'm sure my seat assignment next to this seasoned saint who watched her husband transform into a new man through hardship was God's design for another fill of uplifting grace.

Practical Wisdom for the Invisible War

When considering the theme of forgiveness, it is helpful to recognize there seems to be two types of forgiveness granted by God: judicial forgiveness and fatherly forgiveness.[li]

Judicial forgiveness is granted by God the moment someone is genuinely justified when converted to Christ. It is amazing to think that God grants a full pardon for all our sins past, present and future. As we are justified (or declared righteous) by God, every sin we committed or will ever commit is covered, cleansed, and forgiven. God, as our judge, judicially forgives all our sins forever the moment we genuinely embrace Christ as Savior and Lord. Judicial forgiveness becomes clearer as we unpack the meaning of our justification and hear what Jesus accomplished for His people on the cross. The writer to the Hebrews says:

"But when Christ had offered for all time a single sacrifice for sins, he sat down at the right hand of God…"
Hebrews 10:12

"For by a single offering he has perfected for all time those who are being sanctified."
Hebrews 10:14

Paul reminds us of the power of our received justification and the peace of God it brings when he writes:

> *"Therefore, since we have been justified by faith, we have peace with God through our Lord Jesus Christ. Through Him we have also obtained access by faith into this **grace in which we stand**, and we rejoice in hope of the glory of God."*
> Romans 5:1-2 (emphasis mine)

For the genuine Christian, this judicial forgiveness is full and final, and our status before God is irreversible. **Therefore, when God threatens not to forgive us if we don't forgive others, He must have something other than our judicial forgiveness in mind.**

In Matthew chapter six, Jesus threatens to withhold forgiveness when his disciples failed to forgive: "...but if you do not forgive others their trespasses, neither will your Father forgive your trespasses." This withdrawal of forgiveness should be understood as fatherly forgiveness. If His justified and adopted children fail to forgive, we forfeit God's fatherly forgiveness or intimacy with our heavenly Father. Relational closeness with God is greatly diminished when we choose to hold onto grudges over giving grace. Not only do demons have the right to torment us until we forgive from the heart, but we lose out on emotional closeness with our Father. This is how we must understand the act of God withholding forgiveness.

It is frightening to see how the seeds of an unforgiving spirit can slowly grow and germinate so much darkness within us until we truly learn to forgive from the heart. We must be wise to take ourselves back to the cross of Christ and see the magnitude of our sin the grace of Jesus covers. This is always humbling, but it is also empowering to remind ourselves of the magnitude of grace already given to us, so we can freely give much smaller grace to others. It also reminds us how costly is the grace of forgiveness. It cost Jesus His life to let us go free from the punishment we deserve. It often costs us emotionally, spiritually, and even financially to let people go free from the punishment we want to inflict. Yet this is the only path to true freedom.

If we are misers with His grace, we can expect to live in misery!

QUESTIONS FOR REFLECTION AND DISCUSSION

1. Why is refusing to forgive from the heart and releasing someone from the pain they caused you so antithetical to the Christian faith?

2. Is forgiveness a process or an event?

3. Why do you think the Lord gave the command to forgive in the middle of a prayer He intends His people to pray through on a regular basis?

4. Have you ever wrestled deeply with letting go of a hurt or hurts that seemed stuck in your heart?

5. Are you free from all bitterness?

CHAPTER SIXTEEN

A Hope-Filled Dream of Heaven

I know a man in Christ who fourteen years ago was caught up into the third heaven—whether in the body or out of the body I do not know, God knows. And I know that this man was caught up into paradise—whether in the body or out of the body I do not know, God knows —and he heard things that cannot be told, which man may not utter.
—2 Corinthians 12:2-4

THE ABOVE PASSAGE OF SCRIPTURE WAS WRITTEN by Paul the Apostle about his experience seeing and hearing things in heaven that were indescribable and unutterable. The only thing Paul was uncertain about was whether this experience in heaven came to him when he was "out of the body" or "in the body." The revelations Paul received from God about heaven were so powerful that God sent a "thorn in the flesh" hand delivered by the devil to keep Him humble (2 Corinthians 12:7).

One of the many great encouragements God graciously gave me through this painful journey was a powerful dream to give me a taste of my future destiny. While Paul's visions were much more powerful and his revelations much deeper, my dream of heaven nevertheless sank the anchor of hope firmly in my own soul, giving me great encouragement to keep moving forward in my healing journey. God sent this dream as I was teaching my congregation from the book of First Peter. He would send this dream when the winds, waves, and darkness of my storm were quite fierce.

One night, as I fell asleep, I suddenly found myself in the most beautiful place I had ever seen. Instantly, I knew this beautiful place to be heaven. While I didn't see God, angels, or any palaces or streets paved with gold, I knew intuitively I was in God's peaceful eternity. I was surrounded by the most beautiful hues of blue that were eternally deep.

Interestingly, I always wondered as a child how I could be in any place 'forever" (including heaven) and enjoy it, free of anxieties. The concept of "forever" freaked me out! Worry was such a part of me that I wondered how I could be in a place forever without anxiety scratching my soul. The promise of an unspoiled, emotionally unscathed existence in heaven was something I accepted by faith. Many times, as I imagined eternity, I had to go on the fact that since God lives forever and wasn't touched or spoiled by anxiety, I could trust He could so work His magic of permanent peace in me when I arrived for my eternal stay. Yet thoughts of eternity often struck worry pangs in my soul.

Here I was in this dreamy place of beauty and inner rest, which I knew to be symbolic of heaven. In my dream, however, I felt as if I were really there. As God's peace was surrounding me and infusing me internally, I remember saying something to myself like, "I could easily be here and enjoy this place forever." There were two reasons I said this.

First, I felt a sense of cleanliness course through me, washing away all the impurities of my sin and its soul-corrupting consequences. I had never in my earthly life felt so existentially clean from sin and its effects in and upon me! In this whole process God was taking me through, I had "tastes" of inner cleanliness, which was growing in my body/soul. Yet this cleanliness made me feel as C.S. Lewis once put it, "deliciously clean."[lii] Nothing on earth compared with this taste of being so deliciously clean. This inner cleanliness was, no doubt, what God was performing in me in this growth/deliverance process and will be my permanent state of feeling when I arrive in heaven for glorification. Holiness in heaven will not only be the absence of impurity, but it positively will be a felt cleanliness that will send permanent joy cascading throughout the soul!

In my dream also came a total freedom from all the anxieties and fears which had tormented me throughout my life. I was totally free of any anxiety and fear that had bullied me relentlessly from childhood. For a delicious moment in my dream of heaven, I was both clean and free as never before. How beautiful was this taste of how I will feel in heaven for all eternity.

As this dream ended, I awoke to the clear message impressed upon me from the Lord, that this cleanliness and freedom is my ultimate destiny in Jesus. What a hope I could now use as an anchor for my soul in the inner turbulence that seemed to rock my every waking moment. This was what I could look forward to in heaven. With this anchor of hope set in my soul, I could patiently wade through these tumultuous seas, keeping my eyes of faith on this lighthouse of hope towards which I was sailing. To make heaven's hope even more enticing, cleanliness and freedom are only two of the many emotional jewels awaiting me in heaven.

Practical Wisdom for the Invisible War

Another vital piece of armor that needs to be worn as we prepare for battle is the helmet of salvation. A helmet protected a Roman soldier's head so his most vital organ couldn't be damaged by the enemy's weapons. This helmet protects our minds (the front line of enemy attack) as we put on the salvation won by Jesus Christ and the hope this gives us for eternal life. This is why Paul calls the helmet of salvation the helmet of hope.

---

*"But since we belong to the day, let us be sober, having put on the breastplate of faith and love, **and for a helmet the hope of salvation.**"*
1 Thessalonians 5:8 (emphasis mine)

I like how Dr. David Jeremiah puts it:

"The wisdom of God reminds us that we are fighting a battle the outcome of which is settled. When we are standing firm in our faith and being buffeted by Satan, we can remain standing because we know the outcome of the battle is not in jeopardy. We know that Christ is the Victor and Satan is the defeated foe. We know that we are called to defend the name of God in the earth as His image- bearers as Satan tries to cast aspersions on His name and cause His people to lose confidence in Him. We know that Satan's motive in attacking us is to tempt us to 'curse God and die' (Job 2:9). And we know that we do not have to give in. We know our enemy and his strategy; and with the armor of God in place, we can stand firm."[liii]

Dr. Jeremiah also cites Dr. John MacArthur who says, "Living without hope is like running a race without a finish line."[liv] How futile it is to tell a runner to start running without also highlighting the finish line for which he is working. Our finish line is meeting Christ when He takes us home to heaven.

We put on the helmet of salvation as we consciously lean on the promises of Jesus about our glorious future in heaven, which He worked out on the cross and which He will deliver fully when He returns. Yet how easy it is to focus on the severity of the storms we face and not the sustaining grace God promises to give through those storms, nor the full platter of grace to be enjoyed in our glorious future.

1 Peter 1:13 is the verse I would quote to actually put on this helmet of hope, "Therefore, preparing your minds for action, and being sober minded, set your hope fully on the grace that will be brought to you at the revelation of Jesus Christ." Quoting this verse, believing it to become true, meditating on it deeply, along with remembering these tastes of inner cleanliness and freedom which will be enjoyed in their fullness, all protected my mind with future salvation realities. This is how the helmet is actually "put on" as we sail through the storms of life. This is how our hope becomes an anchor for our souls.

QUESTIONS FOR REFLECTION AND DISCUSSION

1. Do you believe heaven is a real place?

2. Read Revelation 21-22:1-5 and write down what you believe will be the five greatest characteristics of heaven.

3. Who does John say enters heaven? (See Revelation 22:14.) Who are those kept outside? (See Revelation 22:15.)

4. What are some of the enemy's lies the helmet of salvation protects us against?

5. How often do you put on the helmet of hope?

PART THREE

More Gnarly Infections of a Soul Boil Emerge

*And he said to them, "Then are you also without understanding? Do you not see that whatever goes into a person from outside cannot defile him, since it enters not his heart but his stomach, and is expelled?" (Thus he declared all foods clean.) And he said, "What comes out of a person is what defiles him. For from within, out of the **heart** of man, come evil thoughts, sexual immorality, theft, murder, adultery, coveting, wickedness, deceit, sensuality, envy, slander, pride, foolishness. All these evil things come from within, and they defile a person."*

— MARK 7:18-23 (emphasis mine)

*Search me, O God, and know my **heart**! Try me and know my thoughts! And see if there be any grievous way in me, and lead me in the way everlasting!*

— PSALM 139:23-24 (emphasis mine)

*The **heart** has many dungeons, Bring the light! Bring the light!*

— MARY OLIVER[lv] (emphasis mine)

Thomas Dages

CHAPTER SEVENTEEN

The Night All God-Given Helps Failed

God whispers to us in our pleasures, speaks in our conscience, but shouts in our pain. Pain is God's megaphone to rouse a deaf world.
—C.S. Lewis[lvi]

WHEN THE APOSTLE JOHN WROTE HIS INSPIRED LETTER to the seven churches in Asia Minor with commendations and censures, he repeatedly closed his teachings with the admonition, "He who has an ear, let him hear what the Spirit says to the churches" (Revelation 2:7, 2:11, 2:17, 2:29, 3:6, 3:13, 3:22). This is Jesus' way, through John, to get His people to tune into and turn up their listening skills to what the Spirit of God is saying. The future existence of many of these local congregations depended on such listening!

I like to call the first week of March 2013 my week from hell. It wasn't as though this week was necessarily worse or weightier with anxiety or sleeplessness symptoms than prior weeks, but God seemed to temporarily suspend human support, neutralize my sleep medications, and remove all my God-given anxiety aids to get my full attention that I might "hear" precisely what He was working to bring to my attention in my broken soul. In retrospect, God had spoken to me in these areas for years, but the issues to which He was speaking were so deeply embedded in me I was unable to see them or hear Him. God, however, being the Great Physician of body and soul, knew exactly how to bring these spiritual cancers front and center in a way that would force me to face them. I wanted off the operating table, but my Great Physician had deeper, even more serious soul surgeries to perform.

Despite all the good happening to me and the encouraging signs of God being presently palpable, I faced the growing frustration of needing to increase my medication to find sleep. This was exceedingly frustrating for me because it felt like I was slowly and steadily going backwards when I was supposed to be on an upward trend of healing. Week after week, I used a little more medication to snatch my needed sleep. I would soon go back to my Christian psychiatrist Dr. Curt Thompson for help in this slow resurgence of insomnia, and he would prescribe Lunesta to help me find the clouds of sleep. While Dr. Thompson's words were comforting that "this was only temporary," I nevertheless felt a deep sense of frustration and anger that I was steadily regressing.

When I called Dr. Thompson this week, however, he was uncharacteristically slow to return my phone call. For several nights I increased my medication on my own with previously prescribed medication, yet my wakefulness only increased. This week nothing seemed to help induce my sleep. Nothing was working: not my return to a four pill sleep cocktail, nor my soothing Christian music, nor putting on any of my pieces of armor (including an array of memorized Bible verses in my quiver). My frustration was mounting that none of my God-given helps were helping. What in the world was going on in me?

There I lay, late at night full of sleep medication, yet wide awake and wondering what I could do to find sleep. Frustration, desperation, and anger began to mount. Questions laced with helplessness began to escalate in my soul. "God, why am I steadily moving in reverse? God, why aren't any of these wise strategies working? God, I've learned so much and it has already been so hard. Haven't I been through enough?"

I cried out in my frustration and wept words something like this, "Lord, what are You trying to teach me? You know I've tried everything, especially the things You taught me. Lord, if there is some heart issue deep inside me that You want to reveal, please show it to me, and I will commit myself with You to deal with it in counseling."

Not a second after this desperate, penitent lament came through my lips, God spoke to my mind. I saw a flash of a picture of an incident with my then 11-year-old son, Nathan, from that very afternoon. God ran the video of Nathan practicing pitching and my incessant corrections to his pitching motion, and the tears that flowed when he didn't perform according to my corrections. Practicing baseball was supposed to be fun for him and for me, his dad. Sometimes they were, but today, Nathan didn't have a fleck of fun. Today, I made many corrections to his pitching motion and Nathan's pitching didn't improve. I let him know with my words of disapproval, but my frustration with his performance mostly came through by my body language and facial expressions. This brought my sensitive son to tears, and these tears brought me to tears as God brought them to mind. I knew I needed to repent and reconcile with my son, and this vignette was pointing to the deeper heart issue God was pressing me to change.

Truth be told, there was a world of anxiety, anger, and intensity I brought to all my kids' practices and games, which God wanted to cleanse and change in me. I needed to reconcile with my son. I would need grace and humility in more counseling to deal with my performance nemesis, which more than nagged me all of my life and was now starting to spread its infection to my kids and my relationship with them. This performance infection in athletics caused ruinous results to many of my athletic endeavors, and now, it was threatening to bring its rot to my relationships with my kids. If I didn't repent and turn from this pathway, my influence was going to spoil their experience of what was supposed to bring us closer together, not relationally drive us apart.

Right there in bed, with this mental picture fresh in my mind and sorrow in my heart, I made a commitment to God that if He would help me fall asleep, I would get up the next day and apologize to my son and deal with this performance nemesis in counseling, which dominated my heart for decades. No sooner had I prayed this prayer than I was swept supernaturally off into a sweet sleep.

THE LANCING OF MY SOUL

A little bit of my own "performance treadmill" history is in order at this point. I grew up believing my performance in athletics and what others thought of my performance were necessary for acceptance and value in the eyes of others. I lived for peak sports performances so others would think well of me. I truly loved sports and competition and mastering skills, like a fireman's carry takedown in wrestling and nailing runners trying to steal second base on the baseball diamond. However, athletic prowess, performance, and the compliments received from others quickly became the fuel driving the engine of my soul. The more I performed well, and the more others complimented my performance, the harder I worked for their affirmation. Somewhere in the history of my sports career, the joy of skill mastery, healthy competition, and sportsmanship took a far back seat to compliments about my performance.

Yet this treadmill of performing well and receiving accolades, while temporarily satisfying and even addicting, was a very low-octane fuel for the engine of my soul. It became a vicious cycle that drove me to work harder for greater performances, even though the accolades and acceptances were short-lived and ultimately unfulfilling to my inner man. Making matters worse, my performance treadmill spawned deep fears of failure and rejection, leading me to significant soul malfunctions in life.

The symptoms of my performance-based identity were present and screaming for years. For instance, I was a good baseball player up through high school and improved vastly as a hitter in college, but alongside my love for the sport was a terrible fear of failure. My fear of failure (what people thought about my performance on the field) grew so much in my mind that I began to squeeze the baseball when throwing it. My fear of making a mistake with an errant throw made me double-pump my throws around the diamond. Even "easy" tosses back to the pitcher's mound were laborious and gradually became torturous. I couldn't relax and enjoy throwing a baseball because mentally, "What if?" fears gripped my mind and made me clench the ball tightly on each and every throw. I short-hopped the pitcher, frequently threw over the third baseman's head, and lost my zip, accuracy, and aggressiveness on the field. I didn't want to make mistakes, so I became a terribly cautious catcher, and a terribly cautious catcher is just that—a terrible catcher.

I slowly became a big "basket case" in catcher's gear. I dreaded playing the game I had loved for so long. This problem surfaced during my freshman year at Taylor University. My teammates and coaches were at a loss as to what to do. How do you help a young man whose tight grip of fear on the ball reflected the gripping fear around his heart?

At the apex of my baseball days at age 23, I was hitting the ball so well, I was even asked to go to Veterans Stadium for a personal invitation tryout with the Philadelphia Phillies. While I loved the idea of taking batting practice at the Vet, I secretly dreaded the thought of possibly getting drafted. Deep down inside, I knew I wasn't major league material, and I actually released a sigh of relief when I hit terribly in practice that day in the fall of 1983. What would it have been like to play minor league ball while trying to hide such an enslavement to fear? If I had been drafted, I'm quite sure it would have been one the briefest stints ever in the low minor leagues!

I practiced a form of Christian cognitive therapy, "telling myself the truth" relentlessly, but it did little for me. No matter the truth I personally preached to myself, I was still driven by fear. Nothing I thought or did released me from this gripping fear. I had issues, for sure, but where were they rooted in the history of my heart, and how could I find release?

Move ahead two decades in my life, and now I'm on the field coaching my son, Nathan, in baseball and my daughter, Allison, in fast-pitch softball. How I loved to watch them play and excel. They were both natural in their own way. Nathan was a strong left-handed pitcher and hitter. He had a natural fluidity and strength to his throwing and hitting. Allison could run, hit, and throw, both overhand and under-hand, and with terrific velocity. While I found myself enjoying their progress and successes as any father would, I also found myself getting "churned up" inside, both before and during their games. When my kids trotted out onto the field, I felt like Smaug, from Tolkien's *The Hobbit*, opening his eye from sleeping in mounds of gold. My performance dragon awakened, stirred, and snapped its tail all throughout my inner man.

Many times, I would work with them to warm them up even before they went to the field for warm-ups! I would relentlessly correct throwing mistakes and incorrect form when we were simply having a catch. At games, I would enter each pitch, as if my focus, concentration, and intensity would help them throw strikes! I would comment on almost every pitch to affirm or give encouragement or direction. I was like a pacing cat in the dugout and my kids were my outlet with their performance. And yes, this was only Little League!

I spent way too much time "fantasizing" about their upcoming performance on the diamond and how they might get scholarships to college, and in my worst moments I even imagined Nathan pitching in the majors or Allison playing for the Olympic team. Many embarrassing things spawn from the heart of man, and most can be hidden from discerning eyes. Game-time possibilities of stardom would take too much of my time awake before going to sleep. Simply enjoying their game and watching them develop, have fun, and grow in their game skills and social skills was a constant sermon on my lips, but the reality was far from my heart.

My friends, my kids' coaches, and their teammates' parents were very patient with me as I really worked at cutting down my intensity level and letting the kids enjoy the game. However, my kids' performances were still of over-the-top importance to me. To my credit, I didn't shame them after a poor performance, and I really did care about the other kids on the team. However, something was getting me way too wound up about their performances at practices and games. I would even go to games prayerfully asking God to give me the strength not to say a word from the dugout and to leave teaching times to after the game. Only once in five years of Little League coaching was I able to accomplish this. Nathan's head coach, Kevin Smith, congratulated me smilingly after that unique game with an affirming, "Well done." However, while my lips remained sealed, my heart was burning with an unhealthy fire.

What drove me for athletic achievement and crippled me with fear was now a haunting specter on the field with my own kids. It was planted in me at an early age and grew insidiously inside me. God had had enough. He knew in my heart I didn't want to be ruled by these heart idols anymore.

The next day I did apologize to my son. Nathan was easy-going and accepted my apology and hug. Yet I knew I needed to go deeper into my heart to find the genesis causing so much chaos in my life.

I had promised God I would enter counseling for the issues He was touching, and enter into more counseling I did. Nine months later, God would lead me to CrossRoads Counseling in Buena Vista, Colorado, and stir the issue that had me stuck on my performance treadmill. Again, through healing prayer, God uncovered an event from when I was in eighth grade that had planted my feet so firmly on my performance treadmill. This would come through another professional counselor who believed Jesus was a "time traveler" and could walk me personally back into my past to locate and liberate me from such experiences that generated chaos into my life. Wil Franz combined a beautiful blend of Christ-centeredness with biblically faithful and psychologically insightful counseling that was sensitive to the ways God works through healing prayer.

During prayer and in my imagination, Jesus took me back to a time in middle school when I was traumatized by the late onset of puberty. I was in my bedroom on the third floor of our house and sitting on the edge of my bed with my pants down, looking at my hairless privates. I was angry at myself, and no doubt God, for not bringing about physical manhood to my life. The truth be told, I was in a rage. The pain of being in my wrestling locker room every day, without hitting puberty, had finally taken its toll. Taking showers, being called "Baby Dage" and one day even being pulled off a toilet by older wrestlers and laughed at, was emotionally torturous to me. In my mind's eye, I saw myself sitting on the edge of my bed with a blotch of blackness in my inner man. I remembered getting up from the edge of my bed, pretending to pick up a baseball bat, swinging it to crack fantasy home runs ,and saying, "I will prove myself by becoming great at sports," and "I will prove myself by how I perform."

With these simple words, a vow was made and my performance idol of attempting to find fulfilment in life through my sports performances was powerfully set in ruinous motion. While athletic achievements would abound, they would abound with a steep price of proliferating anxieties, controlling fears, and deepening anger.

Interestingly, the seeds of my functional god of athletic achievement had grown for years, even prior to this eighth-grade vow. When I was in elementary school, I keenly remember going to bed one night, looking across my bedroom at my trophy shelf, and telling God, "God, you can have everything in my life except for my trophies and sports, just don't take them away!" Granted, I was only 11 or 12 at the time, but that was a warning alarm sounding off the existence of a functional god growing in my heart! My young, immature, and idolatrous heart was telling me "life" was found in the accumulation of trophies, so get as many as you can...and live! My time traveler, Jesus, took me back to this pivotal moment in eighth grade when my idolatrous heart exploded in anger, making a vow that set my life on a path of performance ruin. Locating and confessing this sin was the first step in breaking its power.

Then, the Holy Spirit gave me another redemptive picture in my imagination about my "new" inner man out of which I was to live. Working with the same counselor, the Holy Spirit also revealed to the "eyes of my heart" my Christ-in-me identity. Sitting across from Wil Franz as he prayed, I suddenly saw in my imagination what looked like a stick figure with the slight contours of an outer man. This was a picture of my eighth-grade soul/body. With this picture before the eyes of my heart, suddenly a bright light shot up and through this stick figure and filled it up completely. The Holy Spirit was filling me with His light and presence and showing me pictorially my new inner man filled with the light and life of Christ.

When I told Wil Franz what I was seeing, He told me God had given me a "flood" of revelation. He told me that I had "individuated" (found my unique true self), and the burst of light was God's Spirit filling my inner being. This was my new identity, replacing my performance driven identity, which I had passionately pursued to find life in my inner man. Now, the Holy Spirit was giving me a beautiful picture of the light and life of Christ in me. It was not enough simply to see and renounce my vow of performance idolatry, but I needed a replacement identity out of which I could live.

THE LANCING OF MY SOUL

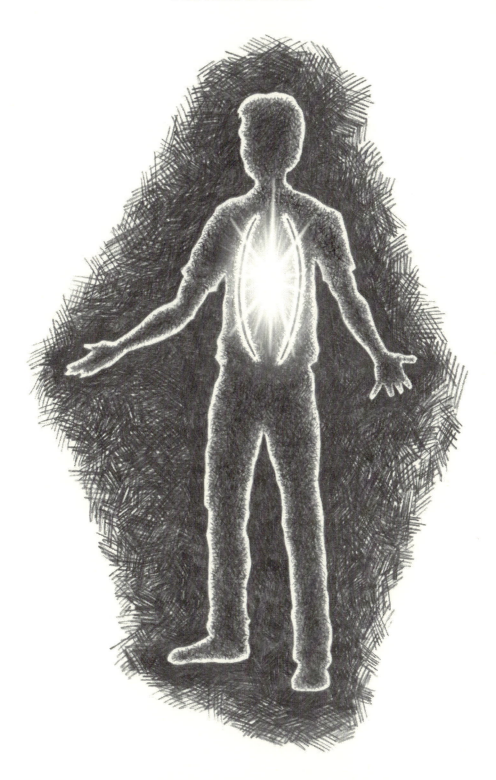

This replacement identity grew as I practiced renewing my mind, not only with the rational truth of Scripture, but with the redemptive images God had placed by the Holy Spirit in my imagination. I would "retreat" into this picture the Holy Spirit planted in me countless times for experiential growth of Jesus and the release of His emotional riches in my inner man. The more I did this by faith (believing what the Holy Spirit brought to my mind was my true me), the stronger my inner man (being built upon Christ) became.

Yet God wasn't done with His powerful pictures in my imagination. While in personal prayer the following week, after retreating into the picture of Christ's light bursting forth in my inner man, God then brought to my mind a picture of brown chunks falling off me. I clearly saw pictures of brown chunks breaking off me and falling away from me, as though they were breaking off me and floating away into space. The brown chunks, I came to realize, were sinful habits and propensities, which would naturally fall off me as I practiced living out of my new "Christ in me" identity.

This is exactly what happened. My sinful propensities didn't suddenly vanish, but as I imagined the truth of "Christ in me" as the deepest part of me, and lived by these redemptive realities in my soul, it became substantially easier to let go of sinful habits that had formerly locked me in bondage. The more I lived by faith out of this new identity, pictured through healing prayer, the more issues of bondage began to break off me. This included my performance treadmill that had exhausted and utterly controlled me for nearly forty years.

Learning to retreat into Christ in me gave me a newfound power to resist the temptation to live in my performance fantasies and live in all the riches of Christ in me and started the process of teaching these stabilizing truths to my kids. Forgiveness of others who hurt me now flowed much more easily. Unfair criticism was much easier to handle as my defensiveness lost its grip. When I struggled at

tasks or wrestled with competencies at work and was tempted to fall into self-hatred and self-loathing, retreating into "Christ in me" stabilized and grew His love and strength in my soul. Going to my kid's games was accompanied by a newfound joy in simply watching them compete and grow in their competencies and skills. Trying to control how they performed and getting upset inside began to fall off of me as Christ and His life settled deeper into my inner man. It was still a war with my flesh, but my retreats into "Christ in me" would give me more and more victories over my performance dragon.

I even began to notice that my own grip on the baseball started to ease up when warming them up or simply having a catch with them. It was amazing the "little yet big" things that I could start to enjoy as I started living out of my "Christ in me" identity the Scriptures so clearly spelled out and now pictorially planted in my imagination. This all didn't happen instantaneously, but this new pictured identity of "Christ in me" as the deepest reality in my soul jump-started all of these changes and filled me up with Christ's life in the interior of my inner man. I found I could retreat into this picture of Christ bursting forth in me whenever I wanted, and the more I did so, the riches of his life became experientially mine more and more. This was the Holy Spirit's work in my imagination serving as a foundation for a deeper mind renewal.

I end this chapter with wise words from Richard Plass and James Cofield that sum up what God was doing in my life.

"In other words, our true self is not an essence that is interchangeable with anyone else. Living in fellowship with Christ does not result in a generic me desperate to confirm my worthiness. The gift of our individual true self rests in the distinctiveness we have as embodied souls. Union and communion with Christ leads us into the real, particular me that God longs for each of us to be. And In living who we are created to be we find life. This is what Soren Kierkegaard meant when he said, 'And now by God's grace I shall become myself.' We become our unique self as we, by grace, discover our true self in Christ."[lvii]

God shouted to me in my sleepless suffering. His voice made me eager to be all ears to what He was saying and doing in the deepest places of my soul!

Practical Wisdom for the Invisible War

Apart from initial salvation in Jesus Christ, and all the riches one receives when embracing Jesus by faith, nothing is more impactful upon the emotional wholeness of a person's life than learning to live out of their Christ centered identity. It would take until the sixth decade of my life for God to help me see this new "Christ in me" identity with my mind's eye and learn to feast emotionally on "Christ in me" in the interior of my soul.

I was granted the greatest discovery for my inner man's wholeness and psychological health. It's the Spirit of the living God inhabiting the deepest part of me. While the pervasiveness of my sin was most humbling, the depth of "Christ in me" as the deepest part of me was even more enlightening and enervating.

The New Testament teaches that a person who is "in Christ" by faith has access to the spiritual wealth of Jesus to grow their inner being. Maybe this is why the Apostle Paul tells us over 160 times, in slightly different ways, that we are "in Christ."[lviii] The parallel truth of "Christ in me" stemming from this union is staggering for those of us emotionally wounded, empty, and controlled by sin's dominion.

God had brought about amazing surgical cuts and salves for my soul, but now, I needed to act upon them and work with God to build upon my new identity. While God breaks through to us in many ways, the following are the surgical tools He used for building the inner me!

- **I had to trust the Spirit to take me to past places that needed His healing touch.** Waiting in prayer expectantly for the Spirit to move is not something that happened very often in the counseling I had received. Such powerful vows need to be located in our past and broken by the power of Christ. Jesus our "Wonderful Counselor" (Isaiah 9:6) can take us back to the historical roots of our spiritual tumors causing such chaos in life.

It would have taken the best human counselor hours upon hours, thousands of dollars, and many tips with guesses riddled with mistakes to maybe accomplish what Jesus my "Wonderful Counselor" did in several moments of healing prayer. While this doesn't negate the important role human counselors can play in helping hurting people, it does highlight that the best counselors rely on the workings of the "Wonderful Counselor" to identify such vows that need to be broken and highlight the power of a Christ-centered identity.

- **I needed to respond in confession and repentance to what the Spirit revealed.** "I will prove myself by how I perform" was an inner vow needing to be identified, confessed, renounced, and broken. My vow firmly planted my feet on a performance treadmill and turned up the speed as I made countless choices to follow this false god of my own making. This is why Richard Smith says we need to be careful about the oaths we speak which can hold power over us: "When we make vows, these must be fulfilled. Christ strongly urged us not to make any promises at all. Not because swearing to do something is sinful, but because God holds us accountable for our words."[lix]

- **I had to retreat often into my "Christ in me" identity.** A retreat is a place we go to for rest and restoration. It is a place to slow down and hear the voice of God for the strengthening, healing and deliverance in the inner man. I now had more than propositional truth for my restorative retreats. I needed to retreat into my "Christ in me" identity every day and live in His riches in me, moment by moment, for His emotional wealth to rise in my soul. The more I nurtured this new identity, the easier it was to get off my performance treadmill.

For some, a steady diet of simply believing and acting on the riches of the "Jesus' riches in me" will build a slow, steady, and strong foundation. For others plagued by vows, serious traumas, and strong idols of performance, the Holy Spirit's power to break off the reinforced concrete that has settled over and into the soul is desperately needed.

Sometimes, we really do need the jackhammer of God to crack the reinforced concrete of sin and lies of darkness controlling our souls, so that Jesus is free to release and grow His life in our souls.

QUESTIONS FOR REFLECTION AND DISCUSSION

1. How was sleeplessness a part of God's plan to get me to listen to Him?

2. How do idols or functional gods become drivers of our souls?

3. How do personal vows become drivers of our souls?

4. Why are confession and renunciation of vows and idols necessary steps in healing?

5. Have you ever identified the functional god(s) or vows driving you heart and causing chaos in your life? What happens if you never discover these?

CHAPTER EIGHTEEN

Severing Thick Roots of Obsessive Compulsiveness

Seems like all I can see was the struggle
Haunted by ghosts that lived in my past
Bound up in shackles of all my failures
Wondering how long is this gonna last
Then you looked at this prisoner and said to me, "Son
stop fighting a fight that's already been won"
I am redeemed, You set me free
So I'll shake off these heavy chains
And wipe away every stain, now I'm not who I used to be
I'm redeemed
I am redeemed
—*Big Daddy Weave*[lx]

MY WEEK FROM HELL CONTINUED AT 5:00 A.M. when I was rudely awakened to an obsessive-compulsive fear. It came crashing down on my conscience, startling me out of my sleep. There I was, sleeping as peacefully as an insomniac can, when I suddenly awoke to a seemingly crazy fear trying to compel me to obey its directives. Just a few days after God started making surgical cuts in my heart to free me from my performance treadmill, He also started making surgical cuts to free me from my slavery to obsessive-compulsive fears.

We had recently had several new windows installed on the back of our house, and the repairman had not finished caulking. It took several days for the repairman to finish the job. However, it rained in the meantime, and even though the repairman had taken measures to dry out any possible moisture inside, my "What if?" fears now ran wild. "What if moisture got inside, and what if mold was now growing there?" These fears spoke fearfully to my heart at 5:00 a.m.! Fear struck deeply as I pictured black mold invading our home. My OCD placed the directive before me: "You must check and make sure moisture and mold are not growing by taking the window out." While my reasoning told me the worker had taken safeguards when he returned to prevent such moisture and eventual mold, my "checking and making sure" syndrome told me I had better take the expensive route and take the window out. Darkness, anxiety, and "What if?" fears ruled me.

OCD is a spiritual/emotional/physical disorder in which a person "obsesses" about doing things a certain way (like washing hands, checking doors, counting numbers in their head) in an attempt to stave off fears of what might happen if one doesn't carry out these compulsions. Establishing attempted control over an object or an environment is a huge part of OCD behavior and leads to a proliferation of anxieties in the soul. As I have now heard several times in my life, "Control is an illusion," and many OCD people are stuck in OCD precisely because they stubbornly live in this illusion of attempted control.

For instance, as a pastor, entering a hospital was a common arena of work and a favorite place for my OCD to surface. I not only routinely washed my hands (a good idea in a hospital setting), but in worst-case scenarios, I would wash my Bible as well (the Pharisees would have been proud of me), while imagining MRSA existing wherever my mind wandered or my hands touched. My "What if?" fears imagined MRSA everywhere, from elevator buttons, to rails on beds, to machines keeping vital signs, to a hazardous material disposal boxes. Everything I touched or whatever touched me made me wonder if MRSA was now on me! So I washed fastidiously and sometimes furiously to make sure I didn't get infected and then infect others. Washing is good, but people plagued with OCD go way overboard.

I remember making a hospital visitation when a nurse came over to me wearing her protective gloves, and she actually picked up and moved my Bible, which was placed on the nurses' station countertop. Internally, I almost went through the roof when her protective gloves touched my Bible. Where had her gloves been? What had she touched? What contagious bacteria were on her gloves that were now lurking on my Bible? When I questioned what she had touched with her gloves and why she had touched my Bible, she looked me right in the eyes and said, "Are you a believer? Then you need to trust the Almighty that He is in charge!" While what she said was true and beautifully said, her words hardly made a dent in my fear-enslaved heart. My "What if?" fears didn't want to budge, and my control to hyper-wash easily won. I still washed my Bible completely with antibacterial soap, and probably washed my hands after washing my Bible. Her powerful one-line sermon brought me to temporary shame for such little faith, but "Fear of MRSA" on my beloved Bible, possibly getting onto my skin, held onto me like a tick burrowed into my flesh. **I needed to trust God's care and control but was stuck living in mine!**

My bouts with OCD started early in life, swirling around my heart in many different forms, ebbing and flowing in their craziness and intensity. The roots of my OCD were as strong and as old as my performance-based identity. Both spawned great anxiety in my life, so much a part of me that their anxieties now seemed normal. It is kind of like having a smelly dog in your house. You, as the owner, get used to your pet's smell, but all your neighbors and friends and home visitors sure do take notice of the odor, which hits them the moment they walk in the door.

My earliest remembrance of OCD symptoms, the feeling of a need to control aspects of my environment for my security, started in grade school when I felt compelled to count to ten as I drank from the drinking fountain. For some reason, it gave me a sense of security when I could drink water and make it to ten. No big deal here, I just took a few seconds longer than most kids at the water fountain.

However, my first serious compulsive fear occurred one day as our family was driving in our station wagon. I was sitting in the back seat and as a car passed us, a terrible fear shot through me. "Dad has to pass this car in return." My fear told me I **had** to tell dad, and dad **had** to pass that car in return. The strength of this fear and the "need" for Dad to speed up and pass was so strong and sudden it resulted in my first remembered panic attack. It rushed upon me and seized me with formidable strength.

I grew up hating elevator rides because of the control I lost when the doors shut. My "What if?" fears exploded in my mind about the possibilities of being abandoned, getting permanently stuck, and catastrophes happening outside in the world around me that would leave me stuck inside forever. Early on panic attacks would sometimes seize me. I would pray and quote Scripture on the way up and when the doors opened, I would flee for my temporary salvation.

However, my OCD was rooted not only in my apparent attempt to control and lack of trust in God's care, but also my attempts to keep myself in God's love by my own crazy works instead of trusting in the finished work of Christ for my salvation. A strong current of works-based righteousness flowed strongly in my heart. My experience of God's complete acceptance of me in Jesus was constantly called into question in my conscience, and I performed so many rituals to "make sure" I didn't give God any reason to use anything against me in judgment. Although, I was and still am convinced I was justified by God's grace through faith alone, I certainly wasn't living as such.

Growing up, I was hypersensitive to the pain of animals, even bugs being crushed by the car as we traveled down the highway. I felt hyper-responsible for making sure they were dead when we passed them on the road! I remember a fishing trip I took to Wyoming in my late 30's, and how I was tempted to drive 50 miles back to a place where I had lost a fish in marshy waters. I felt compelled to ensure the fish made it back safely to the main lake. I didn't make the trip, but it was only because my fishing partner would have thought I was crazy. This hypersensitivity and hyper-responsibility was very much tied into doing extras to crazily keep myself in the love of God.

Tax time was always more than laborious for me. While I have always believed and practiced honesty, I was far too obsessed and hyper-responsible about making small mistakes. The fear of my failing to report the smallest source of income or include something in my housing allowance that wasn't supposed to be there was a heavier burden than necessary. One year, shortly after getting married, I found a mistake of some $40 of income I failed to report. I remember doing the right thing by filing an amendment. Deep inside, I not only wanted to do the right thing with the IRS, but even deeper still, I feared what God might do if I failed to take this extra measure and file an amended return. **I wasn't living by the results of what Jesus accomplished for me on the cross (what I theologically believed), but by what I could do to "make sure" I stayed safe in God's love.**

When my OCD was at its worst, I would back out of my driveway worrying I was going to back over a person. If my OCD got the best of me, I would actually get out of the car and check to ensure there wasn't a body under my car! At times, I would take extra measures and look multiple times to "make sure" no one was underneath the car! There were several times in parking lots when I felt I couldn't stop looking under the car from different angles to verify no one was really underneath! When I saw a shadow under the car, I had to make sure it wasn't a person. I even looked around the corner of my tires to make sure I didn't miss a body!

Fortunately, my life only ebbed into these worst cases sporadically, but I always felt like I was on the edge ready to fall into these serious compulsions at any moment. My life cascaded in and out of various levels of misery, weariness, and anxiety. Life for me was ridden with anxiety and exhausting.

Every ten years or so, at the craziest point of my OCD weariness, taking Zoloft brought incredible relief. This medication alleviated my OCD symptoms almost to the point of non-existence. The higher the dosage, the more palpable the results. Fifty mg. would help, 100 mg. would alleviate almost all symptoms, and 200 mg. would wipe away symptoms even in my crazy phases. Yet as medically miraculous and merciful as Zoloft was to help me retain needed serotonin, it left my spiritual and emotional heart issues largely unaddressed. Zoloft didn't rewire my thinking with thought patterns of trust in God and His grace already given me in Christ.

Then, my five-a.m. attack came during my week from hell. This wasn't a general anxiety, but a specific fear making its compulsive demands. As the picture of black mold grew in my mind, fear burned and spread like wildfire in my conscience. Fear pressed upon every cell in my soul. I felt compelled at the moment to have the window removed to make sure everything was dry and I wasn't responsible for mold growing in my house. Even though I tried to reason with myself (my wife tells me that reason never works during an OCD attack), that the rain had to come at a severe angle to get into the small cracks, and that the worker already dried out the window of possible moisture, nevertheless, I felt compelled to relieve my conscience and confirm everything was dry and mold-free.

Would I obey my OCD directive and take out the window to make an expensive check or resist this fear by sending it away?

As I went downstairs for breakfast the next morning, I was torn between checking to make sure the window was clean and dry or resisting this compulsion. During breakfast, I tried to be led more my rational thinking than simply obeying my fears. However, my rational thinking was bulldozed by my OCD fears. I went back and forth and wondered whether my reason or fears would win. I debated at breakfast and as I drove my son to school. I was caught in a vicious OCD attack.

It was as I drove my son to school when a decisive deliverance to this OCD episode came. Deliverance came through the words of a gospel song highlighting God's grace already given me in Christ. As I listened to K-LOV on my car radio, the words of Big Daddy Weave cascaded over the airwaves, bringing light to my mind and releasing fear from my heart.

Then you look at this prisoner and say to me, "Son
Stop fighting a fight that's already been won"
I am redeemed, You set me free
So I'll shake off these heavy chains
And wipe away every stain, now I'm not who I used to be
I am redeemed
I'm redeemed.[lxi]

The Spirit of God seemed to sing to my heart and send a shaft of light to my soul. Since I was redeemed by the blood of Jesus, I could let go of the chains trapping me in the exhausting lie that I needed to do everything perfectly to stay in God's love. Redemption in Jesus meant I was already forgiven, justified, accepted, adopted, and purchased by Jesus off the slave market of sin, secure in his love and FREE forever from condemnation. I could let go of all fleshly strategies to make sure I stayed in God's love. As the light and love of God flooded into my soul, the compulsion to take the window out suddenly "broke" off my soul. The song reminded me that I was redeemed by **His** work on the cross, and now, I didn't have to rely on my crazy ones! Suddenly, my freedom in Jesus set in and I was free!

For decades I had slowly become a monstrous legalist who overemphasized both divine law and human law to keep me safe in God's love and to make me more like Jesus. While this looked commendable from the outside because of its religiosity, it degraded the gospel of grace and profoundly proliferated my fears and anxieties. For decades I was secretly standing on my crazy works, and this toxic confidence in my crazy works had to go.

Maybe this is why Alister McGrath labels legalism as "the dark side of Evangelicalism."[lxii] It is dark because it degrades the grace of the gospel. It is so easy for Christians to slip into, and leads to fear and religious bondage, all with the appearance of piety. What Jesus wanted me to do was to learn to rest in His finished work and trust in His absolute care for me.

"O foolish Galatians! Who has bewitched you? It was before your eyes that Jesus Christ was publicly portrayed as crucified. Let me ask you only this: Did you receive the Spirit by the works of the law or by hearing with faith? Are you so foolish? Having begun by the Spirit, are you now being perfected by the flesh?"
Galatians 3:1-3

Returning home from taking Nathan to school with the redemption of God's grace singing in my heart, I was completely free from any compulsions of checking this window to make sure there wasn't mold. God exposed a key root of this obsessive fear and cut it off by my standing in the gospel of His grace.

Practical Wisdom for the Invisible War

Freedom from OCD is not a simple issue. While the seriousness of my episode was most likely exacerbated by the demonic, I was set free by a powerful encounter of understanding and standing on the grace of the gospel. However, for long-term healing to occur, my brain would have to be rewired by many choices of trusting God's care for me and many choices of learning to stand on these riches of grace already mine in Jesus. I camped out on Romans 5:1-2:

"Therefore, since we have been justified by faith, we have peace with God through our Lord Jesus Christ. ***Through Him we have also obtained access by faith into this grace in which we stand...****" (emphasis mine)*

Remember Hebb's axiom mentioned in chapter 2, "Neurons which fire together wire together." This rewiring of our brain is as necessary for worry and OCD as it is for lust, chronic negativity, and stubborn self-pity. I needed to relentlessly renew my mind in learning to trust God when I wasn't in control. I needed to learn how to stand by faith in the grace already given me in Christ when more OCD temptations accosted me.

While my medication suppressed my symptoms and managed them well, for real and long-lasting change to occur, I needed to learn to trust God's control and care, and trust in God's grace given in Jesus afresh every day.

When walking into a hospital and entering a room to pray for patients, I needed to trust God was in control of every MRSA staph infection I couldn't see. Washing my hands once was wise, but then, I needed to let it go and trust He could manage all things according to His wise plan. I needed to proceed into public bathrooms and not worry about cleaning up after myself with extra measures. No more washing sinks, faucets, or floors around toilets to make sure I didn't leave any bacteria behind that might infect others. God was in control and I could let go of my hyper-responsibility. No more could I obsess about treating every red spot on my kids as if the spots were staph infections. No more caring about hitting moths and bugs with my car and the pain I might inflict on animals.

God wanted me free from such cumbersome worries that I might love people deeply who needed His care through me. After all, when I was wrapped up in my little OCD storms, how could I follow the Spirit and deeply love others?

QUESTIONS FOR REFLECTION AND DISCUSSION

1. Is there a difference between healthy and unhealthy control? If so, how do you discern between them?

2. Do you believe that failing to trust in God's complete control and care for your life can lead to habits of unhealthy control in your life like OCD?

3. What is justifying grace, and how does it lead to eternal peace with God?

4. Can there be a connection between crazy works of OCD strugglers and attempting to add works in an attempt to stay safe in His love?

5. Why does living as though we must add works to stay safe in His love simply escalate our anxieties?

Thomas Dages

CHAPTER NINETEEN

A Petri Dish of Inner Emptiness

...that which we have seen and heard we proclaim also to you, so that you too may have fellowship with us; and indeed our fellowship is with the Father and with His Son Jesus Christ.
—1 John 1:3

I WAS JUST SHORT OF 50 WHEN MY CRISIS HIT. While my life up to that point was more than sporadically filled with God's power for formal ministry and preaching, my interior life was held together by threads and felt in many ways on the verge of crumbling. Dark things, such as subtle pride, an unforgiving spirit, lust in my mind, worry about my future, the need for control to avoid fear, and my need for others' approval, grew from puppy strength into a full-grown mongrel terrorizing the neighborhood of my soul. The Lord graciously showed me how easily such a menace could grow in such an environment of existential emptiness where the power and presence of Christ was theologically believed yet only sporadically experienced. My inner life was a petri dish where dark things grew by not deepening my meaningful fellowship with God and His people.

I'm quite convinced that at the moment I received Jesus by faith at the sapling age of six, my sins were immediately and forever forgiven. At that same faith moment, God clothed me with the righteousness of His Son and declared me justified. The Holy Spirit sent from God came into my life to take up residence within me. Yet it wasn't until I was twenty-one that I began to find and experience the life of God in my soul in any meaningful way. My soul was shallow on intimacy with God and so, the garden of my soul more easily flourished with dark, thick weeds of sin slowly choking me.

My fear or reverence of God kept me at arms-length from much darkness into which many of my peers in high school and college fell prey. I never tried drugs, never had sex before marriage, and never struggled with underage drinking in any capacity. God gave me a boldness to share my faith in a rather large, public high school, and I even won significant awards for leading with exemplary character in sports in both high school and college. In my senior year of high school, I was even voted the guy whom the girls would "most want to bring home to meet mom and dad." During my first 23 years of ministry, I was successful in avoiding what church people would call "the biggie" sins, and yet, my inner life was experiencing minimal transformation in the goodness of God. I had found God in a saving way, but I was living in the shallows of His experiential love.

The Four Biggest Factors Contributing to the Inner Emptiness of my Saved Soul

First, my failure to develop any kind of attachment with my father. Attachment with parents, especially sons with fathers and later in childhood, is vital for the healthy development of a child's soul. Counselors across the spectrum (Christian and non-Christian alike) are discovering how vital attachment to our parents is for the healthy development of a child and for the ability to enter into meaningful relationships later in life. Listen to the words of James Cofield and Richard Plass describing how formative attachment with our parents can be.

> *Learning to relate starts at least as early as the day we are born (and probably in the womb). Our way of entering into and maintaining all of our relationships (not just marriage) is one of the earliest psychological structures formed in us. We come into the world neurologically wired to make connections, to attach to others. When our early connections are healthy, we will find it easier to connect well as adults. To the extent our emotional attachment with our primary caregivers is lacking while we are children, we will find our relational capacity limited as adults.*
>
> *It is virtually impossible to overstate the significance of our learned relational attachment system in the early years and its profound influence on our relational experience as adults. The quality and character of the programming we received early in life establishes a pattern of attachment that controls our relationships later in life.*[lxiii]

In looking back upon my early childhood, teen years, and young adulthood, this vital attachment never occurred with my dad. I want to be careful here because I don't want to dishonor my dad for what he didn't pass down through our father-son relationship. Positively, in regards to our relationship, since his death in 2003, I have become more appreciative of his medical insights into my anxiety, his willingness to pay for my needed counseling growing up, and his example for the family in both attending and serving in church. Dad also provided a wonderful example of persevering in following Jesus when several severe personal calamities struck. Watching dad and mom tithe their money when things got really tight also provided a great example for the faith of me and my siblings. Nevertheless, dad possessed a severe emotional detachment in all his vital relationships.

I do believe Dad loved us, but the only way he seemed to know how to express his love was through financial provision and showing up religiously at our sporting events. While he never physically abused us, his silence and detachment were nevertheless extremely damaging. A story told by my mom about the detachment of Dad's dad with his wife illustrates how my dad was plagued by disengagement in his own family.

Apparently, Dad's mom was so deeply frustrated with Dad's dad and his detachment and silence, one evening she walked down the stairs naked with only her hat on, like she was walking out the door. She pulled this antic to try to rouse his attention. However, not even this antic roused his attention. She was made even more furious by his lack of response. When we heard this story we all laughed, but what desperation my grandma must have felt, and what desperation I often saw in my mom by the disengagement and silence she felt from my dad! All this to say my dad was most certainly relating to us through the attachment pattern he developed as a child and a young adult set in motion by his deeply disengaged dad.

Growing up in the Dages home, I don't ever remember a time when dad locked eyes with mine and said, "Tommy, I love you." **Never once.** One of my brothers half-jokingly said that the only one who got dad's full gaze were his golden retrievers when he got down on the floor to play. Dad pursued the gaze of his dogs in play but didn't work to lock eyes with his own kids. I can't ever remember an instance of dad drawing me close in his embrace and feeling the strength of his masculine arms and soul around mine. **Never once.** I don't remember hearing dad crafting words to speak positively about my future. **Never once!** He seldom talked about issues of substance, rarely opened up to let us know him in any significant way, and didn't know how to engage our struggling souls. He was silent at the dinner table, engrossed in the *Philadelphia Bulletin* or dialed into a Phillies, Eagles, or Penn State football game. His silence emotionally crippled my mom and each one of his kids.

To my dad's credit, after he was physically disabled as a dentist, he did begin teaching a parenting class at our local church, a class he co-taught with my mom, which highlighted many principles of how God works His grace through parents to impact kids emotionally and developmentally. Also to Dad's credit, he did start putting some of these principles into practice...but with his grandkids. His own kids were out of the house and emotionally and developmentally crippled in many significant ways.

Second, my failure to recognize my "inner me." God gave me a discovery of myself at the age of 21 that revealed just how empty I was in my inner being. My life was dark with my first onslaught of depression, and I decided to transfer colleges so I could seek help pushing through this emotional storm upon me.

Leaving Taylor University and coming home to this emotional darkness, however, was the first time I truly sought the Lord's strength, wisdom, and direction in life through prayer and biblical meditation. Getting slammed with a serious depression, changing colleges, and beginning to think God might have a different vocation for me compelled me for the first time in my life to begin seeking Him with all my heart.

I remember being in the back room in my parents' home, seeking God's wisdom for life by reading and reflecting on the book of Proverbs. To be honest, I don't even remember which Proverb I was reading at the time. However, what I do remember was the sudden realization that I possessed an inner being, which was extremely valuable to God. The Holy Spirit of God opened my spiritual eyes to see that how I looked, how I performed in athletics, and who I was did not depend on what others thought of me.

Up to this point in my life, I had given all my attention to developing my outer man, but strangely, I was giving almost nothing to developing my inner man. Intellectually, I had always understood that I and others were embodied souls made in God's precious image, but suddenly, my soul's very existence broke through from the high shelf of my mind where theories are understood and opened the senses of my heart. I sensed delightfully the existence of my soul with its unique specialness for the very first time. It was like God touched the reality of my inner being, awakening me from spiritual slumber. What a sublime and joyous discovery, yet I didn't feel the existence of my own soul until the age of twenty-one.

In short, I saw my life like an oyster shell. I spent all my time, energy, and focus on adorning the outer shell, but now, God opened by eyes to see the precious oyster inside. Yes, God would show me darkness in my inner oyster, which needed purifying, but what an exhilarating discovery to come alive on the inside! I was so busy trying to paint my shell with performance in sports and grooming my physique and looks to feel good about myself that I never sensed the deeper me inside. I felt like the hymn writer of "O Holy Night" (a poem first written by Placide Cappeau de Roguemaure), when He wrote the following words,

---

Oh holy night!
The stars are brightly shining,
it is the night of the dear Savior's birth!
Long lay the world in sin and error pining,
till he appear'd and the soul felt its worth.[lxiv]

For the first time in my life I felt "my inner being" inside, and my heart soared as my soul finally felt its worth!

Third, my failure to experience Christ in my deepest center. My life was blinded to the darkness growing in my soul and the light of Christ at the deepest part of my identity! I was not only unaware of the unique hand-crafted bucket I was, but unaware of how God wanted to massage His presence and soak Himself into the fibers of my wood. What an experiential soul-empowering discovering, again through healing prayer, to see and feel the presence of God emerge in the deepest places of my newly individuated soul! When this happened thirty-five years later in healing prayer, the unique reality of my soul re-appeared, and the presence of His life and light emerged in the same healing episode. In Reformed Theology, we rightly and humbly highlight sin's pervasiveness, but we often miss the deeper spiritual blessings and emotional wealth of living out of "Christ in me" as the deepest part of our identities. It really does humble us before God and others to see the depths of our sinfulness and makes us totally dependent upon God to change us and cleanse us, but just as important is discovering Christ's life in our deepest centers!

Salvation for me growing up focused almost entirely on my legal declaration of my justification or my right standing before God. However, my new legal status before God also immediately immersed me into an intimate union with God meant to rise into a life-changing fellowship with God. With Jesus, I was spiritually married since receiving Him as a child, but I knew very little of the depths of His love penetrating my soul. I would delightfully find that exploring my union with Jesus would well up into my greatest emotional riches.

Fourth, my failure to connect or engage with others. True engagement with others is a powerful medium for God to bring His presence to our souls. God does intend for us to change, but the deepest changes are meant to occur in the context of brothers and sisters who go with us eye to eye, heart to heart, and shoulder to shoulder in the struggles of life. Salvation involves not only knowing and being known by God through His Holy Spirit, but it involves knowing and being known by others who deeply love.

Growing up, neither my family nor my church provided such an environment. Not many families or churches do these days. Spirituality, for me, meant getting "saved," sharing Jesus with others, and staying away from the "biggie" sins. While it is a good place to start, it is no place to stay. God intends Holy Spirit-inspired fellowship to take place in the context of marriage, family life, and the community of believers, as we worship together, teach the Word of God to one another, put its precepts to practice with one another, speak to each other's hurting and stubborn hearts, pray together for one another, and together expect God to do miraculous life-changing work in our souls, churches, and the world. God moves deeply in and through our relationships out of this radical love in which we are known, encouraged, prized, and challenged to follow the ways of Jesus.

Practical Wisdom for the Invisible War

In the Bible, fellowship (sharing life) occurs in two directions: (1) vertical with God, and (2) horizontal with others. Yet how do we foster this fellowship?

- We foster this shared life vertically by consciously recognizing the life of the Spirit within us and learning to take withdrawals from the riches of Jesus in our deepest center. When a person comes to the Lord Jesus, the Spirit of Jesus takes up residence in them, and that person receives a whole new life center out of which to live. Learning to descend into these riches daily is my greatest power source for living.

In her remarkable little book *Experiencing the Depth of Christ*, Madam Guyon emphasizes an inward look which highlights the treasure of Jesus making His home in our hearts, and changing our very identity with His presence, power, and promises. She cites Augustine learning the importance of this inward look: "It was St. Augustine who once said he had lost much time in the beginning of his Christian experience by trying to find the Lord outwardly rather than by turning inwardly."[lxv] Quieting ourselves in biblical meditation by turning Scripture over and over in our minds and contemplative prayer (sensing the loving Presence of Christ within us) nourishes our inner beings like nothing else can.

In the New Testament one of the most profound passages of Scripture that highlight this fellowship with the Spirit of Jesus and the transforming work He does in us is found in 2 Corinthians 3:18.

---

*And we all, with unveiled face, **beholding the glory of the Lord**, are being transformed into the same image from one degree of glory to another. For this comes from the Lord who is the Spirit.*
2 Corinthians 3:18 (emphasis mine)

The implications of our unveiled face, "beholding the glory of the Lord" in this life, are staggering! Certainly, the idea of a direct, unhindered view of Jesus only awaits us when Jesus returns. (1 John 3:2). But what might beholding in this life involve? Dr. Terry Wardle suggests this beholding Jesus involves building a "word portrait of the Lord."[lxvi] By steeping himself in Scripture's focused on Jesus and his love, Dr Wardle's caricatures of God were changed and his experience of Christ's love deepened.

But do we limit "beholding" Jesus by the Spirit to a study of Scripture? While building a word portrait of Jesus with Scripture is a solid place to start and a safe way to proceed, my experiences of Jesus' truth and love during my crises also included direct messages of love by the Spirit (chapter 5) both during and after seasons of healing prayer along with a plethora of redemptive truth pictures given by the Spirit to help me know redemptive truth in profoundly deeper ways (chapters 5, 17,23). We should be careful not to limit the Spirit (who is "Lord") and the way He chooses to communicate Jesus and His redemptive riches to our souls, which are never contrary to Scripture. Beholding Jesus now, by the Spirit, can go much deeper into our souls than what most Christians experience. AMAZING things happen in our souls when we slow down and meditate on Scripture and allow the Holy Spirit to give us direct massages of His love and plant pictures of truth in our minds through prayer.

- We foster this horizontal fellowship as we pursue this shared life of Christ with our families. Yet we must make time for fellowship and make our time count. Taking time to talk and listen to our family members, teaching and learning life skills together, talking about Bible truths and life challenges together, learning the gospel and its unfathomable riches together, praying together, worshipping together, serving together, and simply being together to know and encourage one another. Family is the most important unit God has given humanity for our security, learning, growth, protection, and depth of relationships.

Fathers today must get gripped with the grace that can flow from God into the hearts of their wives and kids through their affirmations of carefully crafted words, focus of their eyes, touch of their gentle hands, strength of their soulish hugs, the love of really listening, and willingness to humbly and genuinely enter into the chaos of each family member's world—even if we don't know what to say.

- We foster this horizontal fellowship as we pursue shared life in the body of Christ. The early Church met daily to share meals, personal goods, communion, prayer, worship, and ministry together. His presence was palpable in the lives they shared. Due to our speed of culture and disruptive nature of our technology, God's people need commitment and wisdom in how to pursue this shared life together in worship services, life groups, prayer times, and service projects. AMAZING things happen in our souls when we do what the early church did TOGETHER in the power of the Holy Spirit!

QUESTIONS FOR REFLECTION AND DISCUSSION

1. How would you describe the depth of connection you had with both your parents?
2. If our souls are experientially empty of Jesus, why is it easier for us to succumb to dark choices, such as lust, materialism, and power?
3. Why is changing our attachment pattern so difficult?
4. Why might a person with a very unhealthy attachment pattern in childhood tend to avoid depth in relationships later on in life?
5. Is it possible to develop an attachment pattern with God the Father by the Spirit of Jesus which significantly enhances our experience of Jesus and soulful relationships with others?

Thomas Dages

CHAPTER TWENTY

At the Crossroads of Decision Making

Sometimes, Tom, you have to take a step backwards, before you can move forward.
— Rev Cliff Swanson

MY LIFE HAD BEEN HELLISH NOW for better than two years. The spiritual attacks from the demonic realm, the relentless crashing waves of anxiety, and two rip tides of insomnia needing heavy concoctions of sleep medications took its toll on my body and soul. These storms surfaced an inner boil that was growing in me and had caused chaos for decades. My church gave me a partial three-month sabbatical the fall after the onset of my crisis in 2010, but now, I again felt as if I was simply getting through my sermon Sunday to Sunday, and I wasn't much good for anyone or anything else. My heart was unintentionally absent from the people I was supposed to be engaging in love. Emotionally, I was elsewhere to my family. My inner boil felt like a stubborn painful darkness that was inextricably part of my own heart's history. It was not going to move on fast anytime soon. How does one fight to carry the weight of pastoring a congregation of people and tend to his family while fighting such strong internal storms?

I found myself at a crossroads, a place where I never guessed I would be. Do I step down from ministry for an extended time of healing, or do I stay put in preaching at the church where God had clearly called me and weather this beastly storm?

God's call for me to preach was clarion and confirmed by many along the way. He clearly directed me after seminary to pastorates in Colorado, Michigan, and Northern Virginia, but now, I faced resigning my current pastorate for a time of desperately needed soul and body rehabilitation. I had heard of many pastors forced to leave ministry because of serious moral failures, but I never met one sidelined from ministry due to the surfacing of severe inner turbulence that felt like it was going to break apart his life.

If I had met someone like me several years prior to my crisis, I would have told them unhesitatingly to stop complaining, stay put in ministry, and move forward in the grace of God. Yet now the storms raged in my own soul, and the advice I would have strongly given others didn't seem so wise. Was I just being a wimpy soldier, or was God moving me to the sidelines for the healing of my soul to prepare me for a different season of ministry?

This was such a monumental and traumatic decision for me. I remember sitting in a Chick-Fil-A restaurant with our associate pastor, Chris Greenwood, and expressing to him my wishes that our elders would fire me, to make the decision of leaving easier. As we ate together, I told him that resigning stirred up such great fear because of what I was taught about staying the course as a pastor. To resign had connotations of quitting and failure, flavored with defeatism. The elders, however, didn't fire me, and they were unwilling by God's providence to give me another, longer sabbatical where I was relieved from all my ministerial responsibilities. Fortunately, God was not done with His strong, gracious ways of guiding me.

My first guidance that I needed to step down from ministry was the internal conviction that I couldn't carry the job of pastoring our congregation and give the people the care they needed. The deep sense that I needed soul restoration and the people of Reston needed a pastor who was more present to their needs became a strong and settled conviction as I prayerfully pondered my situation. I could play the role of hero or emotional martyr if I chose, dying to my dying self, and the church would get a pastor who tried to be "filled with the Spirit," (Ephesians 5:18), but neither my soul, my family, nor my church would get the healing needed with my martyrdom. Certainly, a pastor with more emotional wealth than what I had accumulated in my inner man over the decades would be able to be a deeper reservoir for God's people at Reston.

God's next guidance came through my new counselor, Paige Fishel, who was recommended by Dr. Thompson for her practical wisdom and closer proximity to my house. Paige spent much time listening to my story, both the crises of the last three years and my painful history of fear and anxiety. God spoke His wisdom to my heart as she re-emphasized the importance of renewing my mind with God's truth and continuing to practice my deep breathing exercises, which she took to another level of using my imagination to picture the bright light of God in me as I did so. However, I also sensed the Spirit speaking His wisdom to me through several questions and comments she made in our limited sessions together.

After several sessions together she asked me a powerful question: "What's next for you and your family?" Through this question, Paige was assuming God had something vastly different for me and my family. She was the first one to help me truly consider that stepping down from ministry was the obvious next step for my battle-weary soul. She saw the crisis I was in, as I was now taking again five sleeping pills to get my needed sleep. She knew I was having auditory hallucinations from my sleep deprivation. She saw how my identity crisis ran deeply into the history of my heart. She knew I hadn't had a total sabbatical rest in 23 years of ministry. With one simple question, "What's next?" I found freedom to consider stepping down from formal ministry.

In one of our last sessions together, Paige told me she had read a comment online posted by one of her friends, who liked to start her day with coffee and asking the Lord to direct her to Scripture she could pass to others. The Lord directed this friend to the following words from Jeremiah, and Paige believed these words were for me:

"Thus says the LORD: 'Stand by the roads, and look, and ask for the ancient paths, where the good way is; and walk in it, and find rest for your souls.'" Jeremiah 6:16

As she read this verse about God's "ancient paths" "and "good way" and finding "rest" for the soul, God's supernatural peace flooded my soul.

However, I feared taking such a rest because this might mean resigning from my church, and what would I do if I had to provide for my family outside my profession, training, and experience? I voiced some of my fears to Paige, and she answered, "Tom, where did this peace come from?" When I hesitantly answered, "The Lord," I knew I had to trust His provision and continued guidance. The flood of peace during this interchange with sacred Scripture was God's signature on that moment, and I needed to trust and obey. Yet God was gracious to add more confirmations for my stepping down from ministry for a time of soul healing.

One Saturday night, as I was finishing up my sermon preparation, the Lord communicated to me with unmistakable clarity. I was seated behind my desk reading a Bible commentary, when the commentary "in my mind's eye" rose off my desk right before me…and closed.

While the Bible commentary itself stayed put on my desk, a picture of it rose from the desk and closed before my eyes.

As I sat there, not a verbal word was spoken to me, but I knew intuitively what God was communicating. As clearly and powerfully as He had called me to preach, He was now directing me that my preaching ministry (at least for now) was coming to a close. What a powerful way for God to communicate His will to one of His fearfully quaking children who wanted desperately to do His will... whatever that entailed. My resignation from Reston could now be a step of obedience to the Lord without wondering if this resignation decision was being led by Him or me.

God also would communicate in both little but big ways that this was His will for me and my family as we began to pray and trust Him for more specifics in His plans. They were little ways because they weren't visions that came with unmistakable clarity, but big ways because these accumulated confirmations, together, had a force of their own. Prayerful comments made by caring friends, circumstances which spoke wisdom to my heart, and wisdom from books that seemed aimed at my soul, were like little tiny bursts of wind all pushing the sail of my soul the same direction.

In June of 2013, I attended our denomination's General Assembly at Cherry Hills Presbyterian Church in Colorado. I wanted to go as our church representative to find out what was happening in our larger denomination. I also wanted to see my colleagues and friends in ministry, many of whom I had known for years. My agenda also included checking out Colorado as a place to possibly move my family. I had an old friend, Carey Green, who had recently stepped down from his pastorate in Leadville, Colorado. Carey lived in the beautiful town of Buena Vista, Colorado, located about two hours southwest of Denver. God stirred my spirit to reconnect with this old friend while on my Colorado trip.

Soon after arriving in Colorado, I jumped in my rental car and drove out to reunite with Carey and Mindi Green. What a godly couple. Carey was burdened by God to give families spiritual tools for becoming more Christ-centered and was now focusing on developing ministries that reached across the spectrum of family life. It was beautiful to see the fruit of God working through their parenting wisdom in the lives of their own children. After listening to my war story, he offered himself and his family to help ours. He also told me that he sensed Buena Vista might be exactly God's prescription for me to find my needed rest and spiritual restoration.

Buena Vista is situated at the foot of the Collegiate Peaks, a series of 14,000-foot peaks named after several Ivy League colleges. The physical setting of this small town and its many natural adornments makes it a perfect place to breathe in God's peace, find God's rhythms, and experience God's restoration. The mountains and valleys are the showcase and playground for stunning summertime wildflowers and animals like elk, deer, antelope, and foxes. Running through the heart of Buena Vista is the Arkansas River, recently labeled a Gold Medal trout stream for many of the miles between Leadville to the North and Cañon City to the South. Many of the smaller streams running out of the mountains into the Arkansas are home to cutthroat and brook trout, making it a fisherman's paradise. Not a bad asset for this "fisher of men" who found one of his greatest forms of restoration fishing for beautiful trout!

Interestingly, in and around this small town are many ministry-embattled pastors. I would meet several at various places in their healing journeys. Rest for the body and soul was something Buena Vista uniquely offered more than any other place I had experienced. While I sensed this was the place to which God was gently guiding me, Carey told me to go home and make sure Julie was on the same page.

Back at General Assembly, God spoke gentle wisdom through a book I picked up at lunch time in the church's café. Every day I would go to the café for lunch; there on a table was a book on the importance of God's church being family-centered in ministry. The book was entitled, *Dreaming of More* by Michelle Anthony and immediately drew me into its contents as I ate lunch. Every day I came back to eat lunch, this book both fed me and created an appetite for connecting with my family in ways I had missed. Michelle Anthony's book opened my eyes not only to where my ministry philosophy through the church to the family was shortsighted, but where my own parenting seriously faltered. There were no fireworks from God, just the deep abiding sense of conviction that this pending move was for my restoration and establishing deeper connections with my family.

Back in Reston, I was also helped by casual comments from my son's academic tutor. We had confided some of my struggles and a possible move to Buena Vista, Colorado. She told me that she had brought up Buena Vista on her computer and was looking at its topography, and even zoomed in on its baseball field for Nathan. She commented, "I sense this is the right move for your family!" My brother, Bill, a pastor himself, told me around this time about my resignation and move to Colorado, "Tom, I really believe in what you are doing for your family." In both of these casual conversations the Lord used these specific words as gentle winds on the sail of my spirit.

Practical Wisdom for the Invisible War

There is great power in teaching children God's truth, but this truth is best communicated in love. Up to this point in our lives, our kids heard biblical truth in church, Sunday school, and youth group. However, the place where it was to come most naturally and consistently was in the home, and ours wasn't done with the kind of consistency and heart connection that would make it most effective. As Dad, I made lots of corrections at home, but too often it came on the heels of yelling and done more out of my convenience than for their good!

THE LANCING OF MY SOUL

Love requires listening, quality time, and sacrifice. I was heavy on lecturing, and I needed to build my listening apparatus with them. I began to listen and make sacrifices for my older daughter as she approached me to talk right before going to bed. How inconvenient when it was already late, and I was tired and worried about getting to sleep, and yet how necessary to connect with her dad and express her world of questions, confusion, and her 16-year-old concerns.

As a family we started dedicating one night per week as a family night, where we would play games, watch a movie, or simply spend time together to develop our relationships. Sometimes I spent time giving extended devotions from Scripture and talk about their application to daily life. I read with my kids and looked for opportunities not only to deepen their wisdom, but to get pertinent discussions going. Many questions in life don't have neat and tidy answers, but discussing issues with kids and helping them see these questions from different angles helps kids sharpen their critical reasoning skills. I also found myself sharing many of my personal struggles and the power of God available in putting on His armor in practical ways.

Interestingly, one of the ways God gave me to overcome my own anxieties was to connect to my family's worlds to become genuinely present to them. At the beginning of my crisis when my son was just nine, I lay down next to him to help him fall asleep. It was a night when my anxiety was acute. This night Nathan wasn't satisfied with dad at his side, however, but wanted me to hold him. We put our arms around each other, and Nathan put his cheek on my chest as I held his head under my arm. The moon shone in the window and highlighted his face. A sense of security came from his countenance as we nestled together, and he fell quickly asleep. As I stared into his face, I felt a depth of connection and protection and love which was a gift of heaven, and as we stretched out together in this father-son connection, his and my anxiety melted away. The blessings both my son and I received in this encounter sank deeply into both our souls!

This focused family time would be foundational for my healing as well as their development.

QUESTIONS FOR REFLECTION AND DISCUSSION

1. How are emotions meant to be messengers of deeper issues going on in the heart?

2. Are you genuinely present to those in your immediate family? What are some steps you can take to help you in this matter?

3. Dr. Tim Keller was the first one to introduce me to the term "emotional wealth." What do you think this means? How does emotional wealth grow in us?

4. Is helping your children build emotional wealth one of your primary parenting goals? What are some practical steps you can take to help this process?

5. What happens when you as a parent hammer your kids with truth when it is not done in love?

Thomas Dages

CHAPTER TWENTY-ONE

The Final Decision to Move West

Now the Lord said to Abram, "Go from your country and your kindred and your father's house to the land that I will show you."
—*Genesis 12:1*

I RETURNED FROM MY WHIRLWIND TRIP to Colorado towards the end of June 2013. I sensed an accumulation of strong whispers from God that Buena Vista was where my family and I were to find rest and spiritual rehabilitation and open up a whole new section of life and development in the Dages family story book. We needed to trust God for what He would write on each subsequent page and the chapters that followed.

However, Julie wasn't part of my avalanche of strong whispers yet, and her heart needed to be persuaded by the Spirit on a move that was going to be seismic for each of us. The impact was foreboding enough to strike indecisive paralysis into the strongest of hearts, especially for Julie, since so much of the work of moving would fall upon her, and she was currently running on fumes. We had two weeks to decide, together, if these winds gathering behind us were from the Lord and whether He was calling us to set sail through such high winds to land our family in the small country town of Buena Vista, Colorado.

Vacations at our lake house on Lake Mokoma, Pennsylvania, were usually getaways of relaxation and wonderful times of emotional and spiritual restoration. This one, however, was a getaway with a huge shadow looming large over us. The shadow had to be faced, and the decision of moving or staying made. I could feel the shadow looming over our car ride to the lake. During casual conversations with my wife, the decision cast its shadow. I felt its presence even on the peaceful lake as I fished and in the blueberries I picked and tasted. The shadow loomed as we watched our kids and we wondered, together, how they would respond if we suddenly uprooted them and headed west. So much work and change and adjustments would be involved, and so little did we know what I would do vocationally and how God would provide.

How could I expect God to move in my wife's heart? She had been through an emotional war with me already and stayed strong all the way through. She was working two part-time jobs, taking care of our home, balancing our checkbook and paying our bills, and demonstrating sensitivity to my heart infections now surfacing and spilling out from my inner life. How would the Almighty persuade my emotionally drained wife, who was now emoting such anger, to set sail into new storms with only the faintest silver linings of hope onto which she could hold?

Julie was angry, and understandably so. As we took walks together around the lake, she began to leak her feelings of anger and frustration at where she was emotionally and what a move was going to demand of her empty reserves. She knew I needed this change away from full time ministry into a place of restoration, but it was going to require so much from her that she didn't currently possess. How could we get our house ready to sell? How could we prepare our kids for such a drastic and sudden move? Where would the money come from to support us when I was going to be without work? Would such a time of restoration truly bring change to my heart and freedom from what had held me in bondage for decades? Julie had tasted the rotten fruit of my anxiety and obsessive-compulsive fears for years. Was this retreat into this tiny town in the west a "pipedream," or would it lead to real change in me that would nourish all of our family? These were the spoken and unspoken fears and frustrations that at times erupted from my usually quiet and gentle wife. For the most part, all I could do was listen and attempt to show that her emotions were deeply felt.

Would God speak to her in a dream or a vision? Would he speak to her heart in her daily Bible reading that she did so faithfully? Would God speak wisdom directly to her spirit, which He did on so many previous occasions? I can't tell you the number of times He has spoken directly to me, through her, in quiet yet powerful statements that were direct hits to my soul—and she is not even a preacher! Would God use a forceful vision, or a gentle whisper, or not speak at all and force us to live by faith in what we thought was best together?

God, however, had another gentle wind to blow upon my wife strong enough to move her fatigued, frightened, and deeply frustrated state. Since living by faith in the promises and presence of Christ is the crux of the Christian life, God would move upon her with just enough wisdom and encouragement to face and walk through this storm as we learned to lean upon Him, and each other, more steadfastly. As we walked and talked and prayed and listened to God and each other, the wisdom of God's will emerged in Julie's drained yet still spiritually sensitive heart. This is how God often works with hearts in tune with His.

As we opened lines of communication with each other, the strength of my convictions God had built in me during my trip out west was what Julie now saw. Our walks and talks together not only helped Julie vent her deep frustrations and fears, but they paved the way for her to hear God's wisdom emerging in my heart and trust this move out west was indeed His doing. By the end of our two-week vacation, Julie, although still emotionally drained from years of putting up with my issues, was miraculously ready to move into this new storm, holding on by faith that a new and eventually better season awaited us out west in Buena Vista, Colorado.

Every believer's journey under the gracious Lordship of Jesus is unique. In times of crises we should not be impulsive about critical life decisions, nor should we be impulsive in giving out advice to others. In prayer, deep trust, and asking spouses and wise discerning people, God will give us enough clarity to take our major steps.

Practical Wisdom for the Invisible War

Prayer is a powerful tool couples can use to sensitize them to God's will speaking through the heart of each other. However, most Christians find themselves too busy to personally pray, sidelining prayer with their spouses until a crisis occurs. Such marriages shirk one of the greatest God-given channels of emotional oneness: spiritual power and spiritual sensitivity to God and each other. Marriages that shirk such grace inevitably shrink in intimacy and power and miss out on God's gentle whispers of wisdom.

My wife needed to express what she was feeling that was stuffed in her soul. She needed to know I was listening, something I had not done well in our marriage. I needed to grow in my sensitivity as a husband to love her in a way she needed love.

I knew and taught for decades that one of the top needs of a wife is for her husband to practice this sensitivity by listening well. After all, she is a co-heir with me "of the grace of life" (1 Peter 3:7). She needs to be heard deeply and receive more hugs and affection that don't have hints of leading to the bedroom. This life of loving, listening, sharing, and praying with one another makes marriage deeper and richer and the communications of God much more discernible.

In his book *Sons of The Father*, Gordon Dalby shares a story of how praying together sensitized him to both God and his wife when they both felt right and were strongly at odds over a marital issue. Listen to how God sensitized their hearts to His through prayer. He says, "I took Mary's hand into our bedroom and we knelt at our bedside. 'Father', I prayed, 'I've told Mary my opinion on this and she's told me hers; we've gone over and over this, and neither of us wants to give up to the other. Speak to us; show us how you see all this.'

"I waited, and sensed the Father saying simply, 'Listen to her.' But Father, I protested quietly, I really feel like I'm right this time! 'I didn't say you were wrong,' I sensed the reply; 'I said, "Listen to her."' Puzzled, but at my wits end, I sighed, turned to Mary, and told her what the Lord had said. 'Maybe I've been so anxious to make my point that I haven't really listened to you. Would you tell me once more how you feel about all this, and I'll try my best to listen?' OK, Father, I prayed, I give up to you all my right to win this argument. Now help me listen to her and hear what you want me to.

"Mary hesitated as a flicker of distrust was swept away by love, and then told me again how she was feeling. As she talked, I sensed her pain was rooted long before we met and began to see why this issue was particularly upsetting to her. Many tears and hugs later, we could only wonder together at the Father's love for both of us."[lxvii]

Learning to communicate lovingly together and then praying together is mysterious business, but lots of grace flows from God to hearts individually and horizontally between couples, and from God to the couple as a unit indwelt by God. The sweetness of fellowship deepens all three directions.

This is another form of "all prayer" that serves as a great form of protection and grace for marriages.

QUESTIONS FOR REFLECTION AND DISCUSSION

1. Why is prayer as a couple often so hard?

2. Why might God hinder a husband's prayers if he is not treating his wife with sensitivity?

3. Why is learning to listen carefully to your spouse vital in determining God's will in big family decisions?

4. When was a time in your marriage when you felt God speak clearly to you through your spouse? If you can't recall, what does this tell you about your listening skills?

5. What steps could you take as a couple to help foster better communication and prayer with each other?

PART FOUR

Developing the "New" Me

Therefore, if anyone is in Christ, he is a new creation. The old has passed away; behold the new has come.
—2 CORINTHIANS 5:17

A friend once asked Stradivarius, who perfected the violin, how long it took to make a violin. Stradivarius said, "A thousand years." He went on to say that a violin can be made only from a tree that is tempered by the wind, beaten by sleet, scorched by summer, and blasted by the ice of winter—a thousand years. In other words, it takes a very strong, weather-worn tree to make a violin. A protected tree would never do.

— DR. FRANK MINIRTH[lxviii]

But the one lesson we learn from all available sources is that there is no "quick fix" for the human condition. The approach to wholeness is for humankind a process of great length and difficulty that engages all our own powers to their fullest extent over a long course of experience. But we don't like to hear this. We are somewhat misled by the reports of experiences by many great spiritual leaders, and we assign their greatness to these great moments they were given, neglecting the years of slow progress they endured before them. Frances de Sales wisely counsels us not to expect transformation in a moment, though it is possible for God to give it.

— DALLAS WILLARD[lxix]

CHAPTER TWENTY-TWO

God Develops My Humanity Through Hardship

I believe in miracle, but not too much miracle, for too much miracle would weaken us, make us dependent upon miracle instead of our obedience to natural law. Just enough miracle to let us know He is there, but not too much, lest we depend on it when we should depend on our own initiative and on His orderly process for our development.
—*Dallas Willard*[lxx]

In the days of his flesh, Jesus offered up prayers and supplications, with loud cries and tears, to him who was able to save him from death, and he was heard because of his reverence. Although he was a son, he learned obedience though what he suffered. And being made perfect, he became the source of eternal salvation to all who obey him...
— *Hebrews 5:7-9*

There is not a square inch in the whole domain of our human existence over which Christ, who is Sovereign over all, does not cry, "Mine!"
— *Abraham Kuyper*[lxxi]

AFTER WE MADE THE DECISION TO MOVE to Buena Vista, one of the most encouraging confirmations our family received that this move was God's doing was the decision of the elders to give us a portion of a year's salary in Colorado...when they knew we were not coming back! This was amazing because we were a small church and had grown smaller the last few years of my tenure as pastor. They knew I hadn't had a full sabbatical in twenty-three years, and God was making restorative changes in my heart that would take significant time and rest. They sent us on our way with a commitment to give us 80%, then 60%, and then 40% of our salary so I could focus on soul restoration and not worry immediately about supporting my family.

God carried our family out west, and He used the hands, creative love, and encouragement of His people to do so. Friends at our church helped us pack our moving van, ready our house to sell, and sell it for a reduced cost. One of our friends called almost every day of our road trip out west simply to remind us that we were loved, not forgotten, and Jesus was with us.

As we arrived in Colorado, we stopped off at Julie's parents' home before our final two-hour trip to Buena Vista. Ron and Marian were delighted to have us move out west, as I had taken their daughter away from Colorado some 20 years prior. Now we would be back in Colorado much closer to them in their later years and closer to Julie's sister, who was declining rapidly with multiple sclerosis. God has a way in His sovereign wisdom to orchestrate moves that are good for immediate and extended families. We lived out east for 20 years and blessed my dad and mom in their physical decline, and now in my deep distress, we were able to move back to Julie's roots, to receive from and give love to her family.

It was during our brief stay with Julie's parents that my eye caught a book sitting on their coffee table. It would speak deeply to my heart about more development God intended for my soul. It was a book entitled *Joshua* by Joseph Girzone and told the fictitious story of what life and ministry might have been like for Jesus if He came back to live again among His people in the 21st century as a small-town wood carver. However, this book had a different "salvation" message for my soul than what I was used to hearing or telling. Girzone's *Joshua* spring-boarded me on a trip deep into the humanity of Jesus, how it was developed through obedience and suffering, and how God was taking aim to develop mine.[lxxii]

It was truly amazing that Jesus came out of heaven as fully God and miraculously become fully man, developed His humanity through suffering, died as a substitute on the cross, and rose from the grave after His crucifixion to give life to believing people. Seminary trained me well in understanding the full deity of Jesus. Over the years God expanded my personal knowledge of the spiritual riches and amazing life I possessed through receiving the Lord Jesus into my own life when I was initially justified and forgiven. Now, however, I was getting an intensive theological course on the full humanity of Jesus, how it was developed, and a practicum on God's plan to work the humanity of Jesus into the fibers of mine!

Jesus developed through obedience and suffering.

"For it was fitting that he, for whom and by whom all things exist, in bringing many sons to glory should make the founder of their salvation perfect through suffering."
Hebrews 2:10

Jesus suffered as the Father perfected his humanity through trials; resisting sin at every point. He suffered as He grew in endurance. His training continued with a 40-day fast and perfect resistance to every temptation the devil threw at Him.

While Jesus suffered uniquely and to a depth of intensity as only our Redeemer could, He also pointed to and paved the way for God's salvation to invade and renovate the humanity of those who would receive Him.

Luke tells us that Jesus "grew and became strong, filled with wisdom. And the favor of God was upon him" (Luke 2:40). Jesus certainly grew in physical strength and wisdom, but He also grew in all categories of a fully developed human. His training included studying and memorizing Hebrew scrolls, which He later used to perfectly resist temptations. His growth likely included His carpentry skills as Joseph's apprentice, His emotional development, and His work ethic. Is there any question that Jesus developed a great work ethic under Joseph's tutelage? Is there any doubt Jesus developed excellence in His carpentry skills and learned how to stay after work without being asked? Jesus developed a toughness and tenderness of humanity through His training.

Up to this point in my life, apart from preaching, excellence in high school and college sports, and casts of occasional excellence with a fly rod, I had little to no developed wholeness as part of my holiness. I didn't know how to cook, attempted and fixed a few things around the house, knew very little about what happens under the hood of a car (except how to add oil and washer fluid), and remained technologically challenged in most aspects of computer communication. I was timid of chain saws and all power tools. I was never involved in Boy Scouts, so knew very little about surviving skills in the outdoors. I became adept over the years in turning a Bible passage into a sermon which could hold a congregation's attention for 30 minutes, but I was void of wisdom in living life and excelling in the "nuts and bolts" of so many skill sets a wholesome life demanded. There was little I could do skillfully through my underdeveloped head-hands connection, and so little I could pass on in developmental discipleship to my kids.

In a very real sense, I was being led by the Spirit of God into my wilderness not only to be trained in putting on God's armor and cleansing my soul infections, but to be developed in every aspect of my humanity. And how this development and training hurt at so many levels!

God highlighted to me that I was on this journey of holiness/wholeness not only through Joseph Girzone's book, but through several teachable moments along the way.

The first came as I watched the movie *The Nativity*. I watched this movie several months prior to the onset of my crises just as my own suffering was about to firmly settle over me. It was like a warning sign preparing me for the hard season I was about to endure. It wasn't anything said in the movie, but the simple event of Mary and Joseph starting their trip to Bethlehem, and Joseph's sandals grinding on the hard rock with the first step of his journey. Without an audible word from God being spoken, He seemed to communicate I was about to embark on my own grueling expedition. Mary and Joseph could not escape the difficulty of their journey and as they depended upon God, He would use the toughness of their trek to develop them and then, use Mary as a channel to birth Jesus into the world. What a difficult passage to Bethlehem, what a difficult birth in an animal cave. As Joseph's sandals ground against the rock, God impressed upon me that this, too, was the beginning of an exquisitely difficult season and journey for me.

Second, about halfway through this period of soul stretching and testing, I was in the side yard helping my nine-year-old son Nathan develop his pitching mechanics. I had just taken him through a pitching workout on a very hot and muggy day. I told Nathan after the workout, he needed to go for a short run to strengthen his legs and endurance. We often did this after pitching practice, so he knew the drill, and several minutes later he came back and fell at my feet, hot and wearied from his short run. I began to clarify to him with encouraging words, why this training and running was important for his strength and development as a pitcher. As Nathan worked to catch his breath, I gently reminded my son, "Nathan, the only way you can..." And he stopped me before I could proceed. "I know Dad," he said, "the only way a pitcher can get stronger for a game is by doing hard things." I smiled over my son when I heard him finish my words of wisdom which I must have said more than once!

However, as I celebrated "he gets it," the Holy Spirit turned my statement into a question. He asked me, "Do you get it? Do you get that the only way I can build endurance in you as my adopted son is to take you through training that makes you work, breathe hard, and sometimes painfully so?"

I experienced high school and college wrestling practices and knew the importance of endurance training. There are no shortcuts to getting oneself in better condition than your opponent so you can excel in your skills at the end of the third period. I defeated a Division III All-American in college in the third period because I was in better shape. The Holy Spirit was now reminding me how this endurance and resistance training was necessary to finish well with following Christ.

I did get it alright, but I didn't like it! I was right in the midst of an extended season of exquisitely hard "endurance" training that wasn't going to end anytime soon. This wasn't the middle of a long five-mile run that would end in thirty-five minutes. This was a battle in my soul with no near-term end in sight. This was my own 80-mile trek to Bethlehem, and I was at the beginning of my healing journey, feeling the first scrapes of my sandals against the hard rocks under my feet. Although there would be plenty of God's grace along the way, there was no shortcut to the grit God was building into my soul.

Paul reminds us in Romans about endurance training that sets in after we are justified by God's grace through faith. Endurance is a process that can only be grown as we face the resistance of hardship and keep moving ahead in faith. While God determines the hardships in a unique plan, tailor-made for each of His adopted children, adding the necessary comforts and assistance of His Spirit along the way, none of His children are exempt from this process of developmental wholeness/holiness. Paul, after stating our justification we received by faith, says it this way,

---

"More than that, we rejoice in our sufferings, knowing that suffering produces endurance, and endurance produces character, and character produces hope, and hope does not put us to shame, because God's love has been poured out in our hearts through the Holy Spirit who has been given to us."
Romans 5:3-5

The endurance training producing character is not optional for only a select few of God's special soldiers. Paul implies this training is for all who have truly tasted the gift of justification and peace. Biblically, the process is seamlessly knit into our salvation immediately after it occurs; though God orchestrates when these hard seasons occur. The love of the Holy Spirit shed abroad in our hearts is the comfort carrying us through until we are perfected in heaven. This training can be, and most often is, painful.

For many Americans who seek a soft spirituality by seeking to escape suffering at every turn and who want everything instantly, the demand of discipleship can be quite shocking, especially when we find ourselves thrust into the furnace of God's fierce love.

Third, right before our move, I tried a home project that I would have previously asked someone else to do. We were trying to fix our home to sell it, and the downstairs bathroom sink needed a new drain and pipes. To save money and to try developing my handyman abilities, I tried this task with the help of my son Nathan. It was hard! I wanted at several points to quit and pay someone else to do it. However, I wanted to push through this project to develop my head-hands connection and accomplish this for my sake and my son's.

My first step was to go to our nearby Home Depot and get replacement parts. As we left the store carrying our supplies, Nathan said, "Dad, this is cool, I may want to be plumber!" Our second step was to take out the parts that were broken and rusted together. This meant getting down underneath the bathroom sink, fighting to find a spot to work, getting a hold on parts I couldn't completely see, and using a strange wrench I had never before used. This took countless tries where the grip of my wrench seemed to continuously slip. Nathan held one side of the pipe and I turned the other. About fifteen minutes into the process, Nathan told me, "Dad, I don't think I want to be a plumber!" Yet we kept at it. Finally, the pipe loosened and broke out of the rust, and we were able to disassemble the drain and its pipes.

Then, however, we had to read the directions several times and proceed to put together what we had never done. I have always hated reading directions but had to do so to get the project right. I read and reread directions and finally, after many failed attempts, the drain was in place. About four hours after starting, Nathan and I sat back with the sense of project accomplished! Wow, did it feel good! It also felt good to do something with my son, to give him a taste of all the work and failures needed to accomplish a task. While I may never be "Tim the Tool Man," to start and finish a project with my son was an exercise in developmental wholeness. It developed our souls, helped us face frustration together, and developed our father-son relationship. God was pleased with my holiness (I didn't use any words of profanity in my frustrations) and our progress in developmental wholeness.

One day shortly after we had moved to Buena Vista, God reinforced in my heart that this process of wholeness and holiness was indeed one reason He had brought us to this small town out west. Nathan and I were walking home to the house we were renting. He had just learned how to chop wood when he turned to me and said, "Dad, God brought me out here to make me a man!" I smiled inside and thought to myself, "Nathan, God brought your father out here to make me a man, too!"

Practical Wisdom for the Invisible War

Dr. Bruce Demarest says, "For the Christian, the path of connectedness to God involves the development of a Christ-like mind, will, affections (or emotions), character, relationships and actions. When any of these capacities is undernourished, our spiritual growth will be stunted."[lxxiii] Of course, the soul suffers spiritually in all these areas when Jesus is rejected as Lord and Savior, and the Spirit of God does not bring His life-giving, nurturing presence to our souls.

Dr. Demarest outlines six areas in which an undernourished soul can suffer great pain.

"First, the soul suffers intellectually when we fail to use our minds to know God, His Word, and His world, or when we believe the heart can be satisfied merely by right thinking about God."[lxxiv] While we can't find satisfaction with God by merely thinking correctly about God, developing our intellect and thinking correctly about God is certainly foundational for the next steps to be taken. Dr. Demarest says, "Growing Christians must use their God given minds to explore truth in the Bible and across the entire field of human learning."[lxxv]

"Second, the inner man suffers volitionally, that is, our inner man can become weak and unable to stand up for the Christian convictions we so strongly espouse."[lxxvi] Life and development into Christlikeness is about the myriad of choices we make every day that either weaken our wills or strengthen them to be more like Jesus. We strengthen our wills in dependency upon the Holy Spirit by making choices of correct thinking, behaving, worshipping, repenting, and courageously speaking for Jesus every day.

"Third, the soul can suffer from emotional deadness."[lxxvii] When we don't nurture godly affections like care and compassion for the hurting or when we fail to nurture the expression of heartfelt thanksgiving and praise, our souls languish in emotional deadness. Nurturing God's life in our emotions is big business. Although we are to live primarily by faith in God's promises, our feelings nevertheless need to be nurtured by truth, action, and fellowship with God.

"Fourth, our soul suffers morally when we fail to keep God's wise commandments and we violate conscience (see 1 Timothy 4:2)."[lxxviii] Salvation is not only from the penalty of sin but for power to live a life morally directed by God to obey the spirit of the law, especially to love God with all our inner beings and our neighbors as ourselves (Mark 12:29:30). When we disobey God's clear precepts in Scripture, our souls suffer moral disorders and breakdowns.

"Fifth, the soul suffers relationally without mutually enriching relationships with God and with others."[lxxix] We were not meant to live outside of fellowship (shared life) with God and others. An isolated soul withers like a grape picked off a vine. We were created to live in community with God and others. While God is our source of life, He uses others as resources to bring His life to our souls. Eyeball-to-eyeball, heart-to-heart fellowship is a source of great strength for God's people.

"Finally, our souls suffer functionally when we fail to do what is right in service to God and our neighbor."[lxxx] Here was probably the most undeveloped aspect of my soul, especially in the development of my head-hands connection and the skillsets, or lack thereof, which hampered my service to God, my family, and others.

God's Spirit was beginning a process of working serious wholeness and grit into the humanity of my already saved soul.

QUESTIONS FOR REFLECTION AND DISCUSSION

1. Why was it necessary for the sinless Son of God to be perfected through the process of suffering and obedience?

2. How was the suffering of Jesus unique to His mission of Savior for mankind?

3. Why does God want to develop the humanity of Jesus in the lives of all His adopted children?

4. Why does this dimension of salvation involve time and struggle?

5. Of the six areas of the soul Dr. Demarest highlights, which one represents where you need the most development?

Thomas Dages

CHAPTER TWENTY-THREE

God Develops My Security by Touching My Past Again

Reason is the organ of truth, whereas imagination is the organ of meaning.
—*C.S. Lewis*[lxxxi]

I do not cease to give thanks for you, remembering you in my prayers, that the God of our Lord Jesus Christ, the Father of glory, may give you a spirit of wisdom and of revelation in the knowledge of him, **having the eyes of your hearts enlightened***, that you may know what is the hope to which he has called you, what are the riches of his glorious inheritance in the saints, and what is the immeasurable greatness of his power toward us who believe...*
— *Ephesians 1:16-19b (emphasis mine)*

UPON DECIDING TO RESIGN FROM MY PASTORATE in Reston, I submitted my plans to the elders. One of the elders who walked extra closely with me through the process offered his only hesitation. He said, "Tom, I like everything about this plan except the lack of counseling available to you in Buena Vista." He saw the depths of struggles through which I was passing, the "many things wrong in me," the great help the professional counseling community gave me in Northern Virginia, and the apparent absence of such wisdom in a mountain town of less than 3,000 people.

However, God's plans always have His resources available, and I was surprised to find in this tiny town some of the richest counseling I have ever received. This is where I met Wil Franz and Peter Kuiper at CrossRoads Counseling, who so beautifully blended biblical truth with its natural Jesus-focused, psychological insight, and who practiced healing prayer during counseling sessions. They welcomed the Holy Spirit to continue His healing ministry to my saved, yet deeply struggling soul.

I used to downplay the idea of needing to deal with a person's past hurts and traumas. After all, doesn't God give us the strength in the present to move forward with spiritual power into the future, no matter what transpired in the older chapters of our lives? God has given us His Word, His Spirit, prayer, and spiritual gifts for our powerful living. However, when my inner boil surfaced with such emotional weight and stubborn pain, my thinking about dealing wisely with my past also began to change. God certainly empowers us to move in the present with His grace and power, but His ideal desire is to do so through healing and wholeness in our inner being.

When we are touched in ways only the Holy Spirit can, and are transformed with His inner healing, we are able to work more joyfully ourselves, and our lives can have more of an impact on others. This brings God greater glory through us! His Spirit can bypass much sin and brokenness in us to accomplish His purposes (which He often does), but He would rather work inner healing and wholeness in us, so that like an engine with frequent oil changes, tune-ups, and repairs after accidents, we run smoothly and last much longer!

During my seminary years, I remember hearing a quote from one of my counseling professors, Dr. John Bettler, "You do need to go back to your past when your past controls your present!" However, at that point in my life, I couldn't see clearly the issues in my past that were clearly crippling my present. After all, I was saved from the penalty of sin and making slow progress in several areas of my life. When I preached, the Holy Spirit moved on me with power. However, the fears and anxieties I felt were so much a part of me that they felt normal. I didn't sense a need for going back in my past because I thought I was managing my flesh and wounds and its brokenness without any "major" failures. Now the Holy Spirit was about to take aim at an early trauma that triggered huge currents of anxiety in my life, carrying chaos through the terrain of my soul.

This trauma occurred when I was just two years old. It was so traumatic, I still remember it as though it was yesterday. Our house was a three-story house (not including the basement or attic). My mom was busy raising five children, who spanned only six-and-a-half years from oldest to youngest. My dad was a busy dentist who delegated to mom all childcare and home responsibilities. Apparently, mom would put me down for a nap by taking me up to the third-floor bedroom, out of the way of noise, so I could find my needed sleep. At this age, I also had corrective shoes for my feet with metal braces attached to the top of each foot and connected together to slowly straighten my crooked feet. These constraining shoes were placed upon my feet as I slept.

One afternoon she put me down for a nap time. When I awakened, I wanted out of my corrective shoes and wanted mom badly. I remember crying crazily for her to come to relieve me. My crying turned into screaming, but still, no mom in sight. I screamed at the top of my two-year old lungs, and still, no one came to hold me and free me from my crib and my corrective shoes and fears. This crying and screaming was so intense, and the fear of panic was so strong, that I remember it clearly some 50 years after its occurrence. Physically, in retrospect, it felt like I blew circuits in my brain as I screamed for mom to come free me from my corrective shoes and hold me in her arms. This was kind of like blowing your nose so hard you feel your tiny blood vessels break, yet this experience was much more prolonged and impactful. It was this prolonged screaming with the fear of mom not coming that became so deeply etched in my brain. I don't remember much, if anything, prior to the age of six in my life, but this event was imprinted firmly in my mind. Mom eventually came, of course, but the trauma of such a prolonged agony for such a fragile psyche made a deep impact upon me.

THE LANCING OF MY SOUL

Interestingly, many counselors today, with discoveries in neuroscience, are suggesting that such strong psychological traumas can actually impact the wiring of our brain's neural highways. What was happening at a neurological level when I felt like I was blowing my circuits in my brain with such strong, intense and prolonged screaming? What happened at a psychological level to set in motion coping mechanisms like control to avoid ever facing such abandonment and overwhelming fear again? What happened at a spiritual level where the enemy could seize upon such overwhelming fear and suggest lies to my mind then and later about my safety and security of my personhood?

Is it any wonder I grew up with sudden panic attacks when I found myself in places I couldn't control and from which I couldn't escape? For instance, I grew up hating elevators. Entering elevators and having the doors close upon me triggered all kinds of fear that I might become trapped and never again see the light of day. "What if I get into this elevator and it gets stuck and no one ever comes to get me out?" These thoughts overwhelmed me when the elevator doors opened and then closed. Riding on an elevator was a gargantuan task, and it took all the faith I could muster to step in and do what others don't give a second thought to doing.

I postured myself to always be in control so I never had to face overwhelming fear. I wanted to be in control to avoid overwhelming fear, yet the more I attempted to control what I couldn't, the greater anxiety would grip me. What started out as an understandable coping mechanism for a small child at age two grew into a heart idol and life strategy of gargantuan proportions.

It was during a 30-hour counseling intensive at CrossRoads in Buena Vista that the Holy Spirit moved powerfully in my imagination through healing prayer to provide powerful redemptive pictures, releasing me from my performance treadmill. Wil Franz told me that Jesus was my "time traveler" who could take me back to old wounds and provide redemptive pictures for healing. During this same time period of my intensive, this time praying at home, Jesus my "time traveler" would also touch my trauma sustained at age two.

I remember well meditating and praying through Psalm 23 when the Holy Spirit took me back to my trauma again, this time to show me with the eyes of my heart that He was with me.

"The Lord is my shepherd; I shall not want. He makes me to lie down in green pastures. He leads me beside still waters. He restores my soul. He leads me in the paths of righteousness for his name's sake. Even though I walk through the valley of the shadow of death, I will fear no evil, **for you are with me;** *your rod and your staff, they comfort me. You prepare a table before me in the presence of my enemies: you anoint my head with oil; my cup overflows. Surely goodness and mercy shall follow me all the days of my life, and I shall dwell in the house of the LORD forever."*
Psalm 23:1-6 (emphasis mine)

As He took me back to my screaming crisis at age two, suddenly a hand appeared in my imagination that was no doubt the hand of Jesus symbolizing His presence with me. This hand appeared and was placed upon my tiny chest to bring peace and quiet to my quaking heart. What a powerful symbol of His presence "with me" at this critical juncture, taught by Psalm 23. Then, the hand of Jesus moved off my quaking two-year-old chest and rested upon me as I was praying. This brought quite a bit of comfort to me to see in picture form the presence of Jesus with me both now and then.

When I told Wil Franz about the experiences of Christ in my imagination, Wil emphasized that I could go back to the hand of Jesus upon me, and use this God-given mental picture at any time I wanted to actualize His presence, especially when I feared losing control and being overwhelmed by fear. If a panic attack seized me, Jesus was with me, and picturing His hand upon my chest and His arms around me brought great comfort to me. If I was in an elevator and stricken with fear, He was with me, and picturing His hand upon my chest and His arms around me would bring His comfort to my soul. This truth from Psalm 23 that He was with me, reinforced by the picture of His hand upon my chest, became a great weapon of faith for me to find a safe place with Jesus, wherever and whenever fear would strike.

I would retreat to this picture of His hand upon me and His arms around me and even picture Jesus standing behind me holding me while traveling in an elevator! When I did so, the peace of Jesus often overpowered my fears! Could it be that walking by faith in these redemptive pictures was actually reworking the neural networks of my brain traumatized so long ago? My right-brain imagination was slowly being integrated with my left-brain logic, and "You are with me" would start to become a more settled peace in my inner being. Deep healing began and I was doing more than coping with my mammoth fears. As I quoted Scripture to protect myself from the enemy and retreated into these God-given pictures, my mind was integrated and renewed at its deepest level.

Dr. Terry Wardle delineates three kinds of memories that take place in the brain.[lxxxii] One is semantic memory. "Semantic memory involves remembering concepts, words, facts, data, and other bits of knowledge."[lxxxiii] This memory is informational in remembering facts. If I return from my son's baseball game and my wife asks me how Nathan did during his game, and I respond with, "Nathan had two hits in four at-bats," this is semantic memory. Another kind is procedural memory. This memory involves a procedure of activities that have to be consciously thought about when learning but then becomes instinctive by practice. Learning how to write would be an example of this kind of memory.[lxxxiv] Finally, there is episodic memory comprised of events we experience.

Dr. Wardle then insightfully argues that episodic encounters with Jesus are most needed to heal episodic memories like my two-year old trauma.[lxxxv] Pay attention to Dr. Wardle's words on this critical issue for our deepest inner healing, "I am convinced that episodic memories are the most powerful type of memories we have because they are filled with senses, feelings, images, actions, and meaning. Traumatic wounds are episodic memories, but in this case overwhelmingly negative. It is very difficult to eliminate the effects of a negative episodic memory through procedural or semantic memory. I am not saying these are unimportant to the process, I am simply saying that they are not powerful enough to free a person from unprocessed emotional upheaval caused by a traumatic episode of the past."[lxxxvi]

I was learning that God's truth settles most deeply into the soul when it is understood, believed, put into practice, and seen with "the eyes of your heart" through Holy Spirit-inspired redemptive pictures leading to episodic encounters with Jesus. Much of my life I had stored God's truth in my left brain, which made me a decent communicator, and quoting Scripture at times gave me the upper hand when assaulted by spirits of fear, but truth needed the help of a Spirit-guided imagination for God's deepest touches in my inner being.

Two years later, my daughter Sarah and I went on a college visitation trip and found ourselves in the Pittsburgh airport. As we went from the first floor to the second floor, Sarah naturally moved towards the elevator and I naturally moved towards the stairs. However, I decided to take a step of faith and face my fears by taking an elevator ride. Yet this time, I planned to take Jesus and the image of His hand upon me to remind myself of His presence with me. We stepped inside the elevator and I not only pictured the hand of Jesus on my chest but also envisioned Jesus standing right behind me with His arms holding me around my chest and proceeded to watch the doors close as we took our short ride to the next floor.

Amazingly, I experienced not even a ripple of fear. I turned to my daughter with a huge smile, informed her of how I consciously took

Jesus with me on the ride and how for the first time in my life I had ridden an elevator without even a fleck of fear. Sarah smiled and celebrated with me! I had previously practiced taking Jesus with me on an elevator ride (re-imagining my episodic encounters with Jesus), with lessening pangs of anxiety, but this was the first time in my life traveling in an elevator when fear was nowhere to be found!

Practical Wisdom for the Invisible War

It is helpful to understand that traumas can come in various forms and that the Holy Spirit of God can bring comfort and healing in each of these arenas. These trauma types are taken from Dr. Terry Wardle's Formational Prayer Seminar.[lxxxvii]

The first kind of trauma is called "wounds of withholding." When a child grows up and gets no or little affection and affirmation from one or both parents, this severely stunts the emotional development of the child. The child develops little to no attachment and their inner security and inner stability is severely thwarted. This kind of trauma was severely present in my life as I developed little to no attachment with my father Anxiety flowed from deep within me from an early age as identity, security, and self-doubt swirled in my soul.

The second kind of trauma is called "wounds of aggression". This is the category under which physical, sexual, and verbal abuse falls. Fortunately for me, this kind of abuse was not an issue. However, for many, it was and still is a lingering open and festering wound. Often, abuse can so jade and jaundice a person's self-perspective and so build layers of self-protection and mistrust of God and people, that much counseling (including episodic encounters of Jesus) from the counselor is needed to bring healing to the deepest part of their souls.

The third kind of trauma is an "event trauma." When a two-year-old is frightened for a prolonged time with abandonment, a young boy is severely beaten up in a fight, a person is stuck in a severe car accident, a spouse suddenly leaves, a soldier witnesses unspeakable carnage on the battlefield, or a child witnesses the sudden death of a parent—these are all examples of "event" traumas. These events can be emotionally debilitating, and in my case as a child, I had no ability to regulate or process my emotions.

I used to think PTSD (Post Traumatic Stress Disorder) was a category of fiction. Now, I realize that severe events (even off the battlefield) can do deep damage that can take great grace and time to heal. The more severe the event trauma, the more easily it is triggered by similar situations, and the more easily a person can feel stuck and handicapped or paralyzed. My event trauma at age two could be construed as a moderate form of PTSD. What made it "severe" was the early age of its occurrence and my inability to regulate my emotions with the presence of Jesus. However, I can certainly relate to feeling stuck in fear, and understand more readily both why and how present fears can be so easily triggered by past traumas. For me, elevators triggered my fears of losing control and took great faith for me walk into and ride. As a pastor, I have been deeply humbled and sensitized to the reality of much worse cases of PTSD than my own.

The fourth kind of trauma is "betrayal" trauma. This arises from an abuse of power. A pastor or priest can betray a parishioner on multiple levels. The most common way is to betray a person or their spouse by inappropriate sexual activity or to betray a confidence given.

The fifth kind of trauma is the trauma of "sustained duress." This is known, according to Dr. Wardle, as "the Chinese water torture" of trauma.[lxxxviii] If a child lives under the constant drip of a father who says, "You'll never become anything," these words will have a cumulative negative impact upon the child's soul. If a wife constantly hears how heavy and unattractive she is or a husband how worthless and lazy he is, the drip can make a deep impact upon the soul.

All of these kinds of traumas can impact the emotions of the soul. Sometimes only the Spirit of God can surface the hidden trauma, bring His logical and pictured truth to bear on our identity, and help us walk or live in God's redemptive realities. However, this healing usually takes time, and the power of episodic encounters with Jesus and redemptive pictures of truth in our God-given imagination can be a powerful tool to get the ball rolling.

QUESTIONS FOR REFLECTION AND DISCUSSION

1. Why is semantic memory or procedural memory ineffective for deep change to occur in traumatized individuals?

2. Why do PTSD sufferers find that similar events trigger fears?

3. What is an episodic encounter with Jesus and why is it important for healing in those people who have suffered deep wounds or traumas?

4. Do you believe that Jesus is a "time traveler" who can both take us back to our deepest traumas and give us redemptive truth pictures for our wholeness?

5. Would you be willing with trusted prayer counselors to ask Jesus to take you back to these traumas to identify them and touch them with redemptive truth pictures?

CHAPTER TWENTY-FOUR

God Develops My Inner Identity

God has put more splendor in a single human mind than in all the Milky Way. Therefore, much of what I write is devoted not only to the marvels of God but to the marvels of ourselves, for through the lens of the one we must see the other.
— Tim Stafford[lxxxix]

True Freedom will only bloom in your life when you put on the truth of who God says you are. Knowing who God wants you to be is not the same as practicing who He wants you to be. When life gets complicated and failures abound, turn your heart and mind back to the basics. Remember who you are in Christ, practice being who God says you are, and in time, you will be walking in the...hall of Freedom.
— Dennis Jernigan[xc]

I learned that we are all in the process of becoming in experience who we already are in Christ by position.
— Dr. Charles Solomon[xci]

When my family arrived in Buena Vista, I had plenty of opportunities to tell people why we had moved out west. Since I tend to wear my heart on my sleeve and share too much too quickly with people, I really needed to think through what was appropriate to share as people inquired as to why the Dages family had made such an abrupt move and why I stepped down from full-time ministry. I was in brand-new territory as I entered into not only a new chapter of my life, but an entirely new section of the book of my life story. People (even in the church) were not used to pastors being "out of ministry" unless they were forced out due to some odious moral scandal. I learned how to respond to people appropriately and how to respond to what God was teaching me in my new station of life.

For instance, about a year and a half after we arrived in Buena Vista, I found myself in an emergency room after a minor accident at the state prison where I was employed. As I overheard the nurse in the hallway say something that indicated she might be a Christian, I naturally took my conversation with her towards Jesus. When I told her I had been a pastor for 23 years and intentionally stepped away from ministry, her sudden response was telling: "Are you still a Christian?" I assured her I was, and that I was now closer to Jesus than I ever before! Yet her somewhat startled response and poignant question revealed she was not used to a pastor being in such a station in life.

I told some people, "I got burned out from ministry," others heard, "I needed a break and felt impressed to write a book," and still others, "I needed five sleeping pills to get to sleep at night and a professional counselor told me I needed to step down from ministry for my long-term health and my family." A few I told, "The Lord clearly directed me to step down." All of these and more versions were true, of course, but some needed more elaboration than others. My kids felt more comfortable when I used the shortest, most "vanilla" versions that left out my most vulnerable details.

I distinctly remember someone asking me the all too frequent question, "What brought you out here to Colorado?" and suddenly responding, "To build on my 'Christ in me' identity." As the answer suddenly and strongly came from me, I realized this was one of the main issues of my soul that God was determined to develop during our stay in Buena Vista. This would be the strength and calm for so many of the anxieties cascading through my soul. This was the source for Jesus to release his treasure chest of redemptive riches to build my emotional wealth in my inner man. Entering into my sixth decade of life, The Almighty was taking me through Identity Building 101.

A person's identity (how they view themselves) is foundational to how they spiritually and emotionally develop and how deeply they can love others. Our society and schools send messages to us that we are descendants of animals, worth no more than the street market price of our chemical composition. It sends the message that our value is tied to what others think and so opinions of people master us. Our society tells us that only what we see with our eyes is real, so developing the inner being of our soul is at best marginalized. How we adorn our bodies with expensive fashionable clothes, keep our bodies in tip-top shape, and build our reputations and retirement accounts are treated as essential life matters. Yet these are peripheral life issues and not central ones.

Little time is spent developing our inner beings, tending to our souls, and living according to the truth of what God says about our bodies and souls and His valuation of us. Even for committed Christ-followers, little space is made for God to build Himself in us through small steps of faith and truth, which when accumulated are huge for our developed emotional wealth. Therefore, most of us wear ourselves out on the treadmill of performance and don't know the futile pace with which we are running nor how to get ourselves off the treadmill of performance. Many today are running hard on the performance treadmill, even pushing to higher levels, and don't even know it.

This process of God building my identity was like He had slowly, over the years, laid an offshore oil rig over my life, set the platform, and drilled down into my rocks (everything that was preventing me from knowing my value as an image bearer of God and my "Christ in me" identity), so that the hidden oil representing the riches of the Holy Spirit could freely flow to all parts of my inner man. As He drilled down into me, God used many preachers, counselors, healing prayer sessions, and choices I made to renew my mind which loosened the rocks. This allowed the oil of the Holy Spirit to flow more freely into every nook and cranny of my inner man. As I learned to live out of Christ in my deepest center, Jesus' life and wholeness began to deliciously grow in my inner man.

I used to tell myself that reading my Bible daily was the most important discipline I could do. This was only half true, because learning to live out of my new "Christ in me" identity, which the New Testament so faithfully and strongly teaches, is the most vital principle of wise living I can practice for holy and healthy living. I was here in Buena Vista to practice my new identity in Christ, and everything and every relationship would be impacted by this Holy Spirit building project.

I remember one morning in 2014, when I was in training at the Academy for the Department of Corrections, in Cañon City, Colorado. I had been trying to get up 20 minutes early to spend time with God in the Scriptures. On this morning, however, I was running late and didn't have time for this needed spiritual exercise. I remember sitting on the side of my bed and simply contemplating Christ and the light of the Holy Spirit that burst in and up through my inner man. I immediately sensed deeply the presence of Christ and His power in the deepest part of me and started my day on this power surge of deep spirituality. My day was spent living and feeding off Christ's truth picture bursting up through my soul. I, of course, had anxiety this day, but as I learned to practice "Christ in me" as my deepest reality, I could live from His presence power and promises within me. My day was lived with more spiritual power over my anxiety than what I had previously experienced.

I had not read the Scriptures that day, but I had "pressed into Christ" through my anxiety into the core of my inner being and lived by faith in His riches already planted in me. I didn't get caught up in doctrines I was going to preach to people but I put into practice the most vital New Testament truth for wholesome living. I hadn't studied the Scriptures for an hour but did an exercise of deep spirituality for 30 seconds on the side of my bed imagining "Christ in me." I feasted off this truth during the day, was rewarded with stabilizing spiritual power, and grew incrementally in emotional wealth.

I remember one night while working the graveyard shift at the prison, deeply struggling with a task that tempted me with surges of self-hate and anxiety. I don't remember if I struggled with doing a pack-out of prisoner who was leaving the next day or checking the water temperatures of all the showers in my unit, but whatever the task...it wasn't going my way. Because neither of these tasks are difficult for developed correctional officers, and I was struggling to get it right, surges of self-hate powered through me. I said things to myself about myself that only tore me down with darkness. I had been here spiritually/emotionally many times before in other competency challenges, and I didn't like the inner chaos taking over my inner man.

However, the Holy Spirit reminded me of my need to live out of light and truth of "Christ in me" as the foundation of my inner man. As I allowed the light of Jesus and the truths of His redemptive riches to rise up from my inner man, the self-hate slowly subsided. I proceeded in the present struggle with the task I was struggling to accomplish. I eventually completed the task before me, but more importantly, I did so with Jesus and His redemptive riches surging through my inner man.

My new identity birthed in me a new peace and security as a preacher. I had preached only three times in the last several years, but living in my new identity enabled me to be far less concerned with what others thought of my preaching. For I am accepted in Christ and wildly loved by Him. It really doesn't matter if others think I'm an A or D preacher! After all, it is not what people think of my preaching ability, but whether they meet Christ in the interior of their souls during the sermon that really counts.

Preaching with little self-consciousness was something God was slowly growing in me. Throughout my crisis, I could see delightful changes we were making together. Back in seminary, I remember being asked to preach without notes. I was terrified of failure. I vocalized my fear to my Practical Theology professor, Dr. Timothy Keller, who smiled at me, looked me in the eyes, grabbed me gently by my elbow, and said, "Tom, you are too self-conscious." While he spoke the truth to me in love, the fear was too controlling of me at that time to make a behavioral impact upon my preaching. I stubbornly memorized the sermon and preached that sermon in power but with very little freedom and love.

When my crisis first hit me, and the elders gave me three months rest from preaching, I came across the story of John Wesley, the great 18th-century revivalist preacher. He had, at the beginning of his ministry, arrived at his place of preaching and realized he had forgotten his sermon. Wesley was more than agitated by this predicament and a congregant noticed. She approached Mr. Wesley: "Putting her hand on my shoulder, she said, 'Is that all? Cannot you trust God for a sermon?'[xcii] Wesley, realizing the truth of the statement, entered the pulpit and preached with an unusual freedom that day...without his notes. From that day forward, Wesley preached without taking a written sermon into the pulpit."[xciii]

This story motivated me to begin preaching without notes myself and really trusting the Holy Spirit to make Jesus big to people's hearts. The results were amazing. I made better eye contact with the congregation, people felt more deeply loved, and a new freedom accompanied my preaching. God was doing a deep work in me in the pulpit as a preacher, but I had to prepare and step out in faith...without my notes. When I did, the Holy Spirit seemed to open up the care connection between me and His people, and we both enjoyed it and were nourished more deeply in the process. Learning to bask in my "Christ in me" identity was what allowed me to let go of attempted control and the opinions of people if my sermon fell flat. It freed me up to really preach for Jesus and not worry about what people thought of me and my performance.

As Jesus planted Himself experientially in my heart and I learned to live by faith in his riches, it became easier to take my preaching prowess (or lack thereof) away from center stage and set up Jesus Christ as the centerpiece for the salvation and healing of people's souls. Incredibly, as I went back to these redemptive truth encounters with Jesus over and over, handling criticism, jealousy over another's gifts, forgiveness of past hurts, incompetence at work and impatience with my kids' teenage disrespect became monumentally easier. Because Jesus, by His Spirit, was filling up the empty places of my heart with His presence and riches in me, much darkness began to fall off me, just as my subsequent redemptive picture showed, feeling like old sins began to break off me in brown chunks and float away.

Practical Wisdom for the Invisible War

One of the most important heart issues for a Christian to get clarity on is whether it is proper to love oneself! Is "self-love" a biblical concept important to carry out for the health of one's soul, or is it a sinful concept that engenders more preoccupation with pride?

One reason for the confusion, even among conservative Christian counselors, is that there seems to be two different kinds of self-love addressed in sacred Scripture.

On the one hand, there is the sinful kind of self-love the Apostle Paul warns against in his pastoral letter to Timothy. Paul describes what people will be like in the last days with the following descriptors:

---

*"But understand this, that in the last days there will come times of difficulty. For people will be **lovers of self**, lovers of money, proud, arrogant, abusive, disobedient to their parents, ungrateful, unholy, heartless, unappeasable, slanderous, without self-control, brutal, not loving good, treacherous, reckless, swollen with conceit, lovers of pleasure rather than lovers of God, having the appearance of godliness, but denying its power. Avoid such people."*
2 Timothy 3:1-5 (emphasis mine)

This is certainly not a list of attributes you want in your children's future spouses when they are brought home to meet Mom and Dad. Neither are these the dominant traits a pastor wants filling the people who frequent the pews. This kind of self-love turns us further in on our already strong inward self-bent. When reading self-love in this context, it is obvious Paul was using it to describe the sinful trait of living to please oneself against the attitude of self-sacrificial love that God commands us to give away to others. After all, biblical love (agape) by nature is self-giving, and not self-serving. So "self-love" in this context, and by the definition of love, cuts against the very outward-directed love Jesus wants to grow in His people.

However, Scripture also implies that in loving God and loving others, as found in Mark 12:29-31, a natural self-love is expected in us to carry out the second part of this great command. Here is what the commandment says, "And you shall love the Lord your God with all your heart and with all your soul and with all your mind and with all your strength." The second is this: "You shall love your neighbor as yourself."

The Great Commandment is focusing our attention on the self-giving love we offer to the Almighty and to those He places around us, no matter their skin color, social and economic status, and relationship to us, even our enemies. Yet the last phrase Jesus throws at us, "as yourself," causes problems with our understanding of self-giving love.

However, there is no such reason that this implied love for self is not a natural love for self, which occurs as we accept by faith the new self God brings about in us through Jesus' redemption in our souls. Loving and accepting what God creates and redeems in us (where Jesus is living) is a great way to experience the fullness of his love in own inner being, and with this empowerment will help more steadfastly give out His love.

This is why our personal understanding of a "Christ in me" identity is so valuable. I can "love myself" when I accept by faith what God says about me is true and think of myself as HE sees me. When I accept myself "in Christ" and see my new creation Jesus created, I can love God and others more readily through His fullness in me. This way love is still directed towards God and others, but I'm not loving out of an energy that is mine, but the fullness of Christ in me and gospel riches released in me. I like how Dr. Henry Cloud and

Dr. John Townsend put it, "God wants us to take care of ourselves so that we can help others without moving into crises ourselves."[xciv]

Another way to look at this issue is to understand how sin twists our thinking to love what we are to hate and hate what we are to love. We are to hate our sinful selves, which unfortunately we naturally love, and what we are to love (accept what God has created and redeemed) is what we often sinfully hate.

Love needs a healthy home in one's heart to be given away fully, naturally, and joyfully. When God's love for you is accepted by faith and fills your heart, it is much easier to naturally and fully give it away. In this context, "self-love" is living off of the high-octane fuel Jesus has poured into souls.

QUESTIONS FOR REFLECTION AND DISCUSSION

1. Does Scripture teach that mankind is a descendant of apes or the direct, immediate creation of Almighty God "in His image?" Why does this matter?

2. Have you ever felt a sudden awareness of your worth and value as a person?

3. How can sinful "self-love" be a barrier to loving others deeply?

4. How can natural "self-love" be a fuel for loving others deeply?

5. What does it mean to take "withdrawals" of the life of Jesus in our souls?

Thomas Dages

CHAPTER TWENTY-FIVE

God Develops My Trust

A little faith will bring your soul to heaven; a great faith will bring heaven to your soul.
— *Charles Spurgeon[xcv]*

Trust is not a passive state of mind. It is a vigorous act of the soul by which we choose to lay hold on the promises of God and cling to them despite the adversity that at times seeks to overwhelm us.
— *Jerry Bridges[xcvi]*

WHEN I REVISITED MY FORMER PSYCHIATRIST, Dr. Curt Thompson, and informed him of my plans to step down from ministry and move my family to Buena Vista, he said two significant things that resonated within my soul. He informed me that we have spent decades developing our thought patterns and neural networks that need changing, and God has all day to help us change them. Second, he said, "God has taken many pastors on a similar journey to make them wounded healers for others."

Both of these statements were directed by the Lord because they would help me immensely to be patient with myself in God's restoration process. They reminded me again and again that even though I was out of formal ministry, I could and would still have a significant impact on other people, especially if it was out of my woundedness.

The first year of our stay in Buena Vista, I felt like a man with his head just underneath the water, fighting to get to the surface for occasional gulps of life-giving air. The second year I spent most of the time with my head just above the water but feverishly doing the doggy paddle to simply keep myself emotionally afloat. In my third year, I found myself still fighting to stay afloat but occasionally swimming with a strong stroke. I actually experienced a few times when God's peace, strength, and freedom accompanied my actions and emotions with great pervasiveness. The more I found myself pressing through my emotional turmoil into Christ at the core of my inner being by trusting His presence and promises, the more His love like a fountain of living water nurtured my inner being.

At times, God's Spirit visited me with consolations of comfort, and my responsibility was to simply receive and enjoy. However, most of the time it would take significant work on my part to respond to the internal stressors in ways differently than I had for decades. Letting go of attempted control and learning to trust God was a new framework out of which I lived, but these new holy and wholesome responses were challenged by my already deeply developed neural highways and thought patterns in my brain.

After spending my first year in Buena Vista worshipping God, writing down my experiences, fishing, and taking in fresh and restful Rocky Mountain air, it was time to find employment to support my family. I prayed about getting back into ministry but didn't sense I was close to being ready. I was able to find employment at The Buena Vista Correctional Complex. It was only an eight-minute drive from home, provided a salary that could pay over half of our bills, and offered both health and retirement benefits. It also placed me among many deeply wounded prisoners, some of whom could be helped by a wounded healer placed in their midst. Some of these prisoners were, for sure, wicked and didn't want help out of their twisted and self-serving criminal mindsets. Others, however, wanted deeply to change, yet they didn't know how Jesus could change their criminal thinking and behaving. I was hired by the state for both "custody and control" of offenders and to help offenders succeed upon their release from the prison. God gave me ample opportunities to help them succeed as I sensitively tried to help in their woundedness, surprisingly often through my own.

God was going to use this new job of mine, and the stressors I faced, to help me trust His wise control by letting go of my mine. In many ways, while the emotional pain of my boil abated significantly, and the spiritual warfare substantially subsided, these would be the hardest changes for me to make, since these thought patterns and beliefs were so deeply entrenched in the neurological highways of my brain.

About a year into my tenure at the prison, I got wind of an offender who told someone else that he had a serious case of MRSA infection. The description of how it was oozing out of his sore sent chills through my soul and triggered a furious OCD attack within me. Here I was faced with one of my greatest fears, and I had to work several days per week in a living unit where this offender lived. My fear of catching MRSA from this inmate, by touching something he touched, smothered my soul. My mind imagined everything the offender had touched to be infected now by MRSA, and everything I touched might now infect me. As I walked about the prison doing my job, my mind also wondered who else might be infected and where else MRSA lurked. My fears sprang into hypervigilance in my brain and followed me torturously everywhere I went! So to prevent myself from getting infected and passing the infection to others, I felt compelled to wash my hands and my clothes and my place of work, often repetitiously and sometimes even furiously. I was suddenly caught in the worst OCD storm I have ever experienced.

Three situations made me realize just how bad my OCD had become.

First, I saw a video of an event in my work unit where the camera was on me. As I watched myself on video, I saw anxiety streaming out of both my face and my body. I witnessed myself rubbing my fingers against my thumbs on each hand as though I was making sure they were clean. I had just washed my hands multiple times, probably used hand sanitizer too, yet this nervous reaction was my attempt to bring comfort and assurance to my OCD-ridden soul that I was clean. I saw OCD anxiety expressing itself powerfully through nervous reactions of my body. How ugly did I wear this OCD anxiety and how clearly it was communicated through this video for me to see.

Second, one day after an offender cleaned my office and obeyed my over-the-top cleaning instructions, which included spraying my office chair with strong spray chemicals, he turned to me and said, "You've got OCD bad. Real bad." While it is often hard to hear confrontation with truth from anyone, it was extra hard to hear it from an offender in prison. Yet the Holy Spirit used this gentle confrontation to speak quite loudly to my heart. Yes, I did have a bad case of OCD, and yes, it was "real bad."

The final powerful way God convinced me of the severity of my OCD came when traveling back home after having Thanksgiving dinner with our cousins in Colorado Springs. We stopped at a gas station and as we pulled out, a homeless person approached our car and asked for me for money. I saw a McDonald's just up the road and told him, "I won't give you money, but I will buy you a meal." He smiled and commented, "That would be just fine." When I met him a few minutes later inside of McDonald's and purchased his meal, another homeless person, hearing I had purchased the meal "in the name of Jesus" wanted to hold hands and pray. He didn't ask for money, he just wanted to pray. Since I don't have a problem praying in public, I thought this was cool! Yet when I reached over to grab his hand, I saw he had a huge, raw, open sore that seemed to scream MRSA lingered here. While the sore probably wasn't infected, I certainly didn't want to take my chances. I thought the better part of wisdom would be to pray by grabbing the cuff of his sleeve instead of his sore ridden hand. It was what I did afterwards, when returning to the car which was my flashing OCD indicator.

I opened the door to my car and asked my wife for the hand sanitizer, just in case the man did have MRSA, and just in case it had been on the cuff of his shirt which I had just held. I not only used the hand sanitizer once but twice, and even smeared it twice on the door handle, which I had first touched with my possible tainted hand. If this wasn't enough, I prayed like crazy on the drive home and told God I was going to trust His control to take care of me. However, I still obsessed about it most of the two-hour drive home. When I arrived at home I cleaned the door handle again with antibacterial wipes and sprayed every nook and cranny of the door handle with Lysol, both that night and the next morning before going to work.

When I told my older brother, Bill, who is also a pastor and a correctional officer in North Carolina, about my renewed OCD battles, I remember him saying in regards to infections, "Tom, prisons can be as dirty as hospitals." Then, he followed up with the stinger, "God has you in the perfect place to break you of your OCD." As I thought about my need to train myself to trust His care and complete control, it was the perfect place for God to break me of my deeply entrenched attempted control, which had controlled me now for almost five decades of my life. Attempted control would die a hard death, one Spirit-led choice of trust at a time.

Practical Wisdom for the Invisible War

In holy Scripture, faith is the vital touchstone of true spirituality, both bringing the treasures of salvation to the soul and evidencing that a person is really an authentic child of God. Faith in Jesus Christ is the gateway to salvation, an instrument for miracles, the weapon for conquering kingdoms, the doorway to peace, and the strength to endure through hardships. Throughout the Bible initial faith is treated as a gift given by God but then as a muscle to be exercised for growth.

Paul says another vital piece of spiritual armor for our protection is "the shield of faith." We pick up this shield and hold it out in front of us to protect us from the fiery darts shot at us by the devil and his minions as we practice the following exercises.

First, faith followers of Jesus need to read and know and stand on the promises found in sacred Scripture. We need to familiarize ourselves with God's promises properly understood in the context of Scripture. God's Word is filled with promises for our peace so the peace of God can flourish in our hearts. Certain Scriptures promising peace are favorite places for me to rest my soul. Picking up the shield of faith means we learn how to memorize and stand on the promises of God.

"You keep Him in perfect peace whose mind is stayed on you, because he trusts in you."
Isaiah 26:3

> *"But now thus says the LORD, he who created you, O Jacob, he who formed you, O Israel: 'Fear not, for I have redeemed you; I have called you by name, you are mine. When you pass through the waters, I will be with you; and through the rivers, they shall not overwhelm you; when you walk through fire you shall not be burned, and the flame shall not consume you. For I am the LORD your God, the Holy One of Israel, your Savior.'"*
> Isaiah 43: 1-3a

> *"...casting all your anxieties on him, because he cares for you."*
> 1 Peter 5:7

Second, faith followers of Jesus need to write down to remember when they experience God come through in both big and small ways. This is how we build faith in His "rest-worthiness." When God answers prayer, gives us supernatural peace, closes the door to the howling spirits of anxiety through faith, or supernaturally gives us strength to walk through the storms, it is time to acknowledge that God is faithful to take care of us and truly worthy of our trust. When God moves in our lives and comes through for us, it is time to write it down and remember it for future storms.

Third, faith followers of Jesus need to expect experiences from God that will stretch and strengthen our faith. I learned early in sports that the only way to make muscles grow is through repetitive resistance training. When a muscle group is worked and the muscles are actually fatigued to total exhaustion, then the muscles, after a short rest, can grow to even greater strength. Breaking down a muscle in a weightlifting workout is painful, but when it is done continually with rest in between workouts, the muscle grows with greater mass and new definition. The muscles can now better support the athlete's performance in grueling competition.

Athletes can elevate their performance to new levels of excellence and skill development.

QUESTIONS FOR REFLECTION AND DISCUSSION

1. When was the last time you trusted God in a worrisome situation?

2. Can we expect God to heal our worries and OCD symptoms if we don't learn to actively trust His care and control?

3. Why is it important to meditate on God's goodness and care through His Scriptural promises?

4. How often do you willfully cast your anxieties upon Jesus and actively trust His control and care?

5. How many Scriptural promises do you have memorized to help you stand against fear and anxiety?

CHAPTER TWENTY-SIX

God Develops My Ability to Stand in Grace

*Therefore, since we have been justified by faith, we have peace with God through our Lord Jesus Christ. Through Him we have also obtained access by faith **into this grace in which we stand**, and we rejoice in hope of the glory of God.*
— *Romans 5:1-2 (emphasis mine)*

O foolish Galatians! Who has bewitched you? It was before your eyes that Jesus Christ was publicly portrayed as crucified. Let me ask you only this: Did you receive the Spirit by works of the law or by hearing with faith? Are you so foolish? Having begun the Spirit, are you now being perfected by the flesh?
— *Galatians 3:1-3*

SINCE CHILDHOOD I HAVE WRESTLED WITH THE FEAR of condemnation. Even though I was saved at a young age, the enemy knew how to play on this deep-seated fear. It forced me to pull out my shield of faith and stand on the promise of my justification by faith in Christ before God. Romans 8:1 was a favorite verse of my youthful years, one which I frequently quoted and stood upon by faith when the assaults were strong:

"There is therefore now no condemnation for those who are in Christ Jesus."

However, I also developed some fleshly coping mechanisms that made my fears and anxieties worse. I developed legalistic tendencies (a lifestyle of overemphasis of obeying God's law and man's law) to help me feel better about my relationship with God. Unfortunately, these legalistic tendencies powered by growing currents of self-righteousness actually grew stronger in my soul than resting in grace and the finished work of Jesus. I slowly became dependent on my efforts and even crazy obsessive compulsions in attempts to keep myself squeaky clean before God. This grew into a stronghold in my thinking that God wanted to expose so that I could rest in grace and cease from my crazy works.

Someone has helpfully defined grace as **G**od's **R**iches **A**t **C**hrist's **E**xpense.[xcvii] Scripture highlights faith as the only channel through which a person can receive this grace, and the moment we do so, our condemnation is completely and forever nullified. This is truly amazing grace! Yet grace must be stood upon by faith when false feelings of condemnation come crashing upon us or temptations of works-based righteousness come calling upon our consciences.

Interestingly, if you had asked me the theological question, "How is a person saved?" I would have answered perfectly, "By grace through faith in Jesus Christ." This was what I was taught and formally believed. Yet my heart and much of my life was not functionally operating at such a level. Deep down inside, growing up and continuing through adulthood, I was living by a faulty belief system of accomplishing works rather than learning to stand on grace already granted me by Jesus that would free me to love others more deeply.

In his book *At the CrossRoads*, Peter Kuiper clarifies the distinction between formal and functional beliefs by saying, "Formal beliefs are what you 'know to be true.' Functional beliefs, however, are what you actually live out, what you do and say. That doesn't mean your formal beliefs are wrong, but they may often be inconsistent with how you go about your daily life."[xcviii] He goes on to say, "What makes understanding the belief system so complicated is that your belief system is largely unconscious. Most of the time you're not consciously aware of your beliefs....Since as a child 'you don't know what you don't know,' you assume that all the beliefs you have assimilated are reliable, whether derived from parents, your own experience, teachers, or many others. You automatically trust this internal belief system."[xcix]

On a conscious level, I was living by grace, but on a deeper, unconscious level, I was living by crazy works with crazy attempts to keep myself safe in the love of God.

It was again in prison, working as a correctional officer with so many administrative regulations to follow and having so many bosses to obey, where God got me in touch with my dependency upon my self-effort strategies to keep me safe in His love, so I could learn to put on His armor and find rest in His already given grace. While obeying administrative regulations and what my many bosses told me to do was important for the smooth and orderly operation of a prison, it had nothing to do with the salvation of my soul!

God Exposes My Need to Stand in Grace

Correctional officers at the minimum center where I worked are required to make rounds in units once per hour. There are two floors with three wings in each floor. As we do a round, we walk, smell, listen, and look for things that aren't right. While it is a good idea to look in every cell window, I often found myself questioning myself at the end of a wing whether I did indeed look in each window, and found myself going back to look again, and sometimes even again, just to make sure I hadn't missed any. When I would fight against my fear and resist going back a second or third time, I would invariably go back to make sure I had done everything perfectly.

It was with this obsessive repetition of rounds driving my heart that God woke me up to the fear driving my heart. I began to ask myself, "What will happen to me if I don't obey my conscience to get up and make sure I didn't miss a window on a round?" When the crazy thought, "You might be condemned," surfaced in my conscience, I began to look at the deeper issues driving my heart. One day it suddenly hit me that this ritual of being compelled to do a round perfectly was not God's Spirit leading me, but my fearfully trained conscience compelling me. It also hit me that this making sure I was perfect was what had driven my obedience in many areas for decades.

I resisted my extra measures by quoting Romans.

---

*"Therefore, since we have been justified by faith, we have peace with God through our Lord Jesus Christ. Through him we have also obtained access by faith **into this grace in which we stand**, and we rejoice in hope of the glory of God."*
Romans 5:1-2 (emphasis mine)

I had to treat going back for perfect rounds as a temptation of the flesh and by faith stand in the grace of Christ's perfection already granted me as a child. God granted me freedom back in Reston during my week in hell when my redemption sent a shaft of light into my soul to set me free; now I needed to practice standing on this grace to reverse my OCD and grow in peace and freedom.

Trying to do things perfectly also manifested itself in making sure the time of a completed round was marked exactly in our log book. I had deep fears of estimating rounds completed, and at times, when

I forgot to mark down a round in the book that I was pretty sure I had done, instead of estimating it, for conscience sake, I would leave it blank. I wouldn't estimate the time just in case I had indeed forgotten one and didn't want to be guilty of lying. I was an extreme legalist wrapped in heavy chains of fear, and learning to stand in grace was the only way to break out of such bondage. Again, I found myself fastidiously quoting Romans, so I could train myself to stand in the grace to resist fleshly perfectionism.

---

*"Therefore, since we have been justified by faith, we have peace with God through our Lord Jesus Christ. Through him we have also obtained access by faith **into this grace in which we stand**, and we rejoice in hope of the glory of God."*
Romans 5:1-2 (emphasis mine)

Yet my legalistic fears didn't stop at making perfect rounds or writing down logs of times in the books. Many of my fears followed me into the offender's rooms when I searched for contraband in shakedowns. My fears made me hypersensitive to touching items like their cups from which they drank or even dropping a pillow or blanket or toothbrush on the floor. I would feel hyper-responsible for possibly causing an offender to get sick. While it was good for me to be sensitive to the ways of love, like telling them when I dropped their toothbrush on the floor, I went way overboard by apologizing about dropping almost anything on the floor. However, when I looked at my heart motives for such actions, I found I was driven by fear to be squeaky clean before God and not resting in grace and compelled by love. Again, when tempted to tell an offender of something insignificant because of my hyper-responsibility, I resisted with Romans.

> *"Therefore, since we have been justified by faith, we have peace with God through our Lord Jesus Christ. Through him we have also obtained access by faith **into this grace in which we stand**, and we rejoice in hope of the glory of God."*
> Romans 5:1-2 (emphasis mine)

Learning to stand in grace by faith helped me resist fear, grew my soul in peace, rewired my neural pathways, and freed me to love people deeply. I'm glad God has "all day" because God had lots of legalism and fear to crush into fine powder by the power of the gospel of grace. Yet I had to learn to stand in this grace consistently to win my freedom.

Practical Wisdom for the Invisible War

I remember chatting with a missionary over the phone the first week I faced my ordeal. After I informed him of my middle-of-the-night accusatory thoughts and extreme stress leading to concrete insomnia, he told me in no uncertain terms to "Put on all the armor of God to stand in His strength."

The second piece of armor Paul tells us to put on in order to stand in God's strength is the "breastplate of righteousness" (Ephesians 6:14).

What is the "breastplate of righteousness," and how do we practically put it on?

Righteousness is a big Bible word that has to do with a Christian's "right standing" before a holy God. Jesus, by His perfect life of fulfilling the law of God and by his sacrificial death on the cross, fulfilled all the righteous requirements of God's law. When a person believes in Jesus, he immediately acquires this "right standing" before God as a gift. Jesus places His righteousness as pure white robes upon us, so we are considered clean in God's holy presence. God doesn't see our sin but sees us clothed in the holy robes of Christ's perfections. This is what Paul says in 2 Corinthians 5:21, "For our sake he made him to be sin who knew no sin, so that in him we might become the righteousness of God."

The enemy loves to come to our minds and tempt us to think "this isn't so" and fill us with the burning feelings of condemnation. He loves to shove guilt and shame in our faces, making us think we are guilty and condemned and on our way to hell. This is why he is called "the accuser of our brothers" (Rev 12:10). When he digs up our past and accuses us with past guilt and shame, he wants us to grovel in our sin and manipulate us to lean on our strategies of self-righteousness. This is when we need to stand on Scripture, placing our full confidence in the gift of righteousness God has granted us in Jesus Christ.

We put on this breastplate when we recall these verses and rely totally on the gift of righteousness already granted us through faith in Jesus Christ. This positional righteousness in Christ provides protection against accusations and condemnations sent from the enemy AND wisdom not to adopt a lifestyle of legalism and self-righteous strategies.

QUESTIONS FOR REFLECTION AND DISCUSSION

1. What is legalism and why is it so deadly to spiritual vitality?

2. Why can legalism be so subtle but appear religious?

3. Why does one need to learn to stand in grace and trust to overcome legalism?

4. Why does learning to stand on grace lead to peace and freedom?

5. How might standing in grace free someone to love more deeply?

CHAPTER TWENTY-SEVEN

God Develops My Love

Beloved, let us love one another, for love is from God, and whoever loves has been born of God and knows God. Anyone who does not love does not know God, because God is love. In this the love of God was made manifest among us, that God sent his only Son into the world, so that we might live through him. In this is love, not that we have loved God but that he loved us and sent his Son to be the propitiation for our sins. Beloved, if God so loved us, we also ought to love one another. No one has ever seen God; if we love one another, God abides in us and his love is perfected in us.
—1 John 4:7-12

DIVINE LOVE IS LIKE A STRONG CURRENT flowing from the heart of God the Father through the sacrifice of Jesus on the cross and released into the hearts of His people by the Holy Spirit "like rivers of living water" (John 7:37-39). The Holy Spirit releases His love in our hearts in many ways and in differing degrees, both to confirm that we are adopted children of God and to empower us to love others with this same supernatural love. There is no greater healing agent for the soul's spiritual and emotional maladies than to soak in His love and learn to give it away. Yet we must learn to step into this current by faith, soak in it prayerfully, surrender to it consistently, and give it away sacrificially. Failing to drink in God's love is the number one reason why Christians live in a state of spiritual dehydration and are so pathetically weak in giving out a life of love to those so thirsty around us.

Because God has crafted every person on earth after His triune being, we are inherently social creatures and made for relationships. We were made in love and made for love—to love God supremely and others deeply. However, the energy of sin inside of us, passed down to each person (except Jesus) from the fall of Adam, seriously corrupts and cripples this impulse of self-giving love. We are now turned in on ourselves and caught miserably in our own little worlds of self-serving strategies.

My crisis and the rise of my inward boil revealed numerous nefarious spiritual and emotional infections within, one of them being how extremely weak this current of love flowed through my own soul to others around me. God's love had to flow deeper in my soul and express itself more consistently in all my relationships, especially my significant ones with family and my congregation. One of the reasons I was sidelined from formal ministry, at least for a season, was to rehabilitate myself in this divine love, to learn how to give it out more fully in all the relationships in which I was engaged.

I love the words of Pastor Zeb Bradford Long, who like myself and many other pastors, had to learn the hard way that giving out the love of Christ is the only foundation for ministry. He confessed the following words after being confronted with his lack of love by an elder in his own congregation:

"As I sat in my car, overwhelmed by this experience, one of the elders, a simple man of profound faith, who could have known nothing of what God had just done, came up to me and spoke these words:

"'Pastor, for a long time I've felt like the Lord wanted me to tell you something. I never thought it was the right time. But tonight as I was praying for you, the Lord spoke clearly to me, and I have to obey. He said, you must love us. Don't be so busy trying to change us; just love us. What we need is to be loved. Please just love us!'

"When I heard these words, part of me died. I realized I had completely missed the purpose of ministry. It is not to develop programs, start a new social revolution, or get everybody filled with the Holy Spirit. Rather, it is to love with Christ's love. It is to love so much that we begin actually to live and die with others. When this happens, we discover the meaning of the Holy Spirit's power, for His power is His love in action."[c]

This divine love settling more deeply into my soul and flowing more fully to my wife and kids provided the foundation and framework for how well they would receive love and give it away themselves. I couldn't help but think some kind of formal ministry was in my future, but for now, my love growth was cut out for me. My work was to sit more consistently in this current to soak in its amazing healing properties and rise out of His power to give it away to others. Yet my own soul and my immediate family were my first parish for needed healing.

My son is now 14 years old and still loves baseball, and I still love watching him practice and play. Yet as I watch him practice and play, I still struggle with surges of my performance dragon rising up to take control of my emotions and actions. I must work to kill its passions and choose instead to love him unconditionally with God's help. Last week, I found myself again ferociously attacked by this merciless dragon inside. It was only by swimming in the current of God's love that I found a slow but sure deliverance.

Nathan was the starting pitcher against our rival middle school. It was one of my days off from the prison, so I could travel and watch both games of the doubleheader. However, it was his first year pitching from the major league distance of 60 feet and six inches. He was still struggling with several steps in the complicated pitching motion. He was content this day, as he was the first two games of the season, to throw just hard enough to make sure he threw more strikes than balls. Yet his speed was noticeably slower than when he practiced with me. Today, for some reason, his lack of performance deeply angered me. I found myself angrily saying under my breath, "Come on, Nathan, step hard to the plate," "Nathan, pitch and bend," "Nathan, aim with your eyes, but throw with your entire body."

Making things even worse, as the clean-up hitter, he went 0-5 at the plate. Nathan has a beautiful, powerful swing. During practice the prior two weeks, he had launched two homers over the practice field fence. I had seen one and knew what he could do when he loaded his bat properly and exploded the barrel of his bat through the ball. Yet this day he failed to load his hands behind him, came forward prematurely (something I did all through high school), and so hit dinkers around the diamond. Topping everything off, he got doubled off second base. As I watched him struggle to find confidence on the mound, go hitless, and get doubled off second, my performance dragon flew in my soul with more power than it had flown for some time, snapping its tail and breathing hot fire all over my emotions.

I knew my performance dragon was getting the best of me, but I felt caught in its power and couldn't find deliverance. I had heard my pastor, Zach Bearss (quoting Kay Warren), say recently, "Reality is your friend." Could it be that my unrealistic expectations were serving to empower my performance dragon? Could it be that my unrealistic expectations of my son were feeding this performance dragon? When a teammate's parent approached me and complemented Nathan on the good job Nathan did pitching, I resisted my initial response of, "He can pitch so much better," and said thank you with half a smile.

Yet the real test was how I would deal relationally with Nathan on the ride home together. Here was the acid test of how I would put to death, with God's help, this damaging performance idol wreaking havoc in my inner man. I knew my son wanted and needed affirmation, but I was frankly angrily slow in giving it. I asked Nathan about his favorite part of the game, so I could break the silence. He hesitatingly said something like, "I got a few hard strikes in there after the first inning," and I responded, "Yes, you did." Then there was once again silence. My soul was struggling to give him a compliment. I wanted to give him corrections, yet this was not the time for corrections. I knew that the deepest struggle he had was learning to throw with confidence and courage, and this was going to probably develop slowly.

While Nathan had to develop in confidence and courage, Dad was being developed in how to live out of God's own divine acceptance, so he could pass this onto his son. After more silence, I told Nathan, "Son, I love you and am proud of how hard you worked today on the field!" He seemed satisfied and told me he loved me too, and we sat in silence for the rest of the ride home.

Yet that evening I found myself stewing before going to bed, being extra anxious as I slept, and thinking angry thoughts even as I woke up the next morning. It didn't dawn on me until the next day that what I needed most was to soak in my own Heavenly Father's patient and accepting love which He had lavished on me, even in my manifold sports struggles. I needed to soak in this love and pass such strong love onto my son. We both needed to grow in God's incredible love for us, and God wanted it to flow strongly to Nathan through me!

I remembered how fear so tied me up that as a catcher I couldn't even throw the ball back to the pitcher, and this was in college. Even so, my earthly dad never said a word of correction, and my heavenly Father accepted and cherished me in the midst of my poor performances. How many times had I gone 0-5 against easy pitchers in my baseball career? How many times had I been terribly cautious with my throws?

I decided to soak in God's love for me by prayerfully thanking God for being ever so patient and accepting me with His steadfast love just the way I was and asking for His help to pass on this same love to my own son. I soaked in the words of 1 John 4:7-12 and imagined soaking in the stream of God's love coming from the Father through Jesus' death on the cross and running through me by the Holy Spirit. As I consciously chose to soak in God's love, stewing over Nathan's performance slowed and stopped and my anger dissolved. Acceptance for him, just the way he was, flowed into me. I began to ponder for Nathan's sake how we could develop his confidence in pitching and encourage him to use his same swing in the game that he used in practice. Soaking and learning to swim in my heavenly Father's love for me was the only power to tame this dragon.

My soul was learning how to grow in God's love, but knowing this love was a process I needed to practice. The apostle John gives three essential points about the love of God we need to practice, internalize, and express toward others.

I received this love when I opened up my heart to Jesus a child. This is when I dipped my toe and stepped into the stream of God's love. His love washed over me fully when I surrendered to Him as a young man. Now, God was teaching me how to soak and swim in His love for my healing, the blessing of others, and ultimately, for His honor and praise.

While I was soaking in the stream of God's love, God also began to open the eyes of my heart to see how rarely I deeply connected with the world of my kids. Again, their eyes are the windows to their souls. Locking eyes with them not only allowed me to get glimpses into what was really going on deep inside of them, but also to send them the message that I was wholly present to them and what they wanted to say.

While each of my siblings prayed for me in my severe season of suffering, I discovered emotional riches of Jesus from which each Dages could deeply benefit. We grew up in the same house and were all saved by Jesus from the penalty of sin, yet emotionally, we were all deeply insecure and mostly walked in the shallows of God's love. Now that I was out of formal ministry, I could spend more time talking on the phone to listen, grieve what we missed emotionally, forgive where necessary, and help each other discover how to soak and swim in the depths of God's love.

For years I hammered congregations with truth yet was very light on the expressions of genuine love. I wanted to learn to listen well to their stories with the hope they would feel the love of Jesus flowing through me. Amazingly, as I began to listen well, my eyes opened to the profound brokenness all around me. While I didn't want to shave one hair off the demands of true biblical discipleship, I did want the truth, when I spoke it, to come from a heart filled with the compassion of Christ. This meant learning to listen more compassionately and speak less frequently and more tactfully to others around me.

Finally, God opened my eyes to the healing power of love when it was put into practice. So much of my soul boil was healed as God empowered me to hug my kids, forgive my dad and others from my heart, dial into my children, cherish my wife, give my money to people in need, trust God's control, pray expectantly for God to work in big ways, accept my kids' performances just as they were, and live out of my "Christ in me" identity. Healing from God flowed to my heart most powerfully when I stepped out and obeyed the love impulses on which God prompted me to take action. Yet I had to take myself back over and over to soak myself in the stream of His love.

"Beloved, if God so loved us, we also ought to love one another. No one has ever seen God: if we love one another, God abides in us and his love is perfected in us" (1 John 4:12, ESV).

Practical Wisdom for the invisible War

The breastplate of righteousness is a positional righteousness granted by God that protects us from accusations of condemnation. However, this breastplate also adds protection against the enemy by our practice of right living, especially as we engage in a lifestyle of Spirit-led love.

Areon Potter says it this way, "Christians must practice righteousness, based on the belief we are now God's righteousness. Righteousness becomes a part of our mind, emotions, and will; that is, it becomes an essential element of our personality. In turn, our righteous thoughts, emotions, and decisions of the will are expressed by our physical actions. As a person begins to practice the righteousness of his spirit, he will not think like he did before being born again. Instead he will begin making more Christ-like choices, and his soul will be conformed more and more into the image of Christ. His actions will demonstrate the character of God. That occurs because righteousness is becoming part of his personality. Righteousness becomes a lifestyle. It supernaturally becomes a natural part of the believer through practice."[ci]

The apostle Paul indicates that this second level of practical righteousness provides protection for the believer in 1 Thessalonians 5:8 when He writes, "But since we belong to the day, let us be sober, having put on the breastplate of faith and love, and for a helmet the hope of salvation."

It took my entire Christian life to see that living out Christ's love affords to me as a strong layer of protection against enemy assault. Conversely, when "unrighteousness" or sin reigns in me, it opens me up to the attacks and oppression of the enemy. He is constantly on the prowl looking for entrance points into minds and souls to gain strongholds over his enemies.

We gain God's protection by practicing the principles of righteous living taught by Jesus in Holy Scripture, especially the prime principle of radical, others-centered love.

QUESTIONS FOR REFLECTION AND DISCUSSION

1. What aspect of God's love (His forgiveness of you, His acceptance of you, His delight in you, His commitment to never let you go, His sacrifices to meet your needs, His protection of you, His watchful eye over you) is most meaningful to you? Why?

2. Have you ever had the Holy Spirit impress you with God's love in a significant way?

3. Why is it important to know the love of God deeply if we want to give it away more fully?

4. What are some practical ways of learning to soak in God's love?

5. Is it possible, if your relationship with your earthly father was not healthy, to be re-fathered in your relationship with God? How might this happen?

Thomas Dages

CHAPTER TWENTY-EIGHT

God Develops My Dying to Self

And he said to all, "If anyone would come after me, let him deny himself and take up his cross daily and follow me. For whoever would save his life will lose it, but whoever loses his life for my sake will save it. For what does it profit a man if he gains the whole world and loses or forfeits himself?
— *Luke 9:23-25*

If we are going to substantially change, something will have to die. But our false self never volunteers for its funeral.
— *Richard Plass*[cii]

Christ's glory was specially the fruit of His suffering of the death of the cross. It is as I enter into the death of the cross in its double aspect, Christ's crucifixion for me, my crucifixion with Christ, that the heart is opened for the Spirit's revelation of the glorified Christ.
— *Andrew Murray*[ciii]

WHEN I WAS 21 AND HOME FROM COLLEGE after my sophomore year battling under my first heavy blanket of depression, I self-consciously surrendered my future vocation to the Lord. This was done in the midst of a baseball game. My team (Delaware County Community College) was playing away at Swarthmore College, and we were at bat. As I sat on the bench on this beautiful autumn day, I told the Lord something like, "I am Yours and will do vocationally whatever You want of me."

Up to this point in college, I assumed I was going into a teaching and coaching profession, but all options were open since I left Taylor University to attend Delaware County Community College to seek the Lord and sort out my life. After my prayer of surrender, peace flooded my heart. I stepped up to the plate and sent a high fastball exploding over the left fielder's head. How like the Lord to confirm my self-surrender with the release of inner peace and the immediate connection of a no-doubt home run!

It was at this time when the Lord etched upon my heart the reality of John 12:24 as my lifetime verse, "Truly, truly, I say to you, unless a grain of wheat falls into the earth and dies, it remains alone; but if it dies, it bears much fruit." The death of self to Jesus is what blossoms the life of God in our hearts. The more we die to our sinful selves daily, the more we give God's life in us a chance to grow.

I also remember some six years later following God's call to my first pastorate out west and being terrified of leaving everything I knew on the East Coast. My home of 28 years, my family and friends, the schools I attended, my home church, and another local church were all surrendered to God's call in pastoral ministry in a foreign state where I knew no one. My parents drove me to the airport and as I boarded the plane, fear struck a deep nerve in my soul. As I made my way to my seat, fear told me to get off the plane and stay home. This was more than unsettling. However, I was stuck in a window seat and couldn't get by the person who sat next to me. I was literally crowded into my seat. When I heard the plane door slam shut with a loud thud and lock, I knew there was no turning back. To my delight and comfort, the young man sitting next to me had made a similar move to Colorado a few years back and would be used by the Lord to calm my anxious heart. In retrospect, I was sitting in the exact seat the Lord orchestrated for my courage and comfort. This was another of many desserts for my obedient surrender.

I surrendered in faith to Jesus when I was just six when deciding to follow Him. However, I learned that surrender to Jesus happened more frequently at multiple levels the further I traveled with Him into the Christian life.

While a believer's justification is free because of the work and grace of Jesus that flows to us only through faith, following Jesus daily is nevertheless costly—very costly. It is costly in the sacrifices of service we give, the steps of courage we take, the love we are to give away, and the sinful temptations we are to daily resist. While God's rewards are greater in this life and the next for His followers who make such sacrifices, nevertheless, dying to self is a disruptive daily discipline of our sinful pleasures. As Peter Scazzero poignantly says, "Our superficial theology fails to grasp that Jesus' death and resurrection is not only the central message of Christianity but also the necessary pattern of our lives."[civ]

Now in my new crisis at 50, I was again surrendering to the Lord by learning to daily "cast all my anxieties upon him" so worry wouldn't cripple my soul. I was surrendering by framing each day and committing to living one day at a time in total trust and reliance upon Jesus. I had to surrender in trust, moment by moment, that God was going to see me through this vast array of dark emotions, which at times felt like they were pulling me under. I found that surrender happened occasionally in big momentous decisions but was also happening in small daily decisions as I learned how to walk by faith one step at a time. By faith I surrendered and retreated often into the redemptive pictures God gave me in my imagination, and many times I felt His presence like a nurturing spring flowing into my soul's deepest places.

The Holy Spirit of God is graciously given by God the Father and God the Son to live intimately within His people who turn to follow

Christ. He comes to live in the believer and serves as our source of strength as we live a life of service to God and others. He shapes our lives into the very image of Jesus, which often involves our submission to suffering. He places the Holy Spirit in us to be like "streams of living water" (John 7:37-39). Surrendering in faith daily to Jesus opens the flow of the Holy Spirit to move more freely in and through us.

The Holy Spirit's life-giving ministries to the children of God are many. He teaches us about the person, redemptive work, and precepts of the Lord Jesus. He helps us grasp the riches of our inheritance in Jesus that He wants to release in our inner beings for our growth in emotional wealth. He counsels us in God's wisdom, gives us strength to do God's will, and brings supernatural comfort in times of soul-searing grief, pain, and darkness. He releases His life-giving streams through our souls. Not least of His ministries is helping us resist the corrupting sins of the flesh, which look to wrap us in their gnarly grasp at almost every step of the way.

Paul says poignantly, "But I say, walk by the Spirit, and you will not gratify the desires of the flesh" (Galatians 5:16).

Although Christians receive a new spiritual nature upon coming by faith to Jesus, old habits and lies we've lived by, idols we've hotly pursued, defense mechanisms we've employed, and established neural pathways of thought patterns still reside largely unchanged in our minds, sometimes feeling like they have a vice-grip upon our lives. The Spirit of God helps us renew our inner being by "putting off" these deceptive desires to live by the truth of God's holy and loving ways. This battle inside of us is ongoing until we arrive home in heaven for our final phase of redemption. However, it is the Spirit of the living God inside the believer who both inspires and energizes us to live according to God's precepts with His power. This power is seen positively in the love with which we learn to give and negatively in the temptations of gratification we daily learn to deny. However, we must learn to surrender, in faith and dependence upon God, every step of the way. This is warfare of the soul!

As God was giving me grace to see "Christ in me" as the deepest and truest me, He also helped me fight the impulses of my flesh that had flourished and strengthened for decades. His Spirit lived in the center of my soul, and His holy love was determined to purify my inner being for His glory and my good.

My life needed to be more than resisting sins like behavioral adultery, stealing, and bald-face lying. Now the Holy Spirit was bringing out of me, through the pain of my inner boil, pollutants as rotten to my inner man as the above-mentioned sins but hidden in the sludge on the bottom of my soul. These were pollutants such as self-pity, grinding grudges, worry, the pride of thinking I was better than others, mental adultery, massive attempts at control, living in future fears, and filling myself with performance fantasies. God was cleansing and changing me as I learned to surrender by faith to Him in these matters, moment by moment each day.

I once caught a largemouth bass in the Shenandoah River. It stunned me, not by how big it was but by how unhealthy it looked. It was skinny, pale, and had growths underneath its scales. I thought to myself, "What kind of chemicals must this fish swim in and ingest to look like this?" How different this was to the beautiful Brook and Cutthroat trout I catch in the high mountain streams of Colorado. The vivid colors on these fish and the strength of their bodies when held in one's hand are enough to almost take a fisherman's breath away. What's the difference? To a large extent, the quality of the water in which they swim. God wants the quality of our inner life to reflect the pristine conditions of the high Colorado streams, not the conditions of rivers polluted by chemicals that corrupt the beauty of His creation. By His Spirit in our inner being, He will purify us in the deepest places if we learn to walk by or swim by His Spirit in moment-by-moment sweet surrender.

So what does it mean to crucify or put to death our sin? Sinclair Ferguson provides a helpful definition that balances our effort with God's assistance:

> "What then is this killing of sin? It is the constant battle against sin which we fight daily—the refusal to allow the eye to wander, the mind to contemplate, the affections to run after anything which will draw us from Christ. It is the deliberate rejection of any sinful thought, suggestion, desire, aspiration, deed, circumstance, or provocation at the moment we become conscious of its existence. It is the consistent endeavor to do all in our powers to weaken the grip of sin in general, and its manifestations in our own lives in particular, has. It is not accomplished only by saying 'no' to what is wrong, but by a determined acceptance of all the good and spiritually nourishing disciplines of the gospel. It is by resolutely weeding the garden of the heart, and also by planting, watering and nurturing Christian graces there, that putting sin to death will take place. Not only must we slay the noxious weeds of sin, but we must see that the flowers of grace are sucking up the nourishment of the Spirit's presence in our hearts. Only when those hearts are so full of grace will less room exist for sin to breathe and flourish."[cv]

However, this crucifying of my fleshly desires needed to be done by a complete dependence upon the Spirit of God (the power of Jesus) who resided at the center of my soul. Jesus by His work on the cross completely forgave and justified me, and now, by His Spirit residing in me, He would give me power moment by moment as I called upon Him in complete dependence to surrender to God and resist my ferocious flesh in His strength.

I vividly remember one night when tempted to masturbate there was my beautiful wife lying next to me in bed. While I genuinely didn't want to disturb her, my deeper issue was my own penchant for personal pleasure NOW. The lust in me began to grow and the temptation to satisfy myself also grew. However, the Spirit of God in me urged me to cry out to him for help. The Apostle Paul commands believers when in such temptation distress to "consider yourselves dead to sin and alive to God in Christ Jesus" (Romans 6:11). What a great verse to go to war with based upon the victory Christ won on the cross! I cried out (in my mind) in total dependence upon God for his assistance, and a wave of God's holiness crashed over my lust and ripped it away like a wave crashing on a beach, flowing unstoppable back into the ocean and taking trash on the beach with it.

I wish I could say God's grace took over in such a palpable way every time I fled to Him. In other temptations, sometimes I don't cry out at all, or maybe I wait to long for lust to build and feel like I have crossed a threshold of no return. However, in this instance of temptation warfare, the Spirit's assistance was palpably strong, and He crushed my temptation into fine powder. **Such is the power of God in the moment of total surrender!** The Spirit of God is present and powerful to resist all manner of selfish anger, greed, pride, and all forms of fleshly lust. He helps me say "No" to performance fantasies and "Yes" to living in God's reality. He is always ready and willing to deliver us and weaken the body of residual sin within us. However, we must learn to rely totally and instantly upon Him by running to Him, as soon as we sense temptation creeping toward our doorstep.

Practical Wisdom for the Invisible War

The key to living by the Spirit's strength is learning to "walk" or "live" by the Spirit's desires. Paul says, "But I say, walk by the Spirit, and you will not gratify the desires of the flesh" (Galatians 5:16).

How do we do this? Below are some helpful principles to live by the Spirit.

First, by recognizing the dynamics of the pitched warfare in our souls. The soul of a Christ follower is the battleground of a huge civil war. In *The Christian Life* Sinclair Ferguson reminds us that "the flesh" in this context is not our body, but "the whole man in his creatureliness, weakness and sinfulness."[cvi] This flesh is at war with the Spirit and vice versa. Our new nature as believers is essentially defined by "Christ in us" through the Spirit, but our old habits, lies we've lived by and idols we've sought for life, still have a powerful sway upon our inner being.

Second, by seeing our sin through His eyes of holiness. This is healthy, for it humbles and helps us to see ourselves as God sees us. As the deadly sin of malice grew in my heart, The Holy Spirit graciously dredged this up from the deep and allowed me to see just how hypocritical and poisonous this was in my life. He allowed me to come to a new level of conviction of sin's deadly disease in my own heart. It is humbling to see yourself as God sees you and feel the ugliness of your sin, but humility is part and parcel of holiness. It starts the process of seeing what needs to be cleansed and changed by God's power.

Third, by focusing our minds on the desires of the Spirit. Paul says in Romans 8:6, "To set the mind on the flesh is death, but to set the mind on the Spirit is life and peace." This is the first great work to be done to walk in the Spirit. It takes a constant battle to set one's mind on the higher life of the Spirit. What the mind chooses to focus upon is key to walking by the Spirit's desires. The constant renewing of one's mind is the first step towards learning to walk by the Spirit. Yet the work doesn't stop here. Learning to retreat into my "Christ in me" identity is also a way for me to set my mind on the Spirit and His power within me.

Fourth, by learning to call out to Jesus in the moment we are aware of temptation cuddling up to us and confessing our sin the moment we fail. The sooner we call out to Jesus in complete dependence upon His strength, the easier it is to break free from temptation's grip. Conversely, the longer we let temptations linger, the harder it is to deny oneself of its pleasure. God has provided a way of escape in every temptation we face (1 Corinthians 10:13), but we need to call out and move towards our God given exit sign the moment He shows it to us. Fighting temptation is WAR and we have to learn to fight with urgency in the Spirit's strength!

Fifth, by learning to lean upon God to put into practice the precepts of righteousness taught in Holy Scripture, especially the command of sacrificial love. Submission to the commands of God given in Scripture plays a huge role in how the Spirit shapes us into the image of Christ. As our inner being transforms into the image of Christ, God expects us to take initiative in His great command of loving Him with all our hearts and loving our neighbors as we love ourselves. He will urge us and empower us, but we must practice carrying love through to the finish line. Much growth and "shaping'" takes place in this passionate pursuit of love. Christians miss much growth at this point because we are way too passive in the pursuit of love.

QUESTIONS FOR REFLECTION AND DISCUSSION

1. When you turn to Jesus to trust Him as your Lord and Savior, do your sinful propensities automatically go away? Why or why not?

2. Why are the desires of the flesh often so easy to give into?

3. How actively do you resist temptation by leaning immediately and totally into Jesus and His power within you?

4. When you resist a temptation in God's strength, why is this a form of surrender?

5. When you love in the power of God's love, why is this a form of surrender?

EPILOGUE

My Inner Boil Now and In Eternity

SINCE THE SURFACING OF MY SPIRITUAL BOIL IN 2010, every infection has undergone significant healing—nowhere close to total healing, yet nevertheless wonderfully significant. My severe symptoms have seriously abated, and the life of God has emerged in substantial and palpable ways in my inner being. His presence is hard to describe in words, but His Spirit seems to be a mixture of joy, inner strength, and cleanness cascading through me. Through my soul lancing, God has made space for His life to emerge in me and His life to flourish in the deepest places of my inner being.

The summer of 2016 saw me restored enough in my sleep rhythms to finally put away all my sleep medications. After taking a year off from work in Buena Vista and then working in the State Prison for a year and a half, I began to seriously entertain the idea I might be ready for a return to full time ministry. Interestingly, later that year, the position of Associate Pastor of Congregational Care opened at the church my family was attending. I submitted my application in November of 2016, prayerfully went through the process of interviewing, and in May of 2017 found myself back in my pastoral calling.

However, God's emphasis in ministry for me was now different. I sensed a renewed heart of joy and strength and a new emphasis in my calling for a one-on-one ministry to people, which included listening to people's stories, locating and empathizing with their hurts, and loving them with the compassion and truth of Jesus in ways my prior ministry had seriously lacked. Through my own crises, my eyes were now open to the emotionally hurting people limping into church, and my new heart wanted to help them find the healing touch of Jesus the way He had impacted me.

In my first year on staff, I attempted to visit everyone in this large church in a small town to get to know them. My prayers with people took on a whole new level of sensitivity to their needs and to the Holy Spirit. While I did get back into the pulpit once per month, I spoke more from where Jesus touched my weaknesses and woundedness. My new pulpit presence prompted my wife to tell me, "When you now step into the pulpit, a spirit of gentleness falls over the congregation."

New thought patterns are established in my brain and mind as I continue a relentless renewal process in which I catch lies and consciously replace them with God's truth. Over the long-term, God's peace has become a closer companion to my soul as I saturate my mind with His truth and learn to trust His steadfast love for me.

Learning to picture my new identity with the light of Jesus in the center of my inner man is the most powerful promoter of true and deep emotional health. Learning to take withdrawals of Jesus and His riches in me by faith has become the single most powerful way God has both healed and built my inner man. This soul growth was explosive at first with the redemptive truth pictures God gave me coupled with palpable massages of His love. This is now a steady stream of strength as I take withdrawals of Jesus each day.

THE LANCING OF MY SOUL

Learning to receive God's love and give out His love to others around me is making me more like Jesus than any other discipline. My relationships are more wholesome. My relationships with my wife and kids bring deeper connection and joy to my soul. I am more present with them, more aware of their needs, and more patient with their deep soul struggles, though obviously, there is still quite a way to grow.

I am amazed at how fear of losing God's love drove so much of what I did and didn't do in life. As I have learned to take a stand on the grace of my being justified by the work of Christ on the cross, legalism, fear, and OCD crazy works are dying a delicious death. Only occasionally does riding in elevators cause stress, and when occasional fears flare up, I imagine Jesus behind me with His arms wrapped around me and His hand upon my chest.

Putting on the armor of God has become a way of life that protects me from enemy attacks and strengthens my inner man. One morning several years after we had moved to Buena Vista, God placed a powerful truth picture in my imagination as I was praying. I had not yet returned to full-time ministry but was asked to preach at a church in Denver. I felt stress and spiritual warfare rise against my soul, and through another redemptive picture I saw myself dressed as a strong soldier in all the armor the Lord. I was reminded of my need to live in His strength, not my own. Notice the muscles of this soldier bulging, which symbolically was what happened in my inner man when I armored up and ministered in His strength.

I can only imagine what life in heaven will be like with my unimpeded sight of God, the perfect touch of His love, and my **total** release from all fears. The following words of Jesus from the last chapter in the Bible build hope in my soul.

> *"Then the angel showed me the river of the water of life, bright as crystal, flowing from the throne of God and of the lamb through the middle of the street of the city; also, on either side of the river, the tree of life with its twelve kinds of fruit, yielding its fruit each month. The leaves of the tree were for the healing of the nations. No longer will there be anything accursed, but the throne of God and of the lamb will be in it, and his servants will worship him. They will see his face, and his name will be on their foreheads. And the night will be no more. They will need no light of the lamp or sun, for the Lord God will be their light, and they will reign forever and ever."*
> Revelation 22:1-3

Peace and wholeness to those who now come to Jesus as Savior and Lord, learn to seek Him for His life in this life, and patiently wait for His full healing in heaven!
Thomas Dages
October 2018
Buena Vista, Colorado

Thomas Dages

APPENDIX

Thomas Dages

THE LANCING OF MY SOUL

A SALVATION CREED

I BELIEVE IN ONE TRIUNE GOD consisting of three persons, God the Father, God the Son and God the Holy Spirit. This God is supreme, all-powerful, most holy and just, abounding in grace and perfect in measureless love. He is also completely faithful to all His redemptive promises given in sacred Scripture of the sixty-six books of the Old and New Testaments to redeem His lost and sinful people.

I believe the Savior to be the eternal Son of God, who journeyed into this world and miraculously put on flesh to become man. Scripture says, "Though he was in the form of God, he did not count equality with God a thing to be grasped, but made himself nothing, taking the form of a servant, being born in the likeness of men. And being found in human form, he humbled himself by becoming obedient to the point of death, even death on a cross. Therefore God has highly exalted him and bestowed on him the name that is above every name, so that at the name of Jesus every knee should bow, in heaven and on earth and under the earth, and every tongue confess that Jesus Christ is Lord, to the glory of God the Father."[cvii]

I believe in one Savior for mankind, Jesus Christ, whose perfect life, sacrificial death on the cross, and resurrection from the dead is sufficient to redeem and raise to life all who trust Jesus and turn from their sin. Today, Jesus is alive, ruling the universe from the right hand of His Father's throne.

I believe God the Father and God the Son have poured out the Holy Spirit on God's people. The Holy Spirit dwells with us and inside of us. He grants us a new nature. He seals us for our protection. He emboldens us as His witnesses. He empowers us to hate sin and love what is holy and good. He fills us with his strong and steadfast love that it might flow freely and powerfully into the lives of others. He comforts and counsels us through the many trials we are called to face. He fills us with His presence that we might shine like stars in a dark world-all for God's glory.

I believe our spiritual growth of being conformed to the likeness of Jesus is wholly the work of God in us (1 Thessalonians 5:23-24) yet demands our wholehearted dependence on and obedience to our Savior and His commands—especially His command to love. While good works are useless for meriting salvation, they are necessary in demonstrating the fruit of salvation.

I believe that prayer, in the name of Jesus, empowered by the Holy Spirit, is both a rich sense of communion with our Triune God and an instrument of great power to accomplish God's will.

I believe Jesus Our Lord is coming again. He will, with His resurrection body, break through the clouds, shining more brilliantly than the noonday sun. He will return to reward His redeemed people with unimaginable joy and glory and punish eternally those who have loved their rebellion and rejected His many overtures of love.

Even so, come Lord Jesus!

Pastor Tom Dages
Originally Written Dec 12, 2012
Updated Apr 11, 2019

BIBLICAL AFFIRMATIONS CONCERNING GOD AND DIVINE HEALING TODAY

1. I affirm the absolute sovereignty of God over all matters of life (Daniel 4:34-35, Ephesians 1:11). History is **His-story** unfolding His redemptive plan to save a world of lost people through the work of Christ into an eternal relationship with Him (Acts 4:27-28). God's sovereignty includes the election of those who are saved (Ephesians 1:4-6), the rise and fall of kingdoms and leaders (Daniel 4:17), nature (Jeremiah 14:22), disasters (Isaiah 45:7), decisions freely made by people (Proverbs 16:1), answers to prayer (1 John 5:13-15), and even diseases with which people are born in which God surprisingly claims full responsibility (Exodus 4:11). God's sovereignty includes His control over everything that happens to a believer which He uses for His glory and our good (Romans 8:28-29). His sovereignty amazingly includes the devil and the evil he viciously throws at us,

which God permits and works according to His plan (Job 1:6-12). As Martin Luther stated, "even the devil is God's devil." However, while He controls all things through what He positively ordains and or passively permits, God is neither the author of sin nor can He tempt people to sin (James 1:13). Knowing this biblical teaching on God's sovereignty develops a humble sense of submission in our hearts as we take our life situations to Him in prayer.

2. I also equally affirm that every person is responsible to God for the vast array of life choices we make. Each of our choices of responding in penitent faith to the gospel of grace determines whether we inherit salvation or stay in our sins and suffer condemnation (John 3:16, 18). Our many life choices subsequent to this seismic choice of salvation—to walk in the Spirit or the flesh, to engage in good works, to develop our talents, to share the gospel in word and deed, to love God with all our hearts and our neighbors as ourselves (including our enemies), to have compassion on the poor, will not only validate our saving faith but impact the rewards we receive on the day of judgement (1 John 4:17, 1 Corinthians 3:12-15). Scripture is clear that while we are justified by faith alone (Romans 3:28, Romans 5:1, Philippians 3:9), we are judged by our works (Matthew 16:27, Revelation 20:11-15). Knowing this biblical teaching on man's accountability to God for all of life's choices keeps us circumspect throughout life on the various choices we make.*

3. I affirm that faith plays a vital role in both expecting and praying for miracles, healing and demonic deliverance (Matthew 8:10-13, Matthew 9:29, Matthew 17:18-20). While faith does not

---

* While no one knows where the issue of God's sovereignty and man's responsibility actually come together in life circumstances (the issue of concurrency), the Scriptures affirm both realities and therefore we must equally teach both as Biblical truths.

dictate healing, its lack often did and does prevent divine healing from occurring (Mark 6:5-6). Our faith in Jesus through humble prayer can be so powerful that at times it can even appear to change the mind of God (2 Kings 20:1-6). Knowing what the Bible teaches on the power of God operating through faith encourages us to pray with greater expectancy and consistency.

4. I affirm that learning to pray "all kinds" of prayers in faith is one of the greatest sources of receiving God's wisdom, spiritual power, and healing (Luke 11:9-13, Matthew 18:18-20, Ephesians 1:16-23, Ephesians 3:14-21, Ephesians 6:18, James 5:14). Knowing the power of learning to go deeper and wider in prayer and that God has ordained prayer to unleash His power on and through His people, we will labor to learn about and practice prayer and teach others to do the same.

5. I affirm that learning to listen to God for both the caregiver and care receiver is one of the most critical disciplines for effective healing prayer. Jesus listened to the Father perfectly during His entire life on earth, and yet our listening skills to others and God are extremely dull and need to be trained. Knowing what the Bible teaches on the importance of listening to God and the hearts of others, we labor to hone our listening skills and teach others to do the same.

6. I affirm that people finding salvation through faith in Christ by His work on the cross serves as the start of the greatest experience of healing this side of heaven. The crucifixion of Jesus on the cross provided the potential for spiritual, emotional, and physical healing (Isaiah 53:4-6, Matthew 8: 16-17, 1 Peter 2:24-25). The spiritual healing of reconciliation with God, adoption into God's family, justification or our declaration of righteousness, and redemption

from the penalty of sin happens immediately through faith. Healing from physical diseases can also occur by faith but isn't fully guaranteed until heaven (Revelation 21:1-5). Knowing the power of this initial salvation which the Bible teaches, encourages us to take part in the ministry of evangelism to help people enter a saving relationship with Christ where God commences an incredible healing journey.

7. I affirm that soul transformation and emotional healing runs concurrently with our growth in Christ and is normally incremental and progressive as we learn to renew our minds with truth and to pay attention and respond to the issues the Holy Spirit reveals in our hearts through activities like redemptive-counseling, studying, and applying Scripture and attentive prayer (Romans 12:1-2, Proverbs 20:5, Phil 2:12-13, 2 Corinthians 3:18). Knowing this biblical teaching on healing and growth in Christ after initial salvation gives us an impetus to hunger for spiritual growth and learn to listen to and cooperate with the truth issues the Holy Spirit brings to our attention about our hearts.

8. I affirm that God uses gospel centered, biblically faithful, Holy Spirit sensitive, psychologically insightful, medically astute counseling to bring the healing touch of Jesus to the deepest places of our body-soul complex. Counselors educated in these areas and trained in prayer will be most effective in bringing the wisdom of God to bear on our deepest and most complex problems. Knowing the importance of discovering truth in these arenas and learning to prayerfully sense the wisdom of the Spirit, we will strive to grow in knowledge in each of these arenas and teach others to do the same.

9. I affirm that Jesus can be our time traveler by the ministry of the Spirit (2 Corinthians 3:18) and can take us back in the past to

identify emotional wounds and traumas and touch these uniquely so that we can move forward with greater emotional wholeness in the present. Knowing the power of Jesus as our time traveler, with His counsel we will step out in prayer and faith for His healing power and presence.

10. I affirm that discovering our identities in Christ (and Christ in us) and learning to live out of this new identity and all the spiritual riches Christ has provided in salvation which the New Testament so forcefully and repetitiously teaches is the foundation for growing in emotional wholeness. Knowing this biblical teaching on the importance of discovering and living out our Christ centered identities, we will labor to teach and counsel people to discover and appropriate their spiritual riches in Christ, which significantly impacts our emotional and physical wellbeing.

11. I affirm that miracles and healing are for today as Jesus ushered in His kingdom with His first arrival. Today God uses miracles and healing as tools of His compassion, a powerful witness of the resurrection of Jesus, and to validate the message of the gospel (Acts 3:4-7, Acts 8:4-8, Luke 10:8-9, James 5:14-15). Knowing this biblical teaching on miracles and healing encourages us to look to Jesus for His healing touches of spiritual, emotional and physical maladies which afflict us.

12. I affirm that the baptism of the Holy Spirit happens when a person is initially saved and is baptized with the Holy Spirit into the body of Christ (1 Corinthians 12:13). However, subsequent experiential encounters with the Holy Spirit and His love and power and gifts as sometimes demonstrated in the book of Acts (Acts 8:17, Acts 19:1-7) should not surprise us. To be filled with the Holy Spirit or controlled by the Holy Spirit is a continuous command (Ephesians

5:18) and directly impacts our growth in holiness and wholeness. A continuous being filled with the Holy Spirit helps deepen the roots of spirituality so that we bear more and more fruit of the Spirit, which serves as the foundation of operating wisely in the spiritual gifts God grants us and discerning of the spiritual experiences we encounter. Knowing that the command to be filled with the Spirit is in the continuous tense, we will labor to teach people what it means to be controlled by the Spirit and not the flesh.

13. I affirm the existence today of all the gifts of the Spirit listed in the New Testament (Romans 12:3-8, 1 Corinthians 12: 4-11, 27-31, 1 Peter 4:8-11). While the Word of God is complete and completely true and serves as the only standard for faith and practice, all the gifts of the Spirit are needed today as they were in the New Testament for a fully empowered church to do God's work of building His Kingdom, growing His people, and setting people free from the forces of darkness. Knowing this teaching on the present reality of all the gifts of the Spirit in Christ's church encourages us to seek the gifts God offers and use them to magnify Him and serve His people in the fullness of His strength.

14. I affirm that while faith and our speech are vital to stepping into God's purposes for us (2 Corinthians 4:13-15), our words of faith don't create reality. Our speech and words are powerful and influential in shaping our lives and those around us (Proverbs 18:21), yet they are not magical. Knowing what the Bible teaches about the power of words, we are careful with them, especially to speak God's promises in Scriptural context and not to make unholy vows which God holds us to. However, we are also careful not to grant our words more power than what Scripture read it its entirety, and in context, gives them.

15. I affirm that God permits suffering in His sovereign plan to bring about Christlikeness and Christian growth in ways not possible with instant emotional or physical healing. We often find the treasures of Christ developed in ourselves as we traverse through darkness and press into the light of Christ within us while learning total dependence upon God for His strength (Isaiah 45:3, 2 Corinthians 12:8-10). Knowing this biblical truth on growth through suffering and struggle compels us, after praying for healing without success, to learn how God may be using our suffering to chisel us uniquely into the image of Jesus.

16. I affirm that the greatest miracles involve God developing His love in His people. We are never more like Jesus as when we learn to forgive those who hurt us and love the most difficult people in the hardest circumstances. These hard seasons are intended by God to develop deeper levels of love in and through His people. Knowing this biblical teaching on development in divine love helps us make learning to love God and others our highest life priority (Mark 12:28-31).

17. I affirm that God uses medical doctors and good medication along with nutritionists and many other health care providers to provide natural healing, pain management, and necessary surgeries and treatments for our well-being. Knowing the biblical teaching on the helpfulness of medicine, seeking wise medical intervention is encouraged and most certainly not a lack of faith nor a denial of divine healing.

Thomas Dages

POEMS

THE CLIMB

By Allison Dages

The Lord has His way
For He molds us like clay
And one day
All things are made good
And all the turmoil is understood
Here is the Dages story
And God in all His glory
Chose to refine a man's soul through unrest
Following the will of the Lord made him blessed
The mountains tugged at his heart
Buena Vista was a new start
A place of heartache and sleepless nights
Then renewal and the Spirit's move to new heights
With the presence of God
His rescue produces abundant laud

THE FEAT

By Sarah Dages

The trauma of the enemy striking
Unrelatable pain without likening
Satan's contempt sent to enslave
With plans to make men crave
But the wealth of God is incorruptible
Not subject to evil so rupturable
The Spirit's power at work to breathe
Breathing mighty grace able to relieve
A grace that empowers, a grace that unshackles
The fetters of fear and the enemy's tackles
Miraculous intervention from the throne room
Mediation poured out from the Bride Groom
A step by step journey marked with mercy
Overflowing from depths of living water for the thirsty
Inner healing and strength streaming forth from the Spirit
Growing attentiveness to hear and to feel it
Granting courage and insight to be renewed
To put on His armor to fight the feud
Anointed favor propelling provision
To follow the lead of His profound vision
A provision that casts away anxiety
Often ridding normal of its propriety
Giving freedom to change and to go forth
To a new place of reward and worth
Spirit, You lead me to Your mountain so holy
To Your land flowing with milk and honey

BIBLIOGRAPHY

i   Dr. Terry Wardle, *Draw Close to The Fire* (Abilene: Leafwood Publishers, 2004), p 164.

ii   Edward T. Welch, *Running Scared: Fear, Worry, and the God of Rest* (Greensboro: New Growth Press, 2007)

iii   See i, p 17.

iv   Nigel Mumford, *Hand to Hand* (New York: Church Publishing, 2006), p 65.

v   Dr. Curt Thompson, *The Anatomy of The Soul* (Carol Stream: Tyndale House Publishers, 2010), p 65.

vi   See v, p 65.

vii   See v, p 31.

viii   See v, p 65.

ix   Dr. David Jeremiah, *Spiritual Warfare: Terms of Engagement* (San Diego: Turning Point, 2011), p 16.

x   See ix, p 36.

xi   See ix, p 24.

xii   See ix, p 37.

xiii   Areon Potter, *From Darkness to Light: Demonic Oppression and the Christian* (Mustang: Tate Publishing and Enterprises, 2006), p 181.

xiv   John Bevere, *Honor's Reward Devotional Handbook* (Palmer Lake: Messenger International), p 83.

xv   Dr. Bruce Demarest, *Satisfy Your Soul: Restoring the Heart of Christian Spirituality* (Colorado Springs: NavPress, 1999), p 14.

xvi   See xv, p 143.

xvii   See xv, p 146.

xviii   See xv, p 146.

xix   See xv, p 148.

xx See xv, p 148.
xxi Jerry Bridges, *Trusting God* (Colorado Springs: NavPress, 2017), p 112.
xxii Charles Haddon Spurgeon, GoodReads, Accessed 10/4/2019, https://www.goodreads.com/quotes/98356-our-anxiety-does-not-empty-tomorrow-of-its-sorrows-but
xxiii See xiii, p 187.
xxiv Frank Peretti, *This Present Darkness* (Carol Stream: Tyndale House Publishers, 2002), p 73.
xxv See xv, p 250.
xxvi Dallas Willard, *Hearing God: Developing a Conversational Relationship with God* (Downers Grove: InterVarsity Press, 2012), p 140.
xxvii Dr. Rebecca Brown, *Prepare For War* (New Kensington: Whitaker House, 1992), p 274.
xxviii Beth Moore, *Praying God's Word Day by Day* (Nashville: Broadman and Holman Publishers, 2006), p 3.
xxix David Powlison, *Power Encounters: Reclaiming Spiritual Warfare* (Ada: Baker Publishing Group, 1995), p 35.
xxx Dr. Terry Wardle, *Healing Care, Healing Prayer: Helping the Broken Find Wholeness in Christ* (Abilene: Leafwood Publishing, 2003), p 220.
xxxi See xxix, p 221.
xxxii See xxix, p 221.
xxxiii Henry T. Blackaby and Claude V. King, Experiencing God (Nashville: Broadman and Holman, 1994), p 31.
xxxiv See xv, p 208.
xxxv See xv, p 208.
xxxvi See xv, pp 208-209.
xxxvii See xv, p 209.
xxxviii Robert Lowry, "Nothing but the Blood," Public Domain, 1876.
xxxix Laurie B. Klein, "I Love You Lord," House of Mercy Music, 1978.
xl Naida Hearn, "Jesus, Name Above All Names," Scripture in Song, 1974.
xli Reinhard Bonnke, *Evangelism by Fire: Keys for Effectively Reaching Others With the Gospel* (Lake Mary: Charisma House, 2011), p 31.

xlii Henry W. Wright, *A More Excellent Way: Be in Health: Pathways of Wholeness, Spiritual Roots of Disease* (Thomaston: Pleasant Valley Publications, 2003), p 238.

xliii Henri J. M. Nouwen, *The Wounded Healer: Ministry in Contemporary Society* (New York: Image, 1979).

xliv See xxix, p 225.

xlv C.S. Lewis, *The Voyage of the Dawn Treader* (New York: Collier Books, 1970), PP 89-90.

xlvi See xv, p 63.

xlvii See xv, p 63.

xlviii See xv, p 14.

xlix Andrew Murray, *The Ministry of Intercession: A Plea for More Prayer* (Abbotsford: Aneko Press, 2016), p 56.

l Dr. David Burns, *Feeling Good: The New Mood Therapy* (New York: Harper, 2008), p. 42

li Dr. John MacArthur, *The MacArthur Study Bible* (Nashville: Thomas Nelson, 2013), p 1403.

lii See xliv.

liii See ix, p 90.

liv See ix, p 90.

lv Mary Oliver, *Red Bird: Poems by Mary Oliver* (Boston: Beacon Press, 2008), p 73.

lvi John Baker, *Life's Healing Choices: Freedom from Your Hurts, Hang-ups, and Habits* (New York: Howard Books, 2013), p 40.

lvii Richard Plass and James Cofield, *The Relational Soul: Moving from False Self to Deep Connection* (Downers Grove: InterVarsity Press Books, 2014), pp 88-89.

lviii John Stott, *Life in Christ: A Guide for Daily Living* (Grand Rapids: Baker, 2003), p 38.

lix Richard D. Smith, *Freedom From Words of Power* (Bland: CM Publications, 1994), p 4.

lx Big Daddy Weave, "Redeemed," Fervent/Curb, 2012.

lxi See lvii.

lxii See xv, P 54.

lxiii See liv, p 25.

lxiv Adolphe Adam, "O Holy Night," Public Domain, 1847

lxv Jeanne Guyon, *Experiencing the Depths of Jesus Christ (Library of Spiritual Classics, Volume 2)* (Jacksonville: Christian Books Publishing House, 1981), p 11.

[lxvi] Dr. Terry Wardle, *Wounded: How to Find Wholeness and Inner Healing in Christ* (Abilene: Leafwood Publishers, 2005), p 180.

[lxvii] Gordon Dalby, *Sons of the Father: Healing the Father-Wound in Men Today* (Davidson: Civitas Press, 2011), p 104.

[lxviii] Dr. Frank Minirth, *Choosing Happiness Even When Life is Hard* (Ada: Revell, 2011), p 16.

[lxix] Dallas Willard, *The Spirit of the Disciplines: Understanding How God Changes Lives* (New York: Harper One, 1999), p 70.

[lxx] Dallas Willard, *Hearing God: Developing a Conversational Relationship with God* (Downers Grove: InterVarsity Press, 2012), p 77.

[lxxi] James D. Bratt, *Abraham Kuyper: A Centennial Reader* (Grand Rapids: Eerdmans Publishing, 1998), p. 488

[lxxii] Joseph F. Girzone, *Joshua: A Parable for Today* (New York: Simon & Schuster/Scribner, 1995).

[lxxiii] See xv, p 51.

[lxxiv] See lxvii.

[lxxv] See lxvii.

[lxxvi] See xv, p 52.

[lxxvii] See xv, p 53.

[lxxviii] See xv, p 53.

[lxxix] See xv, p 54.

[lxxx] See xv, p 54.

[lxxxi] See xv, p 147.

[lxxxii] Dr. Terry Wardle, *Strong Winds & Crashing Waves* (Abilene: Leafwood Publishers, 2007), p 112.

[lxxxiii] See lxxvi, p 112.

[lxxxiv] See lxxvi, p 112.

[lxxxv] See lxxvi, p 113.

[lxxxvi] See lxxvi, p 113.

[lxxxvii] Dr. Terry Wardle, *Formational Prayer Seminar* (2013), pp 6-7.

[lxxxviii] See lxxxii, p 7.

[lxxxix] Tim Stafford, *Knowing the Face of God* (Grand Rapids: Zondervan, 1986), p 169.

[xc] Beth Moore, *Praying God's Word Day by Day* (Nashville: Broadman and Holman Publishers, 2006), p 87.

[xci] Dr. Charles R. Solomon, *Handbook to Happiness: A Biblical Guide to Victorious Living* (Carol Stream: Tyndale House Publishers, 1999), pp 5-6.

[xcii] John H. Armstrong, *Five Great Evangelists* (Fearn: Christian Focus Publications, 1997), p 121.

[xciii] See lxxxvi, p 121.
[xciv] Dr. Henry Cloud and Dr. John Townsend, *Boundaries: When to Say Yes, How to Say No to Take Control of Your Life* (Grand Rapids: Zondervan, 1992), p. 61.
[xcv] Charles Haddon Spurgeon, GoodReads, Accessed 10/4/2019, https://www.goodreads.com/quotes/190659-a-little-faith-will-bring-your-soul-to-heaven-a.
[xcvi] Jerry Bridges, *Trusting God* (Colorado Springs: NavPress, 2017), p 200.
[xcvii] Jerry Bridges, *Transforming Grace: Living Confidently in God's Unfailing Love* (Colorado Springs: NavPress, 2008), p 23.
[xcviii] Peter Kuiper, *At The CrossRoads* (USA: Baxter Press), p 24.
[xcix] See xci, pp 24-25.
[c] Zeb Bradford Long, *Passage Through the Wilderness: A Journey of the Soul* (Grand Rapids: Chosen Books Publishing, 1998), p 102.
[ci] See xiii, p 187.
[cii] See liv, p 150.
[ciii] Andrew Murray, *The Spirit of Christ* (Fort Washington: Christian Literature Crusade, 1963), p 43.
[civ] Peter Scazzero, *The Emotionally Healthy Leader: How Transforming Your Inner Life Will Deeply Transform Your Church, Team, and the World* (Grand Rapids: Zondervan, 2015), p 277.
[cv] Sinclair Ferguson, *The Christian Life: A Doctrinal Introduction* (Carlisle: Banner of Truth Trust, 2013), p 162.
[cvi] See xcix, p 157.
[cvii] Philippians 1:6-11.

Made in the USA
Middletown, DE
12 March 2021